GCSE

SOCIAL AND ECONOMIC
HISTORY

REVISE
GUIDES

Brian Turner

Longman

LONGMAN REVISE GUIDES

Series editors: Geoff Black and Stuart Wall

TITLES AVAILABLE:
Art and Design
Biology
British and European History
Business Studies
C. D. T. – Design and Realisation
Chemistry
Computer Studies
Economics
English
English Literature
French
Geography
German
Mathematics
Mathematics: Higher Level and Extension
Physics
Religious Studies
Science
Social and Economic History
World History

FORTHCOMING:
C. D. T. – Technology
Commerce
Home Economics
Human Biology
Integrated Humanities
Music
Office Studies and Information Technology

Longman Group UK Limited,
Longman House, Burnt Mill, Harlow,
Essex CM20 2JE, England
and Associated Companies throughout the world.

First published 1989

British Library Cataloguing in Publication Data

Turner, Brian
    GCSE social and economic history. –
    (Longman GCSE revise guides)
    1. England. Secondary schools. Curriculum subjects: History.
    GCSE examinations.
    Techniques
    I. Title
    907′.5

    ISBN 0–582–03852–9

Produced by The Pen and Ink Book Company,
Huntingdon, Cambridgeshire

Set in 10/12pt Century Old Style

Printed and bound in Great Britain by
William Clowes Limited, Beccles and London

CONTENTS

EDITORS' PREFACE

Longman Revise Guides are written by experienced examiners and teachers, and aim to give you the best possible foundation for success in examinations and other modes of assessment. Examiners are well aware that the performance of many candidates falls well short of their true potential, and this series of books aims to remedy this, by encouraging thorough study and a full understanding of the concepts involved. The Revise Guides should be seen as course companions and study aids to be used throughout the year, not just for last minute revision.

Examiners are in no doubt that a structured approach in preparing for examinations and in presenting coursework can, together with hard work and diligent application, substantially improve performance.

The largely self-contained nature of each chapter gives the book a useful degree of flexibility. After starting with the opening general chapters on the background to the GCSE, and the syllabus coverage, all other chapters can be read selectively, in any order appropriate to the stage you have reached in your course.

We believe that this book, and the series as a whole, will help you establish a solid platform of basic knowledge and examination technique on which to build.

Geoff Black and Stuart Wall

ACKNOWLEDGEMENTS

The author is indebted to the following Examination Groups for permission to reproduce past examination questions. Whilst permission has been granted to reproduce their questions, the answers, or hints on answers are solely the responsibility of the author and have neither been provided nor approved by the Groups. The Groups accept no responsibility whatsoever for the accuracy or method of working in the answers given.

London and East Anglian Group (LEAG)
Midland Examining Group (MEG)
Southern Examining Group (SEG)

The author further acknowledges the many helpful suggestions and improvements made by Gordon Halliday.

Brian Turner

GCSE IN SOCIAL AND ECONOMIC HISTORY

GETTING STARTED

The purpose of this book is to help students entering for the GCSE examination in Social and Economic History to develop more fully the knowledge and historical skills expected of students entering that examination. If you follow the advice given and the practical tasks set in each chapter, you should be able to show the examiners how well you have mastered the knowledge, understanding and historical skills expected of successful candidates in the GCSE. It cannot be guaranteed that you will achieve the highest grades possible, but if you follow the advice given you should achieve a higher grade than you might otherwise have done.

This book is not a comprehensive textbook, it does not replace the textbooks that are normally used in schools and colleges. It does, however, offer an up to date explanation of the major historical problems and issues covered by the syllabuses of the GCSE examination boards. Unlike most textbooks it also provides advice on how to study and suggests useful techniques for revision and for taking the exam itself. There are also examples of common errors by students, model answers and opportunities to practice the skills and knowledge tested in the examination.

Many students will have ample opportunities to discuss their work with teachers and other students. Do not be afraid to do this; teachers are almost always willing to help those who show interest and enthusiasm for the subject and need help to understand particular problems. Most teachers will, when asked, give guidance on where a student's work is at fault, or how even a good answer could be made better. Students studying on their own outside the classroom should find this book especially helpful, since the worked examples and examiner guidance will provide a model to follow, and against which you can judge the quality of your own work.

INTRODUCING GCSE

THE NATIONAL CRITERIA

The GCSE examination has been described as a revolutionary new system of examining. In some ways it is, but in many ways, especially in History, GCSE has been a gradual development out of the previous public examinations. The experience and best practices of these examinations have been used to create a single system of examining students over almost the whole band of abilities. The Schools Examination Council (SEC) asked committees of practising teachers, historical researchers, examiners and others, to develop what they described as the *National Criteria for History*. The National Criteria represent the standards that are widely regarded as the essential features of that subject, and with which pupils at 16+ should be familiar. Although each examination board is responsible for developing its own syllabuses, *every History syllabus* must conform to these National Criteria and must provide effective ways of assessing the skills and abilities specified in the criteria.

The National Criteria for History do not specify particular areas of subject knowledge that *all* students must learn; instead they provide broad *aims* and outline the skills and abilities which students at 16+ need to have if they are to understand, practise and enjoy the study of the past and to appreciate how modern societies are a product of their History.

History syllabuses are required to:

- stimulate interest in, and enthusiasm for, the past;
- promote knowledge and understanding of the past and its links with the present;
- link this knowledge with the historical evidence on which it is based;
- develop skill in locating, handling and understanding historical evidence and its limitations;
- develop understanding of cause and consequence, continuity and change, similarity and difference;
- appreciate the development through time of social and cultural values;
- provide a sound basis for further study and the pursuit of personal interest.

This in fact describes what has been the best practice of history teachers for many years. These aims will, however, only be achieved if students acquire the *skills* needed to put them in to effect. One thing the GCSE does stress is that each syllabus must *test* whether students have indeed acquired the abilities and skills set out in these aims. In other words, all syllabuses must meet a clearly defined set of *assessment objectives*.

In order to obtain a certificate, all GCSE candidates are required to:

Assessment Objectives

1 Recall a substantial amount of historical knowledge and to write about it clearly.
2 Understand and make use of the ideas of cause and consequence, continuity and change, similarity and difference.
3 Look at events and problems from the past in the way that those living at the time would have looked at them.
4 Show skill in studying historical evidence by
   i) understanding and extracting information from it;
   ii) interpreting and evaluating it – distinguishing between fact, opinion and judgement; pointing out deficiencies in it as evidence, e.g. gaps and inconsistencies, and detecting bias;
   iii) comparing various types of evidence and forming conclusions based on this comparison.

These appear in slightly different form in the syllabuses of each Board, but effectively mean the same and are given in the same order.

STANDARDS

One problem that worries employers, parents and students is the value of the grades awarded and the equivalence with previous examinations. An approximate equivalence between grades in GCSE and the previous GCE O-level and CSE grades is that:

GCSE			*GCE O-level/CSE*
A	is equivalent to	→	A
B	is equivalent to	→	B
C	is equivalent to	→	C and CSE grade 1
D	is equivalent to	→	2
E	is equivalent to	→	3
F	is equivalent to	→	4
G	is equivalent to	→	5
	← Ungraded →		

The responsibility for ensuring that the new grades are equal to the standards of the 'O' level examinations still rests with the GCE Boards and the new grading procedures are, if anything, even more rigorous than before. In time it is intended that *levels of competence* will be established for *each of the skills* specified in the National Criteria. The grade then awarded to each candidate will be determined by the level of performance in each skill. This is not possible at the moment and of the seven letter grades, A to G, so far only two have been described in terms of actual achievement. These are Grade F, the level expected of the *average pupil,* and Grade C, which is the minimum level expected of anyone going on into more advanced courses. The lowest grade 'worthy of recognition' is grade G; a performance below this is ungraded. The GCSE system of examinations and grading should ensure that a more reliable grading system develops, based upon defined skills and levels of attainment.

GRADE CRITERIA

Grade F
Candidates will be expected to:

- recall and display a limited amount of accurate and relevant historical knowledge; to show a basic understanding of the historical concepts of cause and consequence, continuity and change, sufficiently supported by obvious examples; to identify and list differences and similarities;

- display knowledge of other people based on specific examples of situations and events;

- show ability to comprehend straightforward evidence; to extract partial and/or generalised information;

- demonstrate the obvious limitations of a particular piece of evidence; to list some of the evidence needed to reconstruct a given historical event;

- make simple comparisons between pieces of evidence; to list the major features of two or more pieces of evidence without drawing conclusions from it;

- to communicate in an understandable form; to use simple historical terminology.

Grade C
Candidates will be expected to:

- recall and use historical knowledge accurately and relevantly in support of a logical and evaluative argument; to distinguish between cause and occasion of an event; to show that change in history is not necessarily linear or 'progressive'; to compare and contrast people, events, issues and institutions; to demonstrate understanding of such concepts by deploying accurate, though limited, evidence;

- show an ability to look at events from the perspective of other people in the past; to understand the importance of looking for motives;

- demonstrate comprehension of a range of evidence either by translating it from one form to another (e.g. explaining accurately the information contained in a bar graph) or by summarising information given in a document; to answer accurately and fully questions demanding specific information to be extracted from the evidence;

- demonstrate the limitations of a particular piece of evidence; e.g. to point to the use of emotive language and to generalisations based on little or no evidence; to indicate the other types of evidence that the historian would need to consult in relation to the topic and period in question;

■ compare and contrast two or more different types of evidence and write a coherent conclusion based on them; all aspects may not be taken into account;

■ communicate clearly in a substantially correct and appropriate manner, making correct and appropriate use of historical terminology.

Precisely how much *weight* should be given to *each skill* is left to the discretion of each Exam Group. The Groups may also choose the *methods* they will use to assess levels of competence. In practice, they all tend to use broadly the same methods. Some Groups do indicate the weighting for specific skills in each element of assessment, and these will be found in the syllabus. Table 1.1 gives some indication of what happens in practice. Note that just knowing the facts without understanding them, as in some quiz games, is *not* very important. What GCSE History examinations try to test is how well you can behave like a detective. In other words, can you understand the clues or evidence left by the past and apply it to explain what has subsequently happened?

SKILL(S)		% of Total Marks
1	Simple recall of facts	25% maximum
2	Understand and use ideas of cause and consequence, change and continuity, similarity and difference	30%
3	Evaluation and interpretation of evidence	25%
4	Empathy	20%

Table 1.1

3 ASSESSMENT METHODS

The SEC requires that each syllabus not only assesses every skill described in the National Criteria, but that it uses work done *during the course of study* ('coursework'), as well as written end of course examinations, in assessing overall achievement. The National Criteria and Grade Criteria give all Exam Groups the same *objectives* for their syllabus and establish agreed *levels of attainment* for each grade. But the boards do use different combinations and weightings of *coursework* and *examinations* (see Table 1.2). Again, there may be considerable differences in the types of examination question set by the various Exam Groups. It is therefore absolutely essential that all students make themselves familiar with the assessment procedures for their particular syllabus, and also with the question types to be used in each part of the assessment. Schools should have copies of syllabuses, specimen papers and the GCSE examination papers from 1988 onwards. Students should ask to see these. If it is not possible for you to obtain copies from your school or college, then write to the Exam Group whose examination you are entered for and ask for copies; you should be able to obtain copies for a small charge. The addresses of the GCSE Exam Groups are provided at the end of this Chapter.

EXAM GROUP	COURSEWORK		EXAMINATIONS	
	%	No. assignments	Paper 1	Paper 2
LEAG	30%	4 (3 from 1990)	45% 1¾ hours	25% 1½ hours
MEG	30%	1–2	40% 1½ hours	30% 1½ hours
NEA	30%	4–6	30% 1½ hours	40% 2 hours
SEG	20%	2	50% 2 hours	30% 1 hour
NISEC	Modular scheme including some Economic and Social History			
WJEC	Modular scheme including some Economic and Social History options			

Table 1.2 Assessment in GCSE Social and Economic History Syllabuses

In some cases, Exam Groups offer a special format for 'mature students' and for those who cannot submit coursework. This usually involves an additional paper based upon unseen evidence.

4 COURSEWORK

Coursework has a number of different purposes; it ensures that:

■ students undertake tasks and develop the skills specified in the syllabus;

■ skills not easily tested in written examinations are assessed;

■ the final grade awarded is based upon assessments done in a number of different ways and at different times.

Although all Exam Groups allow teachers to set work of their own choosing, they clearly indicate the *kind of skills* that must be tested and in some cases give precise guidelines on how coursework must be marked. It is likely that, in future, the Groups will give *even more guidance* on marking coursework and on the kinds of assignment that have proved to be effective, both in terms of teaching particular skills to students and in assessing how well students have learned to apply these skills. All the Groups publish subject reports after each examination and these usually include useful advice and information on these matters. Only in special circumstances is it possible to *avoid* submitting coursework; if candidates fail to submit coursework, they will not normally be awarded a certificate, no matter how well they did in the written examinations. However, all the Groups have special procedures for dealing with absences due to ill health, or learning problems caused by disabilities of various kinds. If any of these circumstances apply, then students should make sure that the Exam Group is informed of these by the school or college.

Requirements for Coursework

Coursework will account for a significant percentage of the final mark, so it is important to do it as well as you can. Coursework will also prepare students for the kind of problems they will meet in the examination. The number of assignments that have to be submitted for coursework is actually quite small, but in most schools and colleges teachers will set many more exercises than the minimum. They can then select the best examples of work by a candidate. The Groups will *not* accept work that has been corrected and revised several times, nor will they accept fair copies of marked work. Candidates also have to sign an *authentication certificate* to say that it is their *own* work which is submitted. There is a deadline for completing coursework and all the coursework for every candidate must be collected by the school or college so that it can be marked and later moderated. Normally it would be necessary for work to be completed and handed in to teachers during the April just before the examination in June.

The coursework done by students is initially marked by teachers at the school or college. Where several different teachers and classes are involved, the Exam Groups normally expect that the marking of each teacher is carefully checked by others.

All Groups have arrangements whereby the work of students has, at some stages to be sent to a *moderator* who checks upon the marking of the centre (i.e. school or college). Moderators can, if necessary, recommend that marks are altered to bring them into line with the marks of other candidates in the same school, or in other schools. The work of moderators is checked in the same way as that of examiners. So coursework is treated like the written examinations which are sat at the end of the course, the aim being to ensure that work of the same quality should get the same mark.

COURSEWORK ASSIGNMENTS

As has been explained before, whilst a good factual knowledge is helpful, the GCSE examination is *not* like a quiz game. Students have to be able to place knowledge in context and to use knowledge about the past as pieces of evidence. All the syllabuses permit teachers to undertake practical field study activities or to study some aspect of local history, but this is not a requirement. Most teachers will set coursework assignments of different kinds, probably trying to test a *few* skills rather than every skill in the same assignment. In most cases, coursework assignments will test how well you can *use* different kinds of evidence and how aware you are of different motives and attitudes in the past. In order to do well, you will not only need *knowledge* of the subject and an ability to express your ideas clearly, you must also be able to extract information from different types of evidence.

You must learn to read the information given to you very carefully. Many pupils find it helpful, as they read through a passage, to underline the important words and ideas. Some evidence will be visual, in the form of pictures, photographs, diagrams, maps, graphs or tables. This too must be carefully looked at both to understand the information it contains and to judge how reliable such information is.

Useful points to remember

You must always think like a detective. Always 'read' the source several times. Then ask yourself the following questions:

- What *information* does the source contain?
- Is the source *reliable*, is the information likely to be accurate?
- Was the evidence produced by someone for a *particular purpose*?
- Can the *information* in the source be confirmed by other evidence/sources?

- Does the source date from the *time it refers to*, or was it written/produced some time *after* the event it describes?
- Does the source report *fact* or merely somebody's opinion/interpretation?

If you get into the *habit* of asking yourself these questions, they will become automatic and you will be in a better position to answer particular questions set either for coursework or the examination.

5 > WRITTEN EXAMINATIONS

At the moment, *written examinations* are the most important part of the assessment procedures, receiving the largest proportion of the total marks available. Of course examinations are really only a test of the knowledge and skills developed *during* the course of study, and which have already been examined in coursework. If you have taken an *active* part in the course and done your work properly, you should already be reasonably well prepared for the examinations. All you have to do is to *show* the examiner how much you understand and how well you can apply your skills and knowledge to different issues and problems.

In many ways it is the examination format that has changed most with the arrival of GCSE. All the Exam Groups use a *variety* of examination techniques to find out what the candidates can do. In most examinations at least one paper (or a very large part of it) will involve the *comprehension and interpretation of source material* given to you. Other questions (or parts of questions) will require you to *apply* your knowledge of a subject, to describe, explain or make some kind of judgement based on evidence. The questions will not only be of different *types*, they will also vary in *difficulty* and carry different marks. Specific advice on how to deal with these and how to revise for your examination is given below. However, it is important to realise that every student should be able to find questions that they *can* answer. For the most able students the problem will usually be to ensure that they cover the *whole* of the paper and do not waste time writing too much detail, especially when a question is given only a few marks and only a short answer is required.

The format of the examinations varies between Groups, as can be seen below. Some Groups have already published alterations both to syllabus content and examinations that take effect from 1990. It is possible that others will do so in the near future.

6 > ASSESSMENT FORMATS

LEAG

Two examination papers plus coursework.

Paper 1 *(1¾ hours)*	Weighted at 45% of total marks. Questions in Part 1 (20% of total marks), are short answer type with stimulus material of varying kinds; answers are written in the question booklet and candidates have to answer all the questions from 10 of 20 sections. Questions in Part 2 (25% of total marks) are structured essay; candidates answer two questions from a choice of 20.
Paper 2 *(1½ hours)*	Weighted at 25% of total marks. Candidates answer 2 questions from a choice of 10. Questions are data response, basically testing comprehension of sources and ability to compare and contrast sources and make deductions based on knowledge of sources and the topic.

For 1990, there is a major revision to the LEAG syllabus that effectively reduces the subject content to be covered to a more reasonable length and allows teachers to choose various ways of covering a range of material. The revised examination also removes the quiz-type short answer questions. Factual recall and understanding will form part of the questions in Paper 1, arising out of stimulus material.

 Format for 1990

Paper 1 *(2 hours)*	Weighted at 40% of total marks. Questions will be based upon stimulus material and be in two parts. The first part of each question will be short answers testing basic knowledge and understanding. The second part will be short/structured essays to test the use of key concepts i.e. objective 2 of National Criteria (see page 2).

Paper 2 *(1½ hours)*	Weighted at 30% of the total marks.
	Questions will be based upon a number of different types of evidence (as for 1989) and each question will be a series of sub-questions testing comprehension and understanding of evidence and the ability to use evidence i.e. National Criteria objectives 2, 3, 4.
Coursework	The mark weighting stays at 30% but the total number of assignments to be submitted is reduced from 4 to 3 and greater direction is given as to suitable tasks and marking.

MEG

Two examination papers plus coursework.

Paper 1 *(1¾ hours)*	Weighted at 40% of the total marks.
	The examination content is based upon the Core content of the syllabus; this is effectively the classic Industrial Revolution 1750–1850. The topics examined are: population, agriculture, industry and transport. The examination is in 2 parts: Section A: 15%, short answer questions testing basic factual recall. Section B: 25%, choice of two structured questions from 4. Aim is to test basic knowledge and concepts i.e. National Criteria objectives 1 and 2.
Paper 2 *(1½ hours)*	Weighted at 30% of total marks.
	The examination is based on 9 optional topics, 4 of which follow on from the Core content of Paper 1, the others are social history topics 1750 to present day.
	One question is set on each topic; candidates must answer 2 questions. The questions will present source material of various kinds and sub-questions are set to test National Criteria objectives 1–4.
Coursework	30% of total mark weighting.
	Minimum of 1 assignment which must assess each of the National Criteria objectives. The assignment can be broken up into particular elements to test each specific objective.

Some changes are introduced from 1990, that alter slightly the presentation of syllabus content of the Paper 1 Core content. As with LEAG, the 30 short answer questions disappear as a separate part to the examination which will presumably incorporate factual recall into the questions based on stimulus material.

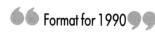 Format for 1990

Paper 1 *(1¾ hours)*	Weighted at 40% of the total marks.
	6 questions based on stimulus source material set on the Core content, candidates answer 3 questions. Aim is to test National Criteria objectives 1 and 2.
Paper 2 *(1½ hours)*	Weighted at 30% of total marks.
	The examination is based on 9 optional topics, 4 of which follow on from the Core content of Paper 1, the others are social history topics 1750 to present day.
	One question is set on each topic; candidates must answer 2 questions. The questions will present source material of various kinds and sub-questions are set to test National Criteria objectives 1–4.
Coursework	30% of total mark weighting.
	Minimum of 1 assignment which must assess each of the National Criteria objectives. The assignment can be broken up into particular elements to test each specific objective.

NEA

Two papers plus coursework.

Paper 1 *(1½ hours)*	Weighted at 30% of total marks.
	All questions are compulsory, and are based upon the content for Theme 1 – 'Industrialisation and Urbanisation'. In 1988, the examination paper was a series of questions generally getting harder on two topics, 'Enclosure' and 'New Towns'. Candidates were given a selection of narrative and illustrations as sources. The questions

tested basic comprehension of the material, contextual knowledge and elementary evaluation. All answers were written on the answer book underneath the questions.

Paper 2
(2 hours)
Weighted at 40% of total marks.

Candidates answer a total of 5 questions based on the other two Themes of the syllabus, 'Responses to Industrialisation' and 'Social Improvements'. The examination paper is in 3 sections.

Section A: 2 compulsory questions based on a variety of sources. The sub-questions test basic comprehension and evaluation of the material.

Section B: Candidates have a choice of two questions; both are based on sources and become progressively more difficult, moving from simple recall and comprehension to explanation.

Section C: 1 answer from a choice of 5 straight essays requiring the candidate to comment upon a statement or explain why a particular change happened.

Coursework
30% of the total mark weighting.

For 1989, candidates have to submit 4 assignments covering all of the National Criteria objectives. The syllabus does offer suggestions as to types of work to be undertaken, but contains no detailed advice on marking, unlike other Boards.

The NEA syllabus appears to be extremely long and contains a lot of content. The examination papers appear to be more of a lottery than other Boards since the choice of questions is probably more limited than with other Boards. It is possible that some alterations may be made, but so far none have been notified. I would strongly recommend that candidates entered for this examination obtain copies of both the syllabus and the papers set in 1988.

SEG

Two papers plus coursework; external candidates may be permitted to sit an unseen evidence paper based upon the syllabus content *in lieu* of coursework assignments. Like the MEG, the SEG examination is based upon a compulsory core of Themes and a range of optional topics.

Paper 1
(2 hours)
Weighted at 50% of the total marks.

2 sections based on compulsory Themes; these cover the classic Industrial Revolution but take the themes of Agriculture and Industry, Communications and People in Society up to the present day.

Section A (25%): 1 multi-part compulsory question arising out of Theme 1 'Agriculture and Industry'. For question 2, there is a choice of structured essays on Theme 1.

Section B (25%): Candidates answer 2 questions from a choice of 6 structured questions. These use a limited amount of stimulus material to test comprehension of data and the ability to present reasoned explanations of events.

Paper 2
(1 hour)
Weighted at 30% of the total marks.

12 structured questions are set on a range of optional 'Topics'. Candidates have to answer 2 questions which are based upon understanding given evidence and generally requiring contextual knowledge and judgement; some questions require an empathetic response.

Coursework
20% of the total marks.

Candidates must submit 2 carefully prescribed assignments; one to test Object 3 and the other Objective 4. The Board publishes a detailed marking scheme and booklets offering advice on setting coursework tasks.

Criticisms of the quantity of content in the SEG course and the attempt to assess empathetic understanding under examination circumstances may lead to minor modification, but as yet no proposals have been made and the syllabus and examination are fairly straightforward.

WJEC AND NISEC

Both these Boards offer an interesting set of syllabuses since they have sought to incorporate the ideas of the Schools Council Project into a *modular* syllabus which permits a variety of different types of study to be undertaken. Both include local studies and an element of straight Economic and Social History. Students entered for these examinations ought to obtain a copy of the syllabus and to check with their teachers which options they are going to study. In both cases, substantial parts of the material presented in this book will be relevant, but this material is only a small part of the overall course offered by these boards.

7 > TYPES OF QUESTION

There are FOUR main types of question used in GCSE History examinations, each designed to test different skills.

MULTIPLE CHOICE AND SHORT-ANSWER QUESTIONS

These questions test overall factual knowledge. Some Groups do this in a section of the examination paper. You either choose the correct answer from a list of alternatives or answer a question briefly with a single word or a sentence. Other examinations ask short-answer factual questions as part of a sequence of questions on a particular topic. For GCSE History examinations, factual recall questions rarely count for more than 25% of the total marks.

STIMULUS AND DATA RESPONSE

These questions test how well you can use different types of historical evidence or data. You must know how historians use sources such as maps, written records, illustrations, and perhaps even artefacts. You should also know how to use and interpret graphs and tables to report findings. Several questions will usually be set on the same data; some will test how well you understand and can extract information contained in the source; others expect you to make comparisons and to point out differences between the sources. Most important of all you will be asked to express an opinion on the value to the historian of a source or of the information contained in it. Your answer must be based on the information given about the source and your own knowledge.

ESSAY TYPE QUESTIONS

Some essays are a single question, but more often they will be broken down into different parts and marks given for each part. Often, even essay questions are based upon a short piece of data. The aim of essay questions is to let you show more detailed knowledge of a topic. They give you the opportunity to explain why something has happened, the results of a particular event or the importance of a particular person.

EMPATHY QUESTIONS

These questions test how well you understand the *motives and attitudes* of people in the past. You should be able to show that people in the past not only had very different ideas from those of today, but that often various groups or individuals within the society *at that time* had different ideas. This may be tested as part of an essay question, or as part of a stimulus or data response question.

There has been a great deal of debate about empathy in History; it is in my view rather simple. Historians *use evidence* in trying to reconstruct the past and to explain what has happened in exactly the same way that a modern detective does. In fact, many of the techniques that are used by forensic scientists to help today's detectives are used by historians. We can never be certain what happened in the past and we can never run the experiment again, as physical scientists can, but on the information available we *can* describe accurately what happened and try to understand why people thought and acted as they did. In this way we can suggest possible motives for why people behaved in the way that they did. This is called *empathy*; it is not an exercise in fantasy or fiction, it is using the best information we have to make a sensible choice between possible alternatives.

8 > EXAMINATION TECHNIQUES

There are eight rules that apply to all examinations:

1 Read the *instructions* carefully and *obey* them.
2 Read the *question(s)* carefully.
3 Choose the questions you feel *confident* about answering.
4 Decide on the best *order* for answering the questions.
5 *Plan your time* carefully.
6 *Think before you answer a question*. For essay answers especially, *plan* your answers in note form.
7 *Answer the question set*; always be relevant.
8 *Check* through your paper.

Almost all questions will require you to examine one or more 'sources'. This means that you must read or examine the sources very carefully since *you will be expected to use information in the sources in your answer*. You must be able to show that you *understand* the material put before you and know both its *value* and *limitations* as evidence.

COMMON ERRORS

Many candidates do badly because they:

- do not answer the *question set*;
- do not *use* the information given in the sources;
- do not *read* carefully the questions or the sources provided. Many students read too quickly. Try to read carefully, making certain you know what the question wants you to do and that you *understand* the information in the sources.

HELPFUL ADVICE

- Where a question is split up into *parts*, note the marks given to each part. Where a question does not show the marks, assume that more marks are given to the later parts of a question. This means that you must not spend too much time on the early parts to a question; most marks are likely to be for the more difficult questions which will probably be towards the end.

- Where questions refer to sources, read or examine each source when directed and note the instructions given in the question. For long written sources, it is a good idea to *underline* those words or phrases which are *key ideas* to understanding the passage as a whole.

- Answer the question set.

9 > SYLLABUS CONTENT

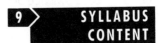

As explained before, this book is not a comprehensive textbook trying to cover all the topics that appear on the Social and Economic History syllabuses. It is attempting to ensure that you have a summary of those topics which are *central* to the subject and which appear on all or most of the syllabuses. The syllabuses published by each Group are long and always give some element of choice, so that you are not normally expected to cover every topic. Precisely how the topics are examined does vary from Group to Group. It is important for you to ensure that you know which topics you *must* cover and those which are *optional*. In syllabuses where a particular *topic* is examined on a specific examination paper (see Table 1.3), make sure you know on *which paper* it will be tested and the *types of question* that will be asked. If you are a student at school or college, it would be sensible to use this book to go over the topics which have been covered by your teacher.

CHAPTER TOPIC		LEAG	MEG	NEA	SEG	NISEC WJEC
2	Population growth to 1870	✓	✓	✓	✓	Modular Schemes.
	Population growth since 1870	✓	✓	✓	✓	You are advised
3	The 'Agricultural Revolution'	✓	✓	✓	✓	to discuss these
4	Agricultural progress since 1870	✓	✓	✓	✓	with your teacher.
	The Great Depression	✓	✓	✓	✓	See also the
5	Industrial changes to 1870	✓	✓	✓	✓	actual syllabus
	Textiles	✓	✓	✓	✓	itself.
	Iron and steel	✓	✓	✓	✓	
6	The 'Transport Revolution'	✓	✓	✓	✓	
	Roads	✓	✓	✓	✓	
	Canals	✓	✓	✓	✓	
	Railways	✓	✓	✓	✓	
7	Transport in modern times					
	shipping	✓	✓	✓	✓	
	motor vehicles	✓	✓	✓	✓	
	railways	✓	✓	✓	✓	
8	Urbanisation and housing problems					
	public health and overcrowding	✓	✓	✓	✓	
	planning and new towns	✓	✓	✓	✓	
	development of council housing	✓	✓	✓	✓	
9	Social problems in an industrial					
	society 1700–1870	✓	✓	✓	✓	
	living standards	✓	✓	✓	✓	
	factory reform	✓	✓	✓	✓	
10	Poverty and social welfare					
	the 'Old Poor Law'	✓	✓	✓	✓	
	the 'New Poor Law'	✓	✓	✓	✓	
	the 'welfare state'	✓	✓	✓	✓	
11	Trade unions and labour					
	unionism before 1850	✓	✓	✓	✓	
	Chartism	✓	✓	✓	✓	
	'New Model' unions	✓	✓	✓	✓	
	'New Unionism'	✓	✓	✓	✓	
	the General Strike	✓	✓	✓	✓	
12	Immigration and discrimination	✓	✓	✓	✓	

Table 1.3
Syllabus Content GCSE Social and
Economic History

10 AFTER THE EXAMINATION

Sometimes students do *not* achieve the grades they expected or needed for a particular job or course and cannot understand why, especially when they believe they answered the questions properly! It is of course possible (though unlikely) that a mistake has happened; if you feel this is the case, then an appeal against the grade can be made by the headteacher of the school and your examination papers will be remarked. However, it is not very often that higher grades are awarded on a remark; this is because great care is taken by the Exam Groups to ensure that mistakes are avoided. We have already seen that the *coursework* assessments marked by teachers will be checked by a moderator. The marking of *examination* papers is also checked several times. The procedure for this varies between the Exam Groups, but the same basic steps are taken. *Chief examiners* produce *questions* and *mark schemes* that are vetted by a *panel of teachers*. All *assistant examiners* receive this mark scheme and attend a meeting where sample scripts are marked; if necessary, changes are made to the *mark scheme* to take account of unexpected but relevant answers by candidates. The work of assistant examiners is regularly *sampled* by Chief Examiners and at least 15% (and usually more) of all scripts are *double marked*. At the end of the marking, all scripts are *checked* at the Board for arithmetical errors by examiners. After a careful study of many scripts and coursework files by Chief Examiners and teacher representatives, *grade boundaries* are decided for the examination as a whole. There is no particular percentage set for each grade *before* the examination; grades are awarded purely on the basis of overall achievement in both coursework and the examination papers. About a week after grading, the Chief Examiners normally carry out a 'borderline review'. This means that scripts around 2% below the grade boundary points are *remarked*, to ensure that no mistakes have been made. Though no system can be absolutely perfect, the Exam Groups do aim for accuracy and fairness. Given the number of scripts and the time limit within which they have to be marked, the number of mistakes is tiny indeed.

11 **USING THIS GUIDE**

As was mentioned above, this revision guide will help you to do better in *the examination* if you follow the advice given carefully; do this and you should also become a better *historian*. It must be remembered that, in many ways, history is *not* like other subjects in which the experiment can be repeated and the information carefully collected. History is about the *past*; historians try both to *describe* what happened in the past and more importantly to *explain* why events happened as they did and the results that followed. They can only describe and explain what happened by piecing together a story from the materials that have survived. Often this evidence is not clear cut; it can be *interpreted* in different ways. Frequently one piece of evidence *conflicts* with another. Therefore to be a historian, you must become familiar with the different kinds of sources or evidence that survive from the past. It is this kind of evidence that will be used in your GCSE examination papers. In other words, historians are like 'time detectives', piecing together the story from the evidence that has been left behind. To do this you must learn to 'read' and understand the evidence, and become familiar with the problems of interpreting this material.

It is no good just learning all the facts. Facts are important, but you must learn how to *use* the facts produced from an investigation of the evidence in reconstructing the past. In order to develop these skills, each chapter begins with a section called 'Getting started'. This will outline the *problems* that historians need to describe and explain. Information is given on the kinds of *sources available* to the historian, together with *examples* of this evidence. These examples of evidence will be presented and discussed in the chapter or will appear in the questions and problems set at the end. Each chapter contains a *summary* of how historians have *interpreted* this data. You will also find examples of the kind of *questions* that could be set at GCSE. There are also examples of the *common errors* made by students and a *tutor's answer* that should provide a model for guidance when answering questions of a similar type.

ADDRESSES OF THE EXAMINING BOARDS

Most teachers give candidates a copy of the relevant part of the syllabus so that they may see precisely what they have to do and how the marks are awarded. Normally teachers will also use past examination papers or specimen questions produced by an Exam Group to ensure that candidates know what to expect. If you do *not* have either of these, copies can normally be obtained for a small charge by writing directly to the relevant Exam Group at one of the addresses below. Write and request an order form to purchase your own copy of the syllabus. You will then have to complete the order form and enclose the cost of the syllabus and postage.

London and East Anglian Group (LEAG)

London	University of London School Examinations Board
	Stewart House, 32 Russell Square, London WC1B 5DN
LREB	London Regional Examining Board
	Lyon House, 104 Wandsworth High Street, London SW18 4LF
EAEB	East Anglian Examinations Board
	'The Lindens', Lexden Road, Colchester, Essex CO3 3RL

Midland Examining Group (MEG)

Cambridge	University of Cambridge Local Examinations Syndicate
	Syndicate Buildings, 1 Hills Road, Cambridge CB1 2EU
O and C	Oxford and Cambridge School Examinations Board
	10 Trumpington Street, Cambridge, and Elsfield Way, Oxford OX2 8EP
SUJB	Southern Universities' Joint Board for School Examinations
	Cotham Road, Bristol BS6 6DD
WMEB	The West Midlands Examinations Board
	Norfolk House, Smallbrook Queensway, Birmingham B5 4NJ
EMREB	East Midland Regional Examining Board
	Robins Wood House, Robins Wood Road, Aspley, Nottingham NG8 3NH

Northern Examination Association (NEA)

JMB	Joint Matriculation Board
	Devas Street, Manchester M15 6EU
ALSEB	Associated Lancashire Schools Examining Board
	12 Harter Street, Manchester M1 6HL
NREB	North Regional Examinations Board
	Wheatfield Road, Westerhope, Newcastle upon Tyne NE5 5JZ
NWREB	North West Regional Examinations Board
	Orbit House, Albert Street, Eccles, Manchester M30 0WL
YHREB	Yorkshire and Humberside Regional Examinations Boards
	Harrogate: 31–33 Springfield Avenue, Harrogate HG1 2HW
	Sheffield: Scarsdale House, 136 Derbyshire Lane, Sheffield S8 8SE

Northern Ireland

NISEC	Northern Ireland School Examinations Council
	Beechill House, 42 Beechill Road, Belfast BT8 4RS

Scotland

SEB	Scottish Examination Board
	Ironmills Road, Dalkeith, Midlothian EH22 1BR

Southern Examining Group (SEG)

AEB	The Associated Examining Board
	Stag Hill House, Guildford, Surrey GU2 5XJ
OLE	The Oxford Delegacy of Local Examinations
	Ewert Place, Summertown, Oxford OX2 7BZ
SREB	The Southern Regional Examinations Board
	Avondale House, 33 Carlton Crescent, Southampton SO9 4YL
SEREB	The South-East Regional Examinations Board
	Beloe House, 2–10 Mount Ephraim Road, Royal Tunbridge Wells TN1 1EU
SWEB	The South Western Examinations Board
	23–29 Marsh Street, Bristol BS1 4BP

Wales

WJEC	Welsh Joint Education Committee
	245 Western Avenue, Cardiff CF5 2YX

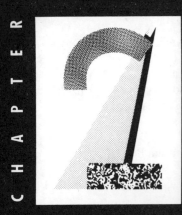

THE GROWTH AND GEOGRAPHICAL DISTRIBUTION OF POPULATION

THE PROBLEM OF SOURCES

WHY THE POPULATION INCREASED

CHANGES IN POPULATION DISTRIBUTION

CONSEQUENCES OF POPULATION GROWTH

GETTING STARTED

Industrialisation has always been linked with the growth of population. Until quite recently, the problem for historians was that they had been uncertain whether the increase in population during the eighteenth century was the *reason for*, or *the result of*, industrialisation. Although there are many sources of information, it is not always in a form that historians find easy to use. Countries that have *not* industrialised are often poor and usually do not have the means to collect the information. For some underdeveloped countries there are relatively few well-educated people able to read and write and the government does not have the means to collect reliable information. A large, well-educated population and an efficient government bureaucracy is often a sign that a country *has moved* from being a poor agricultural-based nation to an industrial country able to expand and grow richer. In 1700, Britain was very much poorer than it is today; average incomes were then about the same in real value (possibly even a little higher) as those in a modern underdeveloped country. By 1850 the situation had changed dramatically. The process of *industrialisation* had clearly begun and major changes were taking place in all aspects of life, including the efficiency of government and the collection of an enormous quantity of information on trade, industry and everyday life.

Today, historians have largely overcome the problems of getting accurate reliable data on population growth in England between about 1600 and 1850. Now, the problem is to explain *why* the changes took place when they did and the *results* of those changes. In answering questions on population and urbanisation, it is expected that GCSE candidates will be able to do most of the following:

- show knowledge of the sources used by historians;
- describe the major trends and patterns in the growth of population;
- explain the reasons for population growth and the changing pattern of geographical distribution of population.

Other issues arising out of the *results* of urbanisation will be dealt with in Chapter 8. Not every syllabus covers these problems, so use the chart in Chapter 1 and refer to your own syllabus to check how much of the period after 1870 needs to be covered.

ESSENTIAL PRINCIPLES

1 > THE PROBLEM OF SOURCES

Some older textbooks explain that the problem for the historian has been the lack of information on population before 1801 and the inaccuracy of *parish registers*. This is only partly true. Often the problem was one of *too much* information, but information of a kind which did not always help historians to answer their questions. As explained in Chapter 1, before events in the past can be explained, historians have to produce an accurate *description* of what they think happened.

Before 1801, exact information on population was indeed scanty. Although *private individuals* such as Gregory King and William Davenant made estimates of the total population based on the numbers paying tax, their figures were little more than guesses. National figures on the size of population were not collected until the first *Census of 1801*. It was not until *1841* that information on ages, occupation or place of birth was collected in a way that historians have been able to use effectively. Unfortunately all kinds of changes have taken place in the collection of census information and its presentation since 1841. It is therefore often quite difficult to make *comparisons* over long periods of time of the numbers of people living in a particular place, or of changes in occupation, or even birthplace. Also the census only gives a '*snapshot*' in time taken every ten years. It does not tell us what happened *in between*. The printed census tables give basic information on the *total numbers* of people living in particular areas; the forms filled in on *each household* do survive, but they can only be examined after a hundred years has passed.

Information from the Census of population

Before 1801 there was little information of any kind available. What historians have tried to do is to combine the information in the *census* together with information collected in the *parish registers* to produce more reliable estimates. The parish registers are books kept in each Church of England parish church, recording the numbers of people who were married, baptised and buried in the church. The registers record the date, names and ages of the people and sometimes other information, such as occupations, or the cause of death. Historians have used this information to carefully reconstitute the history of individual families and to estimate birth and death rates in each parish and then for the whole country. They could then estimate how many *extra* people there were each year and, *working backwards* from the census of 1801, estimate the number of people in 1799 and so on.

Information from Parish Registers

It was not until 1837, when it began *civil registration*, that the government collected for itself information on births, deaths and marriages. When historians have been able to crosscheck census and civil registration information they have found that the figures seem to be fairly accurate from about 1841, and very accurate from about 1861.

...and from Civil Registration

Individual historians did not have the time or money to examine *every* parish register, so that when historians used different ones they often disagreed about probable birth and death rates. Some historians tried to use figures from all the parish registers collected by *John Rickman*, who was in charge of the first census. Unfortunately, when it has been possible to check Rickman's figures, it has been shown that they contain lots of errors, especially in areas such as the Midlands and the North. In these areas many people were *not* members of the Church of England (such as non-conformists, and Roman Catholics) and so were not recorded in the parish registers. Until historians had more accurate information on the total size of population, on how it changed over time and on the trends in birth, death and marriage rates, it was possible to offer two basic explanations as to when and why population increased.

EARLY EXPLANATIONS OF POPULATION GROWTH

1 Increased demand for workers and increased birth rates

After 1750, industrial expansion led to a labour shortage and to higher wages which encouraged people to marry earlier. Without the widespread use of efficient methods of contraception, more children were born and the family size increased. Also young children were an asset who could work in factories and boost the family income. It was even said that systems of poor relief, like the Speenhamland System, encouraged large families because the amount of money given was linked to family size.

2 Improvements in agriculture and lower death rates

Some historians suggested that population growth began *before* 1750 because of good harvests and agricultural improvements which together increased output and lowered food prices. Death rates fell because the population had more to eat and was fitter and healthier. People could not only buy more food, but also industrial products. This encouraged the growth of industry and improvements in technology. Improvements in medical knowledge and improved hospitals led to lower death rates. Also cheaper cotton textiles and soap allowed people to keep warmer and cleaner.

We now know that *neither* of these explanations is completely accurate, although both are true in some ways. Today we have very good estimates of population before 1801 because it is possible to analyse information from hundreds of parish registers with the help of computers. Teams of historians have examined all the surviving parish registers and have carefully selected a sample of 404 registers. All the information on marriages, baptisms and burials was copied and transferred onto computer tape. Using statistical techniques like those used by opinion pollsters to predict the results of elections, historians have calculated the population for the whole country. Working *backwards* from 1871, when the census was very accurate, they have used the birth and death rates calculated from the parish registers to *estimate* the population every year back to 1540. For the years 1871 to 1801, the estimates could be *checked* against the actual census figures, so we know just how reliable the estimates are.

These new estimates are quite different from those made before. They show that population *did not grow steadily*. Before 1650, there was a rapid growth of population, but then it stopped and even fell until the 1690s when it began to grow once more. During the 1790s through to the 1840s it grew especially rapidly. Unlike earlier times, population growth since the 1690s has *continued*, though since the 1840s, the *rate* of growth has fallen. But even today, with a very low rate of growth, there seems to be no possibility of population actually declining, as it did after rapid periods of growth in medieval times or in the late seventeenth century (see Figure 2.1 and Figure 2.2).

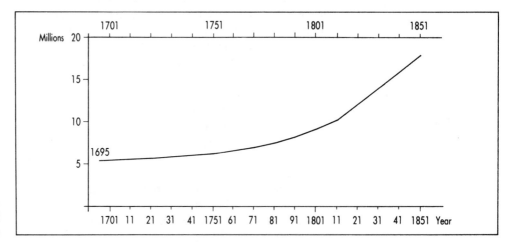

Fig. 2.1 Graph of population estimates 1695–1851 (England and Wales)

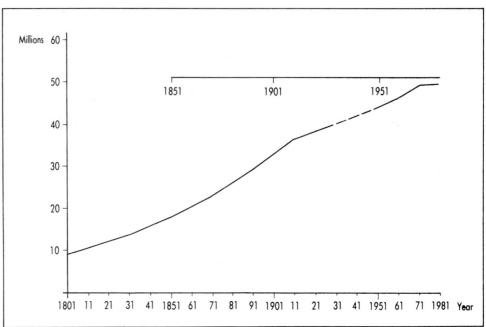

Fig. 2.2 Graph of population growth 1801–1981 (England and Wales)

2 ▷ WHY THE POPULATION INCREASED

There is no *single* explanation for the bigger population. Both an increase in birth rate *and* a decrease in death rate are important, but at different times one was more important than the other. In the eighteenth century about 60% of the increase in population was the result of an *increased number of births*.

THE AGE OF MARRIAGE

The average age of marriage of women fell from about 27 years to 24 years during the period 1650 to 1850 (see Figure 2.3). As little use was made of contraception, the result was an increase in family size of almost two children per family.

Period	Males	Females
1550-99	27.2	24.8
1600-49	28.1	26.0
1650-99	28.2	26.6
1700-49	27.5	26.2
1750-99	26.4	24.9
1800-49	25.3	23.4
1851	26.9	25.8
1861	26.4	25.4

Fig. 2.3 Age of marriage

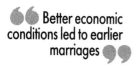

Better economic conditions led to earlier marriages

The reduction in the age of marriage was linked to better economic conditions, lower food prices and better job opportunities. Improvements in agriculture (even before 1750) boosted food production (see Chapter 3) and there was an increased demand for labour in rural districts. This resulted from both the expansion in agriculture and the extensive growth of industrial activities in the countryside before 1750. As will be made clear in Chapter 5, the growth of large scale factories in towns did not take place until after 1790. Small cotton spinning factories and all kinds of domestic outwork activities in weaving, leather working and some metals trades were well established by 1780 in pastoral rural areas in the north and midlands, where there was a large skilled labour force and water power to drive machinery. Large industrial villages are even described by *Defoe* as early as 1724–6 during his travels through Yorkshire and Lancashire.

BIRTH RATES

Since about the 1870s, despite continued reductions in the age of marriage, family size has gradually *fallen* as the practice of family limitation has become more widespread. This began amongst the upper and middle classes but slowly spread to the working classes. After World War I adverse economic conditions, together with the increased activities of groups such as the Family Planning Association, led to a more general acceptance of family

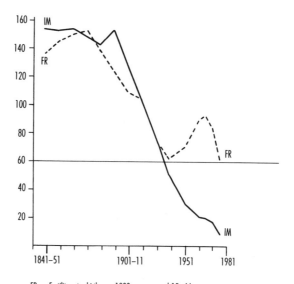

Fig. 2.4 Fertility rate and infant mortality

FR = Fertility rate: births per 1000 women aged 15–44
IM = Infant mortality: deaths of infants under 1 year old per 1000 births

planning. Since 1945, apart from the short-lived baby boom of the late 1940s and 1950s, many changes have encouraged people to *choose* to have smaller families (see Figure 2.4). The advent of the pill in the 1960s has made contraception a more 'certain' process. The desire to *postpone* child bearing to a later age has followed from the extension of higher education and the increase in the number of married women at work. These factors have been reinforced by a change in family values, with married couples becoming more anxious to maintain a high standard of living. All these factors have contributed to a *reduction* in the average family size of all social classes.

DEATH RATES

Death rates for adults did fall a little before 1800, but not by very much. Towns and cities had grown enormously in size from the eighteenth century. In 1700 there were only 68 'towns' in England and Wales with more than 2,500 people; but by 1801 there were 188, and of these 15 had a population of more than 15,000. By 1851, just about half the population lived in urban areas. In 1911 more than 80% lived in towns. The growth of towns led to *higher death rates* because housing and sanitation became worse and disease spread more easily (see Figures 2.5 and 2.6). Before 1790 death rates in *towns and cities* were *higher than* birth rates, with the rapid growth of towns taking place because of massive inwards migration from the countryside.

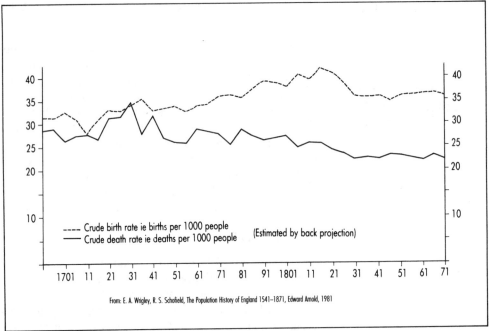

Crude birth rate ie births per 1000 people   (Estimated by back projection)
Crude death rate ie deaths per 1000 people

From: E. A. Wrigley, R. S. Schofield, The Population History of England 1541–1871, Edward Arnold, 1981

Fig. 2.5 Crude birth and death rates 1691–1871

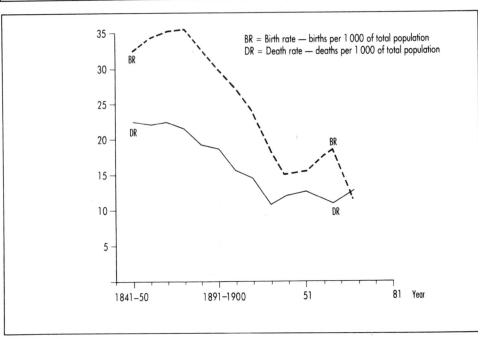

BR = Birth rate — births per 1 000 of total population
DR = Death rate — deaths per 1 000 of total population

Fig. 2.6 Birth and death rates since 1841

Apart from smallpox inoculation, used from the mid-eighteenth century, and Edward Jenner's safer method of vaccination, widely used from the later 1790s, there were no medical advances before the 1850s that helped to reduce death rates on any large scale. The only groups whose death rates fell in the eighteenth century were young adults who benefited from improved food supplies. Death rates among newly born and very young children remained very high and did not change until the late nineteenth and twentieth centuries. Improvements in the environment (see Chapter 8) did however mean a reduction in deaths from killer diseases such as measles.

Infant mortality (that is death before one year old) in 1840 was about 154 per 1000 children born, and rose to 162 in the 1850s, not falling back to 154 until 1900. Infant mortality fell rapidly in the years to 1910, when it stood at 105, and by 1938 it was as low as 53 (see Figure 2.7). Today the figure is just below 12 per 1000 children born.

MEDICAL ADVANCES

Medical advances in areas such as surgery and the development of antiseptics may have reduced death rates in *hospitals*, but only a very small proportion of all deaths took place in hospitals. It was not until the late nineteenth and early twentieth centuries that the work of *Pasteur* and *Koch* allowed doctors to identify the causes of diseases (see Figure 2.8). Slowly doctors came to understand how diseases were spread and took action to prevent this by isolation and by improvements to the environment (see Chapter 8).

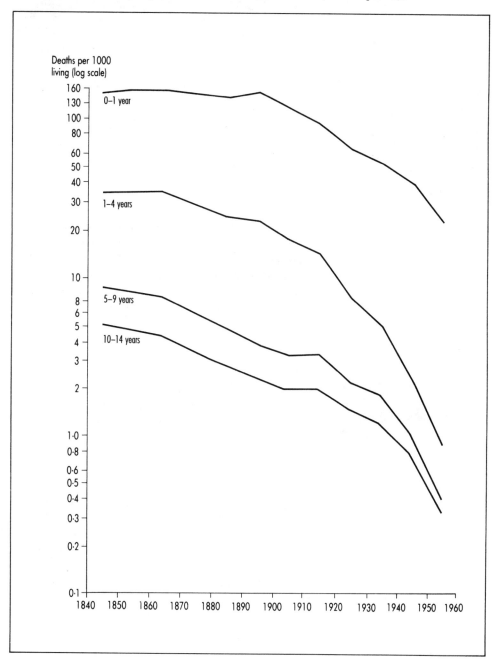

Fig. 2.7 Age Specific Mortality Rates

Death rates* (per million)

	1848–54	1901	1971	Percentage of reduction (1848-54 to 1971) attributable to each category	For each category, percentage of reduction (1848–54 to 1971) which occurred before 1901
I Caused by micro-organisms:					
1 Airborne diseases	7259	5122	619	40	32
2 Water- and food-borne diseases	3562	1931	35	21	46
3 Other conditions	2144	1415	60	13	35
Total	12965	8468	714	74	37
II Conditions not attributable to micro-organisms	8891	8490	4070	26	10
All diseases	21856	16958	5384	100	30

*Standardized to the age/sex distribution of the 1901 population

Standardized death rates (per million) from airborne diseases

	1848–54	1901	1971	Percentage of reduction from all causes (1848–54 to 1971) attributable to each disease	For each disease, percentage of reduction (1848–54 to 1971) which occurred before 1901
Tuberculosis (respiratory)	2901	1268	13	17.5	57
Bronchitis, pneumonia, influenza	2239	2747	603	9.9	Increase
Whooping cough	423	312	1	2.6	26
Measles	342	278	0	2.1	19
Scarlet fever and diphtheria	1016	407	0	6.2	60
Smallpox	263	10	0	1.6	96
Infections of ear, pharynx, larynx	75	100	2	0.4	Increase
Total	7259	5122	619	40.3	32

Fig. 2.8 Causes of Death

Scientists also developed the means to *prevent* or *reduce the likelihood of catching* various diseases by inoculation or vaccination. Medicines to cure patients who had serious infectious diseases were not developed until the later 1930s or even used on a large scale until the 1940s and 50s, as can be seen from Figures 2.7 and 2.8. Despite this, very large scale reductions in death rates did take place before 1900. The most likely explanations for this are improvements in the environment which reduced the spread of infection (see Chapter 8).

3 CHANGES IN POPULATION DISTRIBUTION

The rapid growth of population since the eighteenth century was linked to major changes in *geographical location*. Until about the 1850s almost all regions increased their population, but some regions grew much faster than others and generally towns grew even faster than rural areas. It was not, however, until the 1850s that just over 50% of the population lived in urban areas ('towns') with more than 2,500 people (Figure 2.9). All towns grew in the nineteenth century, but the towns and regions that grew the fastest were those where industry was expanding rapidly (Figure 2.10).

Changes in the geographical distribution of the population came about because of economic opportunities. As rural populations grew faster than the numbers of new jobs, men, and later whole families, were forced to look for work elsewhere. At first people only travelled as far as the nearest town, but once the tie with the countryside was broken, some families moved many times to bigger towns and cities, looking for better prospects. Even as early as the eighteenth century, many poor people had migrated as servants to America. Although this was to become even more important in the nineteenth century (see Chapter 12) most migration was *within* Great Britain. During the nineteenth century, some rural parts of Great Britain even had an *absolute fall* in population, as the numbers migrating to new areas in search of work exceeded birth rates.

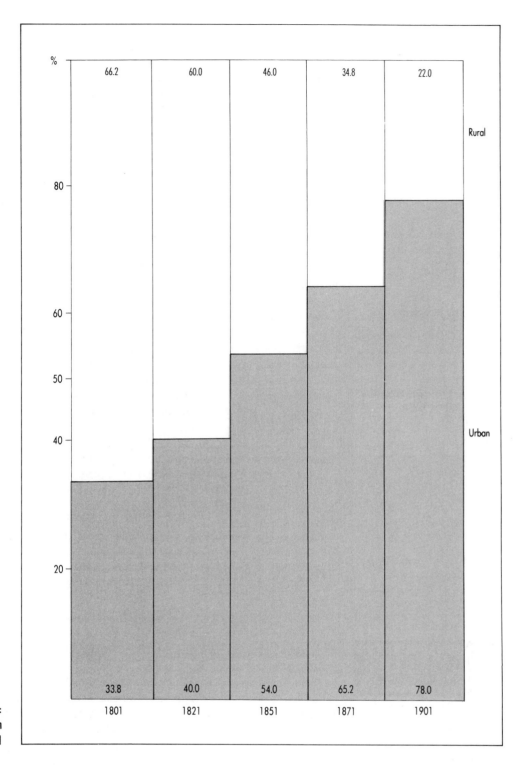

Fig. 2.9 England and Wales: Urban and rural population 1801–1901

	Population (thousands)			
	1801	*1851*	*1901*	*1931*
London	957	2,362	4,536	4,397
Manchester	70	303	645	766
Birmingham	71	233	523	1,022
Nottingham	29	57	240	269
Bristol	61	137	339	397
Sheffield	46	135	407	512
Leeds	53	172	429	483
Glasgow	77	329	776	1,088

Fig. 2.10 The growth of major cities 1801–1931

The rapid growth of cotton textiles and other related industries, such as the dyeing of cloth, and the manufacture of textile machinery, led to new concentrations of industry in the north-west and midlands. The growth of shipbuilding, iron and (later) steel, as well as coal mining, led to new industrial centres in the north-east and south Wales.

In the nineteenth century there developed for the first time *large scale urban centres* based upon concentrations of interconnected heavy industries. Other towns and ports outside these areas also grew, but some areas had special advantages in the location of raw materials (such as coal), climate, ready access to imported raw materials, highly skilled labour and good means of transportation. These advantages meant that industrial location changed and with it the main centres of population. In several regions from the mid-nineteenth century onwards, there developed groups of towns that expanded out into the countryside and gradually merged together to form a continuous urban area known as a *conurbation*.

The rapid growth of heavy industry, especially in the north, did not begin to change significantly until after 1914. The problems of the export staples and the industries linked to them (see Chapter 6) meant that employment in these industries eventually *stopped* growing rapidly. Areas such as Lancashire, South Wales, Northumberland and Merseyside became areas of high unemployment.

 **New industries, new locations**

Before the Second World War considerable growth began to take place in industries such as electrical products, motor cars and consumer durables. This led to changes in industrial location, to new patterns of employment and to shifts in population. The growth regions were concentrated in the midlands, from Birmingham and Coventry, moving south to Luton and London. These trends continued after the Second World War. Though governments since 1927 have adopted many different ideas to stop the continued decline of some regions, they have not been very successful. As a result population began to drift southwards in search of work.

Since the late 1950s, there has been a new trend. Improvements in communications, especially in road transport, and the *growth in ownership* of motor cars, have allowed many people to escape from *living in* cities. They have moved to rural or surburban areas whilst *continuing to work* in the city. This has applied to all the major cities and conurbations. Indeed in many cases *inner* cities have *lost* population. At the same time there has been a growth of *new towns*, as governments have tried to overcome the problems of over-crowding in the cities by encouraging industry and people to relocate themselves in new areas. Continuing technological developments in industry, changes in raw materials, improved communications, and changing patterns of demand for goods and services, all mean that *further* changes in the location of both industry and population are likely.

4 ▷ CONSEQUENCES OF POPULATION GROWTH

As has been shown above, the growth of population began in the late seventeenth century *before* the technological advances associated with industrialisation began to take effect. The problem that has fascinated historians is the social and economic consequences of population growth. It is not possible to make simple direct connections between the two. The changes that took place in population *interacted with* industrial and social change, being both *a cause* and *a result of* such change. A larger population, with changing characteristics of age, sex and regional distribution, created problems and opportunities for industry and society. Changes in industrial structure, and in social values, attitudes and institutions, in turn 'fed back' to population, leading to still further changes in population size and structure. Figure 2.11 tries to show some of the connections that will be examined in later chapters.

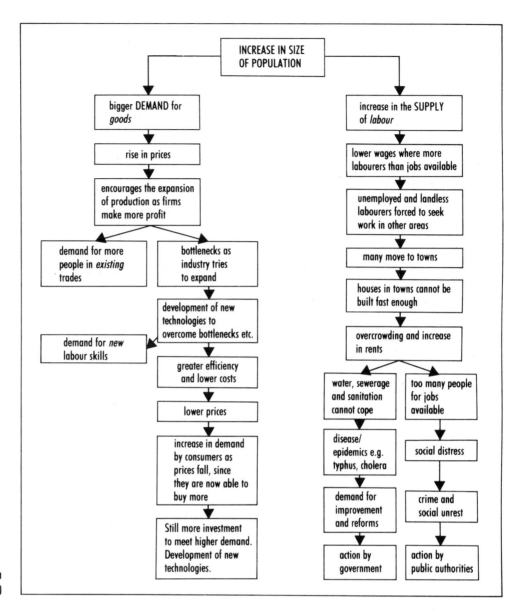

Fig. 2.11 The effects of population growth 1750–1850

EXAMINATION QUESTIONS

Examine Figures 2.7 and 2.8. With the help of these sources and your own knowledge, answer the questions below.

a) In what ways is the pattern of death rates for children ages 0–1 different from that for children aged 10–14?

b) How does the information in Figure 2.8 make it difficult to believe that the reduction in death rates was caused by improved medical knowledge? How might improved medical knowledge have helped to reduce death rates between 1850 and 1910?

c) What does the information in Figure 2.8 suggest were the most likely reasons for reductions in death rates?

TUTOR'S ADVICE

Question a) is testing basic comprehension of the source and you need to pick out the major differences between the two lines on the graphs. Note the shape of the graphs and what is happening to death rates in particular years. You only need to show differences.

Question b) asks for deduction. You may know the dates on which particular medical developments took place. Did death rates begin to fall significantly before or after these developments? Could the medical advance have been responsible for the fall in death rates? How did diseases spread? What actions could be taken to prevent the *spread* of disease even if people did not know how to *cure* a disease?

Question c) asks you to think about the reasons for the spread of disease and to suggest how to prevent such spread, by improving the environment or by the isolation of sick people.

QUESTION

This question is of the structured essay type and is designed to test overall knowledge and ability to present a reasoned argument and explanation.

With the aid of the information in Figures 2.9 and 2.10 plus your own knowledge answer the questions below.

a)   What changes took place in the geographical distribution of population between about 1750 and 1850?

b)   How do you account for these changes?

TUTOR'S ADVICE

This question is about the *distribution of population* and not about changes in size. There is therefore no need to go into detail about the reasons for the growth of population overall! In a), a brief comment that the changes in distribution occurred at a time when population increased rapidly is sufficient. Then describe *how* the geographical distribution changed. Mention the growing importance of particular regions and the increased size of towns and growth of urbanisation.

Most marks would be for part b), the explanation of these changes. Here you need to comment upon the most important features, such as the shift of population to industrial and urban areas in search of work. Explain why some areas were *especially attractive*, leading to migrants from areas where work was hard to come by. You could also mention that good employment prospects encouraged people to marry earlier so that birth rates in some areas were higher than in others.

A TUTOR'S ANSWER

QUESTION

The aim of this question is to test comprehension of sources and to use knowledge of the sources to suggest possible explanations for changes.

Examine Figures 2.3 and 2.4. With the help of this information and your own knowledge answer the questions below.

a)   Describe what happened to the age of marriage between 1700 and 1850.

b)   Why might historians have to be careful in using these figures?

c)   How did changes in the age of marriage and numbers of people getting married affect family size?

d)   Why do historians believe that changes in the age of marriage and changes in birth rates were more important than changes in death rate in explaining the growth of population before 1850?

TUTOR'S ANSWER

Note that the question expects you to use information contained in the sources, together with your general knowledge of the subject.

a)   At the beginning of the eighteenth century, the average age of marriage of *women* was 26.2 years; it gradually fell during the second half of the century to 24.9. Between 1800 and 1849, the average was only 23.4 years. The age at which *men* married was higher, about 27.5 years between 1700 and 1749, falling to 26.4 by 1799 and to 25.3 between 1800 and 1849.

b) These figures are not official government figures collected for the particular purpose of collecting information on marriages. They are *estimates* based upon a large sample of 404 parish registers of the Church of England which record the numbers of people getting married. Usually the age of the couple was given, but not everyone married in the Church of England and the sample can only give us an estimate of the likely ages. In *particular regions* the pattern might have been different. Again, if the source had given the figures for *shorter periods of time*, there might have been a different pattern to the trend.

c) In the eighteenth century, there were no really effective mechanical methods of contraception. By marrying earlier it was probable that women would have their children younger and that more children would be born in the course of the marriage.

d) Increased family size because of *earlier marriage* increased the numbers of children. This, together with a *larger proportion* of women getting married, meant that the number of births per thousand women increased. Unless there was an offsetting increase in death rates, population was bound to increase. Death rates did fall, but only in the older age groups and to a lesser extent than the increase in births and family size. There were no major advances in medicine at this time that affected any of the major diseases that caused deaths. There was also an increase in the proportion of the population living in towns, where environmental conditions were very bad and led to an increased death rate.

AGRICULTURAL PROGRESS AND DEVELOPMENTS SINCE 1700

THE PROBLEM OF SOURCES

LEVELS OF AGRICULTURAL PRODUCTION

INCREASING PRODUCTION

THE ROLE OF IMPROVERS

MACHINES AND LABOUR EFFICIENCY

ENCLOSURE

THE CORN LAWS

THE GOLDEN AGE OF ENGLISH AGRICULTURE

GETTING STARTED

The key issues regarding agriculture before 1850 concern the links between agriculture and industrialisation, and the impact of the changes that took place in agriculture upon different groups in society. As with population growth (see Chapter 2), the basic question is whether improvements in agriculture were the *causes of* population growth and industrialisation, or a *response* to population growth and the increased demand for foodstuffs and raw materials that came with industrialisation. The uncertainties arise largely because of the nature and character of the evidence available to the historian.

Previously, historians have emphasised the rapid changes in agriculture that took place in the period 1760 to 1850, suggesting that these were largely a result of population growth. Historians used the phrase 'Agricultural Revolution' to suggest that there were rapid changes in the methods of production and in land ownership. Modern research has shown that this was *not* really the case. Though the period from about 1750 did see many changes taking place in agriculture, most had *begun* to take place in the late sixteenth and seventeenth centuries. It was the growth in population and rapid industrialisation of the late eighteenth and nineteenth centuries that gave farmers the market opportunities that made it *worthwhile* investing in the new agricultural methods. In other words, changes were gradual or evolutionary, rather than sudden or revolutionary.

This process of change is a constant theme in agricultural history. Historians are concerned not only to *describe when* these changes took place, but also to *explain why* they took place, and why some changes took place more quickly than others. In explaining the reasons for change, we try to decide which were the most important of many different factors. For example, how did changes in *government policy* affect agriculture, or what part did *technological developments in industry* play in improving farm machinery and farming methods?

Changes in farming methods led to changes in the farming community. New farming methods altered the character of work on the farm and were linked to changes in land ownership. These changes fundamentally altered the social structure of farming communities and the pattern of rural life.

Students must be prepared to answer questions on one or more of the following issues:

■ How agricultural output and efficiency increased between about 1700 and 1850.

■ How enclosure was carried out and its effects upon both farm workers, tenants and landowners.

■ Why the Corn Laws were adopted, how they worked and why they were repealed.

■ The extent of, and reasons for, the 'Golden Age' in agriculture between about 1850 and 1870.

As before, in precisely which part of the examination papers these topics are to be tested will vary from syllabus to syllabus. So before you revise for the examination you must check your syllabus and the choice of options made by *your* teachers. Check which topics apply to you before revising.

1 ▷ THE PROBLEM OF SOURCES

ESSENTIAL PRINCIPLES

Agricultural historians have many different *sources* available to them. Often the sheer quantity of information makes it difficult to identify the *general trends* in agriculture. When evidence is from a map or from a description of a particular farm or region, the difficulty often lies in deciding *how typical* this information is of other areas. Agriculture is *not* a single industry. Farmers produce many different products. What a farmer produces is decided not just by the demands of consumers but also by how well particular products will grow in an area.

SPECIALIST FARMING

Even though almost all farmers produced a number of different products, kept animals and grew crops, increasingly they came to *specialise*. As a general rule, farmers in the *wetter western districts* have become *livestock farmers*, especially in the highland regions; whilst those in the *eastern lowlands* have become *arable farmers*. But this division is far too simple for any practical use and geographers and historians have identified many changes in farming regions over time, as farmers changed the crops grown according to *market opportunities*.

Specialisation increased tremendously in the later nineteenth and twentieth centuries as improvements in transport and communications made it easier and cheaper to move perishable goods to consumers. Also, technological developments in industry and improved scientific knowledge led to better tools, fertilisers and even plants suited to particular areas.

To generalise about farming is almost impossible. Farming is not one industry, but many different and often interrelated ones. What is good for livestock farmers for example might not necessarily be good for arable farmers. The varied pace of change between *different farming sectors* and between farmers who produced the *same products* makes it difficult for historians to give simple explanations. Diversity and local circumstances make it very difficult to generalise.

FARMING STATISTICS

Today, the government collects all kinds of statistics from farmers on crops grown, the amount of land used, and so on. In England and Wales this information was only collected from 1866. For a crucial stage in history, the agricultural historian has no regular national figures of production. What we *do* have are lots of descriptions by contemporaries about farming practice. Some of these are *general descriptions by travellers* such as Celia Fiennes (1662–1741) or Daniel Defoe (*c.* 1660–1731). During their travels through England, they recorded what they saw and their diaries and journals give us an invaluable description of many different parts of the country, what they looked like and how people lived and worked. Others are by *farming commentators* such as Arthur Young (1741–1820) and William Cobbett (1762–1835). We also have records of *individual landowners*, such as their account books, maps or tenancy agreements, and these tell us how particular farms were worked.

Although there were occasional *government enquiries* into agricultural problems from the sixteenth century, during the later eighteenth and nineteenth centuries the number of enquiries by *Parliamentary committees* increased tremendously. There are also *official records*, such as enclosure awards, tithe returns and even the records of cereal prices in the major market towns or of the kinds of goods imported and exported. The quantity of information becomes enormous during the nineteenth and twentieth centuries, with many more newspapers, official enquiries and government departments concerned with agricultural problems. Many more books and journals were also published concerned with good farming practice.

Historians *cannot say precisely* when or why changes took place; what they can do is to suggest when a particular idea is adopted and try to explain how and why an improved method of production came to be more generally used. Historians can also use examples of 'best practice' in farming methods to suggest how output per acre could be increased. Using modern estimates of population (see Chapter 2), we have also been able to suggest what happened to total output. Changes in population must have been accompanied by increased agricultural output and the more general adoption of better farming methods. What we *cannot* be is precise!

2 > LEVELS OF AGRICULTURAL PRODUCTION

As was shown in Chapter 2, the population of England and Wales increased substantially during the sixteenth and early seventeenth centuries, and increased continuously after about 1680. Such evidence as we have on labourers' incomes and the consumption of food, indicates that because food intake was quite low, a continued increase in population from 1680 to 1850 could *only have been possible* if agricultural output in England increased, or if there were substantial imports of food. A reduced diet per person would have increased the number of deaths from malnutrition and illness. This did *not* happen.

IMPORTS AND EXPORTS

One potential source of increased food supplies was of course *imports* from other countries. But the trade statistics show that imports of foodstuffs into Britain were insignificant until *after* the Napoleonic Wars. For most of the seventeenth and eighteenth centuries England, and later Ireland, were *exporters* of cereals. In England, from 1673 until 1773 the government gave bounties to farmers to encourage production and grain exports. Imports of corn for example (mostly from Ireland) occur *occasionally* between 1728 and 1757, but only become a regular event after 1765. Even then, in most years before 1793 exports and re-exports of corn or wheaten flour are greater then imports. The same is true for barley and oats.

    Agricultural output must therefore have increased to account for the large increase in population. Since we now have good estimates of population, we can calculate the *minimum amount of extra food needed*. We cannot be certain, but if we assume that the amount of food eaten per person *stayed the same*, then after allowing for imports and exports, grain production must have increased between 1500 and 1800 (see Figure 3.1).

INCREASE IN GRAIN PRODUCTION	DATES
25-40%	1500–1600
25-35%	1600–1700
60%	1700–1800

Fig. 3.1 Increase in grain production 1500–1800

3 > INCREASING PRODUCTION

USING MORE LAND

One simple way to increase production would have been to bring *more land* into use. This certainly happened, especially during periods like the Napoleonic Wars when food prices increased considerably. The land brought in to use could have been 'waste' land; however, so called 'waste' land was usually already used for rough grazing. What was really happening was that *marginal land* was put to *better use*. Some marshlands, such as the fens, were drained from the late seventeenth century, and woodlands cleared and used for arable farming. Again, this was really a *change of land use*, since both the fens and forest areas already produced agricultural products; now however they produced grain and other arable crops.

    It seems unlikely that very much more land was brought into use during the eighteenth and nineteenth centuries, since a great deal of land was taken out of agricultural use and converted to industrial and urban uses. The land under cultivation cannot have increased by more than 7% between about 1690 and 1800, and 5% is more likely. How then did domestic output increase to feed the people?

IMPROVED EFFICIENCY

It can only have been done if farmers became *more efficient* and found ways to grow more food per acre. That is they *increased yield per acre*. The rough estimates from the population figures show that output per acre had to increase by at least 44% between 1700 and 1800 for the population to have been fed even at the *same level*. Since in all probability labourers in 1800 were better fed than in 1700, this is likely to be an *underestimate* of the improvement in yield.

NEW FODDER CROPS

The improvement in output/yield per acre was the result of farmers finding ways to grow more food *without* reducing the fertility of the soil. This was done in two main ways.

Putting marginal land to better use

Firstly, farmers used *new crops* and *developed rotations*, so that it was no longer necessary for part of the land to be left *fallow*. Most of these changes were influenced by the Dutch during the later fifteenth and early sixteenth centuries. They developed a whole range of new 'artificial grasses' (clover, lucerne, sainfoin and rye-grass) and root crops (turnips in the sixteenth century and swedes in the late eighteenth century). Secondly, these crops *increased the supply of animal fodder*. Root crops were especially useful because they were harvested in the late autumn/early winter when the animals fed off the green tops in the fields. Also the roots could be lifted and stored over the winter. Farmers could then increase the size of their sheep and cattle herds and more especially feed them over the winter when fresh grass was not available.

Many of the new crops not only provided more animal fodder but helped to maintain soil fertility. Farmers did not know *why* this happened, just that it *did*. Today, we know that plants such as clover and leguminous plants such as peas fix nitrogen directly from the air and store it in their roots, but this was not discovered until the 1840s. There are indications in the Customs and Excise records of turnip, beets of various kinds, clover and other special grass seeds, being imported into the East Anglian ports during the sixteenth century. Certainly by the 1630s in Essex, Suffolk, Norfolk and Lincolnshire, such crops were used quite widely.

SOIL FERTILITY

The increased numbers of animals, especially sheep, gave farmers more manure which maintained soil fertility. Farmers also used all kinds of rotten materials and nightsoil collected from the towns as fertiliser, but as yet there were no 'artificial' chemicals that could be used. There is however plenty of written evidence to suggest that farmers from Roman times used all kinds of products such as dried sea-weed, soot, and marl (burnt clay and chalk) to improve the quality of light sandy soils or sour peaty lands. Marl was widely used in East Anglia and Cheshire. It bound the soil together so that it held the moisture and became more fertile, especially when farmers added humus or mixtures of straw and manure. On heavy clay soils farmers added burnt limestone and sand to make it easier to work and less liable to become waterlogged. Even today, many small lime kilns can be found on some farms. As canals improved communications after the 1760s, it became easier to buy lime from large scale commercial producers.

Farmers on the heavy clay soils in the midlands found that most of the new root crops did not do well in their heavy, wet, cold clay soils. Root crops need well-drained, sandy soils. Artificial grasses were widely used on the clay lands and some regions specialised in livestock rather than arable products. In many parts of the west country and midlands, farmers close to streams and rivers were also using water meadows. This meant that they flooded their land over the winter, giving a better crop of early grass in the spring for sheep and cattle.

ANIMAL BREEDING

Big improvements took place in animal breeding. Specialist animals were now bred for a particular product, such as meat, wool or milk. Historians gave especial importance to the work of individual breeders such as Robert Bakewell (1725–95), the 'Wizard' of Dishley, Leicestershire. Bakewell pioneered the selective breeding of sheep and cattle; he took sheep and cattle and bred like with like so that *particular qualities* became dominant. Unfortunately in many ways Bakewell was *not* successful; specialist breeds such as his Longhorn cattle did not reproduce very well and had died out by the early nineteenth century. Also his New Leicestershire sheep, though they grew rapidly and put on weight, were not popular because their meat was very fatty.

Surprisingly, although Bakewell's ideas were widely publicised, especially by Arthur Young, Bakewell himself was very secretive about his breeding methods. He covered up what he regarded as failures and did not always explain in detail *how* he achieved his results. Despite this, his ideas were taken up by others. Breeding became more systematic with the development of specialist breeds and stud books to keep track of the breeding lines.

Bakewell was not the only breeder. George Culley (1753–1813) of Northumberland adopted his methods and improved Bakewell's sheep; John Ellman developed the Southdown breed of sheep and David Dunn the Blackfaced sheep. Later in the nineteenth century breeders realised that even better animals could be produced by *crossing* rams of one particular breed with ewes of another. Sheep with particular qualities, but often *without the faults* of pure bred animals, were bred and animals suited to local conditions were developed by cross breeding. Similar developments happened in cattle. In Durham, the Colling brothers began with cross-bred animals with a particular characteristic and then adopted rigorous pedigree breeding to produce specialist Shorthorn meat cattle.

4 ▷ THE ROLE OF IMPROVERS

Early historians suggested that 'Improvers' were important in encouraging the adoption of both new crops and rotations. In fact, the influence of men such as Thomas Coke (1750–1842) of Holkham in Norfolk and 'Turnip' Townshend (1674–1738) has been greatly exaggerated. We know that the basic ideas and most of the new crops were developed on the continent, especially in Holland during the sixteenth century. These ideas were already known in England by the 1630s. Sir Richard Weston for example adopted the methods he saw used during his tours of the Continent on his Surrey estates in the 1630s and 40s. His book *'Discours of the Husbandrie used in Brabant and Flanders'* published in 1649 was widely read amongst the gentry and his ideas were adopted by large land owners, especially after the Civil War and certainly long before 1750. Weston's book was only one among many agricultural manuals. Some, such as *'Markhams Masterpiece'* (1636), were of little practical value but others did offer practical advice on many different aspects of farming. These books included John Norden's *The Surveyor's Dialogue*, (1608), Walter Blith's *'The English Improver'* (1649), *'The English Improver Improved'* (1652), Joseph Blagrave's *'The Epitome of the Art of Husbandry'* (1685) and John Worlidges's *'Systema Agriculturae'* (1698). Walter Blith was probably the most widely read of all and he described the use of water meadows, the drainage of wet soils, the practice of enclosure, and the use of artificial grasses and root crops. In other words Blith and others had already outlined most of the so called 'new' ideas which late eighteenth century 'improvers' advocated during the so called 'Agricultural Revolution'.

> " Early contributions to farming methods "

The improvers were therefore not really offering new ideas at all; rather they were popularisers of practices that had, in most cases, already been proven. Their position as large land owners in a region allowed them to *insist* that tenants adopted the farming methods of which they approved. Many encouraged agricultural competitions and county shows. Knowledge of good practical ideas became more readily available and, with the increased commercial attitude and opportunities of the late seventeenth and eighteenth centuries, more widely adopted.

The problem for the historian is that though many ideas were *known* by at least 1630, it is not clear how *widely practised* they were. Before 1700, it seems that the use of these modern methods and ideas was restricted to particular areas and the larger scale farmers. It was the well read, large scale gentry farmers, trying to farm their land as profitably as possible who were aware of the opportunities and who had the capital to invest in new practices. Their example was often followed by many of their tenants. By 1800 the 'new' methods were used in most parts of England, and a whole host of developments appeared after 1800.

5 ▷ MACHINES AND LABOUR EFFICIENCY

The other major aspect to improvements in farming was a *lower cost of production* as a result of increased labour efficiency. Many of the new farming techniques were *labour intensive*, yet the number of people employed directly in agriculture increased more slowly than production and much more slowly than the growth of population.

FARMING TOOLS

Alongside *better methods* came *better tools* and the need for a more skilled labour force. In the eighteenth century, almost all the tools used by farmers were hand tools. But from the mid-seventeenth century there were considerable improvements in the implements pulled by animals. Horses gradually replaced oxen, and specialist ploughs and harrows suited to particular soils and designed for particular jobs were now available. Most were made almost wholly out of metal. Developments in the iron industry between 1690 and 1800 helped to make tools much cheaper and more readily available.

Attempts to produce drills to sow seeds are recorded in Italy in 1566. But in England, despite all kinds of patents given to inventors in the 1620s and 1630s none seem to have worked. Blith does describe various new ways of sowing, but the first practical device seems to have been that of John Worlidge described in 1669. The most publicised drill was developed by Jethro Tull and described in his book *'Horse Hoeing Husbandry'* (1733). This drill (see Figure 3.2(a)) was pulled by a horse and sowed three rows of seed simultaneously. Tull appeared to have successfully overcome the problem of controlling the regular flow of

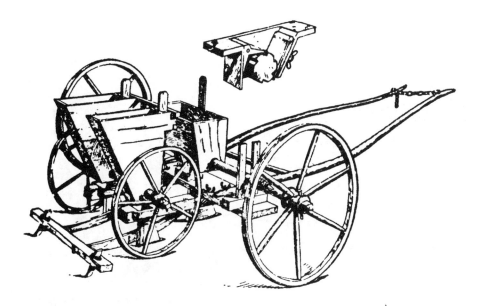

Fig. 3.2 a) Jethro Tull's Seed Drill

Fig. 3.2 b) The Seed Drill of William Ellis

This four Wheel Drill Plow, with a Seed and a Manure Hopper, was first Invented in the Year 1745. and is now in Use with W.ᵐ Ellis at Little Gaddesden near Hempstead in Hertfordshire, where any person may View the same. It is so light that a Man may Draw it, but Generally drawn by a pony or little Horse

Fig. 3.3 Sowing – sheet and hand – sowing corn

From Stephenson's Book of the Farm 1876

seed from the hopper to the furrow by a simple axle and spring mechanism. Tull's system was not however widely adopted in England until the later eighteenth century. It seems there were problems in getting the machine to work properly. However, there were numerous other drills, such as those by William Ellis (Figure 3.2(b)), James Sharpe and John Randall, though many of these machines were expensive to buy and unreliable.

It really required changes in the iron and metal industries before cheap, strong and reliable seed drills were available, as was the case from the 1770s. The big advantage of the seed drill was that because seeds were planted in straight rows, it was much easier to weed. Tull developed a horse drawn hoe. It was found that regular weeding led to better crops and Tull believed that this was because the plough/hoe used for weeding ground up the soil into small particles that the roots could 'eat'. This of course is nonsense and, even in the eighteenth century, many chemists realised that Tull was a bit of a crank. Tull's *explanation* was wrong but his machine and similar *machines* were successful. This was due to fewer weeds removing competition for nutrients in the soil, so that the crops grew better. Also by breaking up the soil, regular hoeing stopped land becoming waterlogged, so that it was easier for the plants to absorb moisture.

Seed drills were much quicker than hand broadcast sowing (see Figure 3.3) and also made harvesting easier, though it was not until the 1830s that the advantages were really noted with the gradual use of reapers. Horse-drawn mechanical reapers were invented in America by Cyrus McCormick and John Hussey in 1833/4 (see Figure 3.4(a)). However, these were not widely used until the 1850s, even in America. In England, even as late as 1875, only about 50% of the land was harvested by machine. Labour was cheap in England and the fields were often too small to make the use of mechanical reapers worthwhile. They were not cost effective in England until the later 1870s.

Fig. 3.4 a) McCormick's Reaping Machine 1851

Fig. 3.4 b) Mowing with the scythe

One of the biggest changes in harvesting came in the 1790s when cheaper scythes became available because of changes in their manufacture. Scythes were much quicker to use than sickles; gangs of men could now cut the corn or hay about four times faster than before (see Figure 3.4(b)).

FARMING MACHINERY

After the wheat had been harvested it needed to be threshed. Just as broadcast sowing was replaced by the seed drill, so by the 1790s horse, and eventually steam, threshers were introduced instead of hand threshing and winnowing. The earliest attempts at machine threshing are described in 1735 in Scotland, but the first really effective thresher was developed in 1758 by a Mr Stirling of Perthshire. This machine used four flails to beat the corn and these were driven by a water wheel. Other effective machines were produced by a Mr Ilderton of Alnwick and Mr Oxley of Flodden during the 1770s. It was not until 1786 that Andrew Meikle used the ideas developed by Ilderton to produce an even more effective thresher. Instead of using flails to beat the corn this thresher passed it between rollers. Water-powered threshing machines were widely adopted in Northumberland by the late 1780s. Portable horse-powered threshers and winnowing machines were in general use throughout England by the 1790s.

Mechanical threshing machines, even when they were hand-powered, greatly reduced the number of labourers required after harvest. In August 1830 there was opposition by

Kentish farm labourers to the new machinery because it took away their main source of winter work. This led to riots and machine breaking. These Captain Swing riots were quickly copied throughout most of the country and a fear of social unrest led the government to begin enquiries into rural poverty and the operation of the Poor Laws.

The 1830s and 1840s saw enormous improvements in all kinds of farm machinery. Specialist agricultural machine companies, such as Ransome's, exhibited ploughs, drills, threshers and later reaper binders at all the major agricultural shows. By the 1840s many pieces of agricultural processing equipment were driven by steam traction engines, but most farmers continued to use hand- or horse-powered machines until the late nineteenth century. Developments in the iron and metals industries also meant that numerous machines for cutting root crops, twisting straw, etc. became available and increased the productivity of farm workers. Even by 1840, whilst mechanised equipment was still limited and most jobs were done using hand tools, these tools were so much better than earlier equipment that the time needed to complete many farm jobs was greatly reduced.

6 > ENCLOSURE

The history of enclosure provides many problems for historians, though the basic reasons for enclosure are reasonably clear. Landowners believed they could increase their incomes and profits if the old communal farming methods of the open fields were done away with and land ownership was made individual. It is *not*, however, clear when these changes took place or what specific factors were involved.

OPEN-FIELD FARMING

In the middle ages, most of the land was farmed communally in 'open-field' villages, rather than by individual farmers owning fields enclosed by hedges or ditches. Slowly the amount of land farmed in this open-field way decreased. By 1530 large areas of land were already enclosed and this continued throughout the sixteenth century. The high price of wool during the sixteenth century encouraged enclosures since most enclosures were for conversion to sheep pasture, through in the 1590s conversion to arable also increased. By 1700 at least half of the land in England and Wales had already been enclosed *by agreement*; during the eighteenth century, most of the rest was enclosed by *Acts of Parliament*. The two major periods for such Acts were from 1750 to 1780 and 1790 to 1830. The first period mostly concerned the heavy clay lands in the Midlands, especially Northamptonshire, Warwickshire and Leicestershire, and the east and south-east Midlands in general. The second period completed the enclosure of the Midlands and also included the lighter, sandy soils of East Anglia, Lincolnshire, parts of Yorkshire, Cumbria and the south-eastern counties close to London (Surrey, Middlesex and Berkshire).

In the open-field system, landowners and tenants/leaseholders had *individual strips* in each of the large fields and also had *shared areas* of pasture, woodland or rough grazing known as 'waste'. They often had rights on these common lands to collect fire wood or to graze a certain number of animals. The fields were farmed communally in a rotation (see Figure 3.5) that was traditional. There was a village *court* that ensured that the rules, customs and traditions of this communal system were kept.

Many historians have suggested that open-field villages were inefficient. Villagers had little choice over which crops to plant or when the sowing and harvesting was to be done. This was decided by the village court. The number of animals that could be kept was quite small and the methods of farming were wasteful. Villagers had to waste time travelling from strip to strip, and land could be wasted on paths and tracks between fields. Any bad farming by one person would also affect everyone. Stray animals helped to spread disease and often ruined crops. The small scale of production limited opportunities for more efficient farming methods using the new implements.

In fact it seems that many of these possible inefficiencies were exaggerated. Many changes *did* take place in the open fields. Strips were consolidated together and some farmers gradually extended their holdings by buying out less efficient farmers. This is called *engrossment*. The new fodder crops and rotations did not require specialised machinery, so it was possible to introduce the new ideas even into the open fields. Of course it would clearly be easier to adopt *new* methods and ideas when every change did *not* have to be agreed upon by the whole of the village.

Criticisms of the open-field system

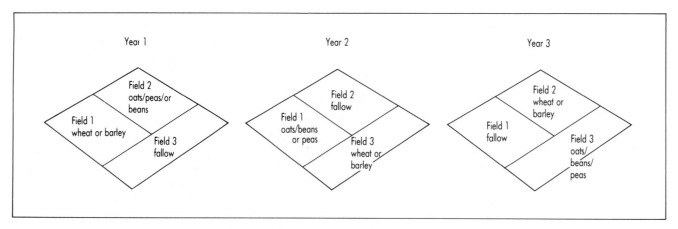

Fig. 3.5 Principle of Crop rotation with Fallow

PARLIAMENTARY ENCLOSURE

As the advantages of the new methods in reducing cost of production became increasingly obvious, so also did the growth of population. Higher prices gave better opportunities for profit to the more adventurous farmers with capital to invest in the new ideas. Large landowners realised that it would be much easier for them to increase rents if the land was farmed by tenants farming *larger areas*; tenants would then have the opportunity to make more profit and thus be willing to pay higher rents. As early as 1604 at Radipole in Dorset, landowners arranged an enclosure by Act of Parliament. Many areas were *not* enclosed even by the middle of the eighteenth century, and attention began to turn to Parliament to speed up the gradual process of enclosure.

In England there were over 5250 private or public Acts dealing with enclosures. About 85% of these took place before 1830, but *General Acts of Enclosure* in 1836, 1840 and 1845 simplified the process of parliamentary enclosure and made it easier to enclose areas *not already enclosed*. In Cambridgeshire, and Oxfordshire over 10% of all enclosures took place after 1830.

Obtaining a Private Act for enclosure

Each Act was passed separately and eventually a customary general routine was established. If at least 80% of landowners and the owners of the tithe petitioned Parliament for a *Private Act*, then it was likely to be approved. Often 80% of the landowners was only one or two people, whereas there might have been lots of tenants and leaseholders. In many cases the tenants and leaseholders counter-petitioned Parliament to try and *stop* the Act being passed. After discussion by a Committee of M.Ps., which sometimes led to amendments, the Act was normally passed without difficulty and became law. Parliament appointed *Commissioners* who were often representatives of the major land and tithe owners. They surveyed the land and established who were the legal owners with title to the land and a share in the common fields. The land was then re-distributed according to the value of the land held by each person, the value of the tithes and the value of commoners' rights. Often, owners took this opportunity to exchange lands and to consolidate their holdings into compact farms. The enclosure was legally binding even on the large numbers of minority farmers and tenants who may have opposed the enclosure.

THE COSTS OF ENCLOSURE

Parliamentary enclosure was expensive, costing between about 28 shillings (£1.40) and £5 per acre in the eighteenth century to cover all legal fees and parliamentary costs. There were also lots of expenses *after* enclosure, for building new roads, hedges or ditches, and for putting in whatever improvements (such as new barns) that the landowners needed. It also took *time* to complete an enclosure, often as long as five or six years from petition to final enclosure. In general it seems that the Commissioners acted fairly, according to the evidence available to them.

Many small landowners were *unable to afford the costs of enclosure* and therefore ended up selling their portion to larger landowners. Often, small owners and especially customary copy-holders or tenants were *unable to prove title* to the land and their right to share in the common fields. They therefore lost all their privileges and were forced off the land, either to become landless labourers or to move to one of the expanding towns.

It seems unlikely that enclosures led to rural depopulation. Enclosures created many jobs since many of the new methods were in fact labour-intensive. The problems occurred where enclosure led to a *change of land use* from arable to pasture, which meant fewer workers were needed in the long term. This did not stop people, like Arthur Young, from

66 Results of
enclosure 99

criticising enclosures which forced many poor people to give up their small-holdings. Many people who had just scraped a living by working as farm labourers and by keeping a cow or pig on the common land, fell into a worse state of poverty when they lost their commoners' rights. Even many wealthy landowners feared that enclosure weakened the social ties between the gentry and the labourer. This was because many farmers began to stop the practice of 'boarding in' and 'payments in kind' to their labourers, and some even hired people on a daily basis. Some of the gentry suggested that this would lead to disruption and social unrest as traditional ties and values were broken.

Though some areas *were* depopulated, especially in the early nineteenth century, overall the numbers of people living and working in rural areas continued to increase until at least 1861. Unfortunately, the population grew *faster than* job opportunities. Even if there had been no enclosure many people would still have found it necessary to move to other areas, such as cities, where there were jobs. Information on enclosure is shown in Figures 3.6 and 3.7.

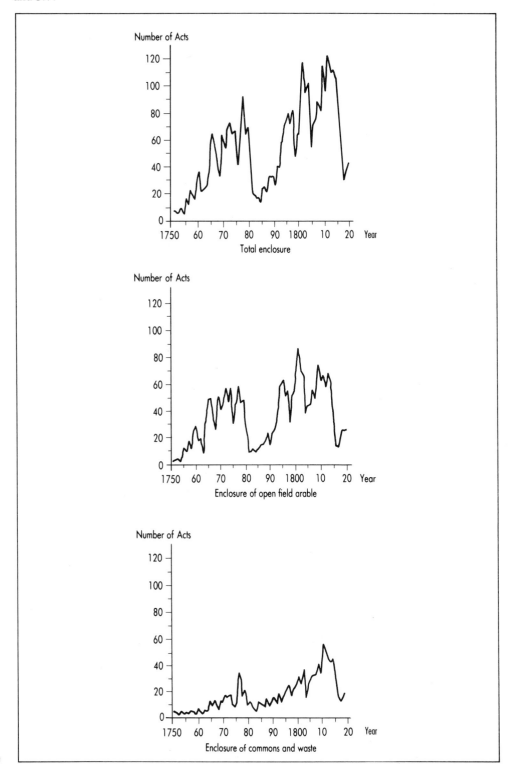

Fig. 3.6 Graphs on enclosure

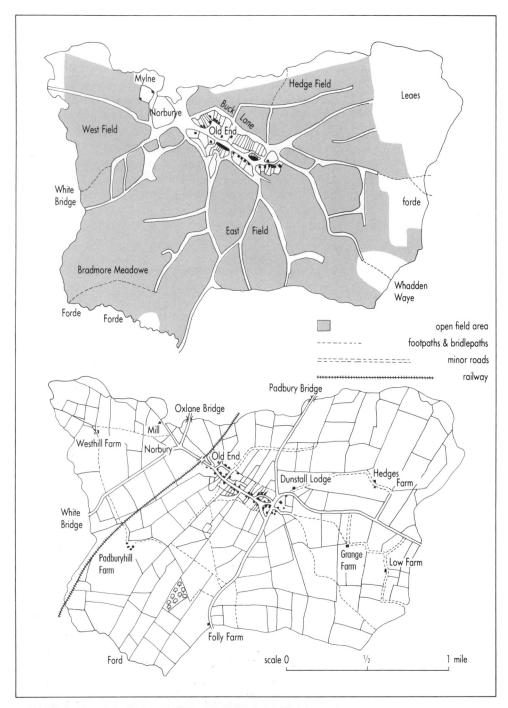

Fig. 3.7 a) The effects of enclosure: above, the open field parish of Padbury, 1591. Below, the parish today showing fields and outlying farmsteads built after the enclosure of 1796.

Fig. 3.7 b) Aerial photograph of enclosure at Padbury

7 THE CORN LAWS

One of the big changes that took place during the Revolutionary and Napoleonic Wars with France (1783–1815) was that Parliament became more interventionist in commercial policies. The wars were also marked by periods of high prices for agricultural products, largely because poor weather led to poor harvests at a time when population was increasing rapidly. These shortages led Parliament to abandon its earlier policies of export bounties and instead to return to prohibitions on exports and to restrictions on imports in order to encourage home production of wheat instead of imports. The need to increase revenue also encouraged the government to impose import duties on foreign grains. In any case, it became increasingly difficult to import cereals from Europe due to the rapid growth of population in Europe increasing demand there, and to the disruption of merchant shipping caused by the Napoleonic Wars.

The period of rising demand for agricultural products and rising prices (see Figure 3.8) encouraged many farmers to invest heavily in enclosure, to plough up marginal land and to borrow heavily to invest in new buildings and equipment. Good harvests in England during 1812–14 meant an increased supply, as the benefits of the earlier increases in land under cultivation and investments in new methods came into effect. However, the boom in agriculture came to an end as the increased supply caused prices to fall; this led to rising protests from farmers burdened with war-time taxes and high interest charges, but now receiving falling profits. Since Parliament was dominated by M.Ps. from the farming districts, various proposals were made to alleviate the distress amongst farmers who complained of excessive taxes and interest charges at a time of falling prices.

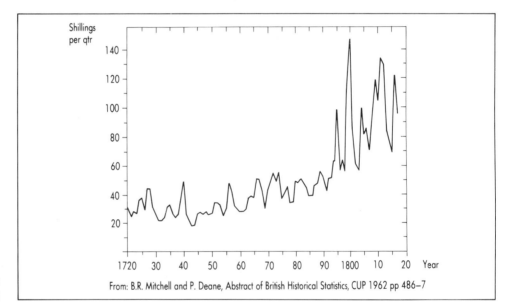

From: B.R. Mitchell and P. Deane, Abstract of British Historical Statistics, CUP 1962 pp 486–7

Fig. 3.8 Graph of cereal prices during period 1720–1820

Eventually Parliament passed the *Corn Law* of 1815 (see Figure 3.9). This Act was supposed to stabilise prices, by restricting imports when prices in England were low, and allowing imports when prices rose. In 1822, and again in 1828, the law was altered to make it more effective and to discourage speculators.

In 1815 Parliament passed a law which became known as the 'Corn Law'. No corn could come into Britain from overseas *until* British grain reached a certain price. These prices were:

Barley	40 shillings a quarter*
Oats	26 shillings a quarter
Rye	53 shillings a quarter
Wheat	80 shillings a quarter

The Corn Law was changed in 1828.
A *sliding scale* of tax was now imposed on corn imports. The *higher* the price of foreign grain, the *lower the tax* imposed on it when it was imported into Britain.

* a quarter being a measure of corn, equal to 64 gallons or 8 bushels.

Fig. 3.9 Details of the Corn Laws

THE ANTI-CORN LAW LEAGUE

Reasons for opposing the Corn Laws

Critics of the Corn Laws, such as Ricardo, said that the law kept prices artificially high. In the 1830s the growth of large scale manufacturers and of a class of landless labourers dependent upon wages to purchase food led to complaints by industrialists that high prices for basic foodstuffs encouraged demands for wage rises. Higher wages increased costs and reduced profits and employment. Such views led to the formation of the *Anti-Corn Law League* in 1838. This was an organisation of wealthy Manchester cotton manufacturers, including Thomas Potter the town's first mayor. The first President was George Wilson, a starch and gum manufacturer who really organised the League and co-ordinated its various publicity and propaganda campaigns throughout the country. The League included radicals and M.Ps. such as Richard Cobden, John Bright and Charles Villiers. With plenty of money and able speakers, the organisation mounted a campaign in Parliament to repeal the Corn Laws and at elections sponsored candidates. They were helped in this by improved posts and communications and new printing technologies. These made it easier both to distribute propaganda and for well known speakers to travel about the country.

The increased representation in Parliament of the urban areas under the 1832 Reform Act, gradually gave manufacturers and the urban interests a bigger voice in Parliament. The speeches of the League campaigners attacked the logic of the Corn Laws. They also criticised the laws for protecting a privileged class, the landowners, against the interests of the workers and manufacturing classes who had to pay higher prices to protect the aristocratic landowners.

It came to be generally accepted that the Corn Laws were *against* Britain's commercial interests; not only did they lead to higher prices and wages in urban areas, but they cut exports of British goods overseas. The *Free Traders* argued very convincingly that foreign producers of cereals in Europe and America could only afford to buy British goods if Britain allowed them to export their products to Britain. It was shown that if each country specialised in the products that they produced best, everyone would benefit. Britain, as the major producer of a wide range of textiles and manufactured products in the 1840s would gain tremendously by specialising on manufactures and exporting the surplus produced. The problem was that the government needed the *revenues* from taxing imports and could not afford to offend the commercial interests of the farming community.

Various reforms were made in 1842 by William Gladstone as Chairman of the Board of Trade after a report by the *Select Committee on Import Duties 1838–42* allowed grain to be imported from the Empire at a nominal rate of duty. It was, however, the appalling distress and starvation caused in Ireland and parts of England between 1842 and 1846, with the repeated failure of the potato crop because of blight, which finally pushed Robert Peel the Prime Minister to change the law. Despite opposition from many members of his own Tory Party led by Benjamin Disraeli, Peel in 1846 reduced the import duty on corn and other cereals to a nominal 1 shilling (5p) a quarter. By 1849 most of the restrictions and prohibitions on a wide range of imports and exports had also been reduced and Britain effectively became a free trading nation.

THE EFFECTIVENESS OF THE CORN LAWS

On paper at least, the Corn Laws would seem to have been effective. Corn imports into England throughout the 1820s, 30s, and 40s were not very great. Certainly cereal prices in many parts of Europe were lower than in Britain and even if allowance is made for transport costs, it seemed that but for the Corn Laws cereals *could* have been imported into Britain at a profit.

In fact it can be shown that the Corn Laws were *not* very effective. The price of corn after 1815 often fell substantially despite the Corn Laws (Figure 3.10). Again after 1815 our *net imports* of wheat and flour were often as large, or larger, than they were *before* the Corn Laws (Figure 3.11):

■ grain prices were collected from particular markets and the prices of corn averaged out over a five week period. It was possible for *corn dealers* to buy large quantities of cheap corn in small market towns. This abuse was made more difficult in 1822 when the number of market towns from which prices were collected was increased.

- a system of *bonded warehouses* was available at the docks. Dealers could import corn into Britain from Europe when prices were low, and keep it stored in bonded warehouses at the dockside. This meant they did not have to pay any import duty until the corn *left* the dock area. They could wait until prices had risen so that *no duty* was payable and then flood the market with the corn released from store.

Fig. 3.10 Average Prices of Corn 1780–1910

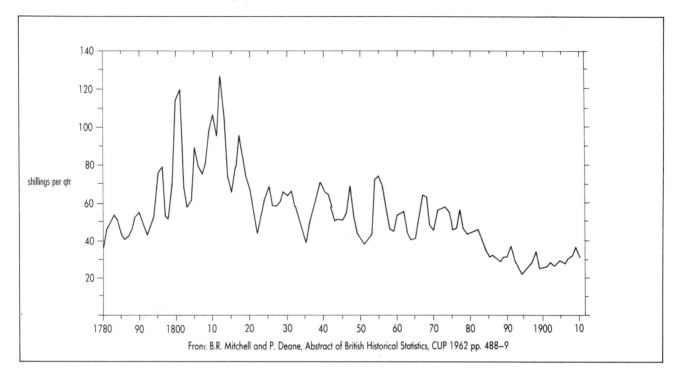

From: B.R. Mitchell and P. Deane, Abstract of British Historical Statistics, CUP 1962 pp. 488–9

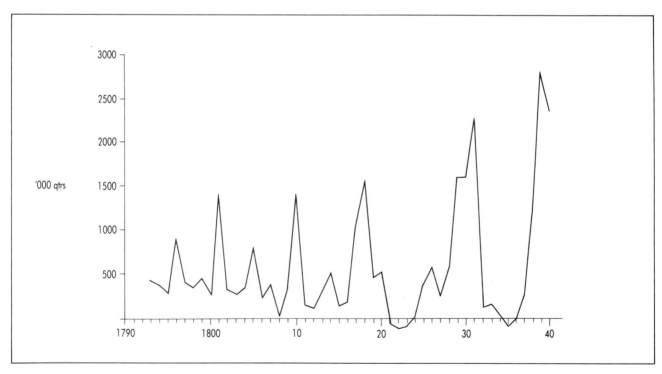

Fig. 3.11 UK net imports of Wheat and Flour (ie imports less exports)

Corn was imported into Britain in 25 of the 32 years between 1815 and 1847, but only in six of those years did more than 50% of the corn imported pay any duty *other than at the lowest rate*, and in 13 of those years 75% of imported corn paid *no import duty at all*. The corn laws did not really keep out foreign corn, except when the home prices were very low and imports probably would not have happened anyway. What *did* happen was that corn dealers ensured that imports only occurred when *prices were at their highest*. They could then make big profits, since the cost of storing corn in the bonded warehouses was not very high. What kept English prices low was *not* imports of foreign corn, but the high levels of domestic production.

8 THE GOLDEN AGE OF ENGLISH AGRICULTURE

The first half of the nineteenth century was a difficult time for many farmers. Corn prices were low and it was often a period of distress for farm labourers who faced low wages and long periods of high unemployment. Some farmers, however, did very well. Those who had invested in new methods and reduced their costs of production found that they could make good profits, even at low prices. Even between 1800–1840, innovation continued and farmers were able to expand production. It was the farmers who did *not* invest in new methods or whose land was unsuitable for the new tools that faced problems. Many farmers believed that the repeal of the Corn Laws would lead to continued depression, but in fact this did not happen. Imports of cereals and flour did increase steadily, but not by as much as many expected and prices did not fall dramatically over the long term. Farmers who invested to reduce costs or who grew less cereals in favour of other crops found that they could make a good living.

Imports did not increase because the growth of population in Europe meant that the large surpluses of cheap cereals that *had* existed were now used locally. In any case, internal transport facilities and dock handling facilities in Europe *could not have coped* with a massive increase in exports, even if surpluses for export had been available. During the 1850s and 60s, wars in Europe also disrupted supplies. As a result of these factors, Britain remained a market still dominated by domestic corn.

Surprisingly, the trade figures show that the onset of the American Civil War resulted in increased exports of American cereals and flour to Britain. This was because there were bumper harvests in America at a time when European harvests were poor. Also, northern farmers in America who had previously sold grain to the southern states now needed to find alternative outlets. The Union government, especially in the early years of the war, encouraged exports in order build up its holdings of foreign currency to buy weapons and uniforms that it was as yet unable to supply from American manufacturers.

There was also an expansion of imports into Britain in the later 1860s when the first series of really poor harvests led to a general increase in prices and to more imports of all kinds of cereals for flour and animal feeding stuffs. However, it was not until the 1870s that British farmers began to experience a massive flood of cheap foreign imports.

HIGH FARMING

Increased demand for farm products

British farmers did quite well in the 1850s and 60s. Demand increased as both population and incomes rose. Consumers began to purchase a wider variety of more expensive vegetables, meat and dairy products. The prices of cereals and grain were at best static, or falling slightly; but for milk, butter, cheese, eggs and meat, prices were generally steadily rising. The growth of large scale urban markets at first only benefited those farmers *close to towns*. But gradually, as railway lines extended from the cities to the rural areas, it became possible to transport perishable goods such as milk even without refrigeration (see Chapter 6). Farmers whose land was suitable for market gardening, or for dairy or livestock farming, and who had access to capital, began to take advantage of the new opportunities.

Other developments *outside* agriculture also helped farmers. Improvements in the manufacture and design of equipment meant better and cheaper machinery and tools. The government, as part of the repeal of the Corn Laws, provided cheap loans for drainage, though Caird and others complained that it was not enough. More especially, many farmers adopted what became known as 'High Farming'. That is, by careful investment in fertilisers, better animal feeding stuffs and improved buildings, they *increased output* and *reduced costs of production*. The typical farm in mid-Victorian England was the *mixed farm*, but increasingly the larger scale commercial farmer was becoming more dependent upon products bought off the farm, so that in some regions *specialisation* was developing.

FERTILISERS AND SEED DEVELOPMENT

Farmers bought fertilisers in enormous quantities. From about the 1790s, it was usually in the form of crushed bones cut up into half inch chips or ground into powder. The bones were supplied by local rag-and-bone merchants. However, during the 1820s most bones were imported from Europe. In the 1830s, the German chemist Leibig complained that English merchants were rifling the battle fields of Europe and ransacking the catacombs of Sicily searching for bones. Imports also came from Russia and South America, with the bones of cattle now added to English imports of hides and tallow. By the 1840s there were also imports of guano (dried bird's droppings) from the islands of Peru.

The discovery of large caches of coprolite (fossilised dung and bones) in Cambridgeshire and Hertfordshire led to local production of fertilisers. In 1842, John Lawes began to use sulphuric acid to make superphosphate from bones and this gave farmers a cheap and concentrated fertiliser that was easy to handle. Later, supplies of phosphate came from Europe, the Caribbean, from various islands in the Pacific and from Africa. Basic slag, or 'Thomas phosphate', was being used from British steelworks after 1885. During the 1850s nitrates were imported from Chile (as saltpetre) and in the 1870s it became possible to process the sulphate of ammonia from gas works. Large quantities of potash were imported from Canada as burnt wood ash and in 1861 potash mines were discovered in Prussia.

These developments were made possible by the research of John Lawes in the 1840s and 50s, who showed the practical effect of *different types of fertiliser* on the experimental farm at Rothamsted. They were also helped by the work of chemists and plant biologists, such as Leibig, who began to show *how* plants grew and what chemicals would promote growth. Imports of fertiliser into Britain increased enormously (see Figure 3.12).

Fig. 3.12 Fertiliser and Feeding Stuff Imports 1810–76

Period	FERTILISERS		FEEDING STUFFS		SEEDS	
	tons 000	value £'000	tons 000	value £'000	tons 000	value £'000
1810–14	26	130	27	220	2	187
1832–6	42	205	61	489	3	196
1851–3	263	3,666	506	4,961	8	483
1872–6	899	7,870	1,747	14,160	15	739

Source: THOMPSON, F.M.L., *The Second Agricultural Revolution, Economic History Review*; April, 1968.

Similarly, imports into Britain of seeds such as clover, sainfoin, turnips, lucerne and later rye grass increased enormously, as did foreign supplies of animal feeding stuffs. Cattle cakes, based on oil seeds such as rape and linseed, had been used quite extensively in Lincolnshire and Scotland in the eighteenth century, primarily to increase the quantity of manure. During the 1830s and 40s farming magazines carried detailed accounts of the relative value of different feeding stuffs, calculating how much extra weight could be put on from particular feeding stuffs and how much extra manure was formed. In this way, there was seen to be a very close relationship between livestock and arable farming. Farmers needed additional cattle *and* fertilisers to keep up soil fertility if they were to keep all their land under cultivation. Mixed farming also allowed them to take advantage of movements in the price of cereals and animal products, shifting the emphasis from one to the other, depending upon prices.

EXAMINATION QUESTIONS

This is a structured essay question to test ability to construct a reasoned and logical explanation.

a)   Briefly describe the improvements that took place in each of the following areas of agriculture before 1830.
  i) New crops and rotations.
  ii) The breeding of animals.
  iii) Farm machinery.

b)   Why do historians find it difficult to agree as to when the 'Agricultural Revolution' took place?

TUTOR'S ADVICE

Note part a) says briefly. There would probably be about 3–5 marks for each part in a), a long answer is not required therefore keep to the point and just describe the main developments. Most marks would be for b) which expects you to note the problems about evidence given in the chapter (pages 30–33) and in particular to mention the difficulty of knowing when ideas became widely adopted. You could draw the distinction between first use and general use and refer to the growth in food production needed to feed the growth in population after 1740.

This question examines the comprehension of maps and diagrams and explanation of developments.

Examine carefully the graphs in Figure 3.6.

a)   During which two periods did most enclosures take place?

b)   Explain why most Parliamentary enclosures took place during these periods.

c)   Examine Figure 3.7, the enclosure at Padbury. Use the information in the Figure to describe the changes that took place in the village of Padbury as a result of enclosure.

TUTOR'S ADVICE

Part a) is straight observation from the graphs. Part b) has most marks and requires careful explanation. You need to mention the growing demand for food and the increase in prices which gave the possibility of greater profits. Mention could also be made of low interest rates which made it easier for large landowners to borrow money to meet the costs of enclosure and improvements. The second period is largely the result of price rises during the Napoleonic Wars when population increased very rapidly and there was greater knowledge of the possible advantages of enclosure. For part c) note the growth in new farms, the improvements in communications, etc.

Source A: Map of an open field village.

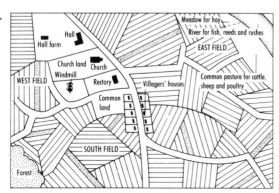

Strips for one villager

Source B: Comments on Enclosure in Cambridgeshire by Arthur Young (1797).

I spoke with a farmer and several cottagers, one of whom said that enclosure would ruin England and was far worse than ten of the present French Wars. "Why my friend," I asked, "What have you lost by it?" "Before the enclosure I kept four cows, but now I do not even keep a goose." . . .

The accounts of such people of the advantages of open-field farming are not to be believed. The past always seems better than the present. On the whole, enclosure has been very good for everybody: the land produces more corn; the farmers are more prosperous; the poor have more bread and employment. . . .

Source C: B. Turner, A Modern Historian, (1987).

Overall, enclosures were to the long-term benefit of the economy. On enclosed farms, farmers found it easier to use the latest techniques and methods because they did not have to get the agreement of their neighbours to any changes. Not only could they farm as they wanted, it was also easier to farm large compact farms than to waste time moving from strip to strip as in the open fields.

The people who suffered were those who could not prove their legal right to graze animals on common lands and those, who after meeting the costs of enclosure, did not have sufficient land to make a living. The effect on employment is difficult to decide. At first, more labourers were needed to build roads and hedges or fences, but in the long-term as population increased many landless labourers were forced to look for work elsewhere. Even Arthur Young, who was generally in favour of enclosures, wrote in 1801 that, "By 19 enclosure Acts out of 20 the poor are injured."

Examine Source A

i) Source A is part of a map of of an 'open-field village'. Explain what is meant by an open-field village.   *(2)*

ii) State 2 ways in which enclosure would be likely to alter this village.   *(2)*

Examine Sources B and C.

iii) What is there in source B to suggest that Arthur Young was a supporter of enclosures?
                                                                                                                                      (3)

iv) "Source B was written at the time enclosures took place, therefore it must be reliable." Do you agree? Give reasons for your answer.   *(8)*

v) Now, using all the sources and your own knowledge, explain the different attitudes towards enclosures about the year 1801.   *(10)*

A 'Student's Answer' with 'Examiner's Comments' is provided for this question below.

QUESTION 4

Study the poster opposite and then attempt **all** parts of the question which follows. This is an example of the kind of election poster which appeared in the late 1830s and early 1840s.

Explain the feelings and reactions of **each** of the following to the poster:

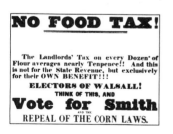

a) a factory owner in Walsall (an industrial town in the Midlands);

b) a neighbouring landowner;

c) a skilled worker in the town.

(Total 30 marks)
(SEG; 1988)

TUTOR'S ADVICE

This kind of question expects you to be *knowledgeable* about the Corn Laws and why they were an important element in Parliamentary elections. It also expects you to be able to understand the likely attitudes of different groups of people to the issue. It is important that your answer is accurate factually and that you show you are aware that opinions were not only different *between* social groups, but that often there were differences of view *within* a social group. For example not all *landowners* were in favour of the Corn Laws; some knew that they did not have to worry about foreign competition because they were efficient farmers. Some *manufacturers* were afraid that if the Corn Laws were repealed then their protection from foreign imports would be taken away, e.g. silk producers who feared competition from France.

A STUDENT'S ANSWER TO Q.3 WITH EXAMINER'S COMMENTS

66 A sensible accurate answer; full marks. 99

66 Good sensible answer; enough up to 'hedges' for two marks so that the rest of the answer though probably true is not really needed. 99

66 Good; extracts relevant information from Source B and fully explains answer using information in source. 99

66 A good answer that shows an awareness of the need to check the accuracy of all sources, despite their age, and to question an author's motive. *Does* question the accuracy of the source and shows an ability to cross reference one source with another. 99

i) An open field village was one where the owners or tenants held land in strips which were dotted about each of the three large fields rather than all being held together in a large group.

ii) Instead of holding strips in different fields, the tenants would be given all their strips in a single block. The big fields would be broken up in to separate farms and the fields enclosed by hedges. Tenants who did not have enough land after enclosure would probably have sold their land to one of the larger farmers and become farm workers or moved to the towns.

iii) Arthur Young shows that he is a supporter of enclosure because although he points out why people were against it, he also says that 'enclosures have been good for everyone'. He says that enclosure made farmers more prosperous because they could grow more corn and that the poor have more bread and employment.

iv) Though it was written when enclosures took place, Source B is not necessarily reliable. Arthur Young may have been biased in favour of enclosure and have selected his evidence to fit in with his opinions. He does not explain why the cottagers are not to be believed and historians would need other evidence of increased output of food and employment to confirm his statements. Source C does confirm Arthur Young's views and also shows that he was aware that poor villagers did suffer. It is likely that a modern historian would have checked up on other sources besides Arthur Young.

66 The student failed to complete part v) of the question, which is poor examination technique. Try to attempt *all* parts of a question. Otherwise you are throwing away good marks. 99

Note: part v) of this question requires an *empathetic* response. This means that you must show an awareness of the different attitudes of the major groups of people affected, namely landlords and tenants, and also how *within* each group not everyone held the same point of view. E.g., some *tenants* were in favour of enclosure because they saw the chance to farm more land and to use more modern methods, giving a higher income; some, mostly *smaller tenants*, were against it, as were those who knew they could not *prove* their title to the land. Such people would lose their right to graze animals on the common, and even if they *did* have a claim to share in the enclosure, the land they would end up with would probably be too small to farm successfully. If they could not get jobs on the larger farms they might have to leave to find jobs in the towns. Most *landlords* were willing to enclose because their rent from the enclosed farms would be much higher; but others recognised the hardship that could result and were concerned that this would disrupt the village way of life and lead to social unrest. Your answer must be based on *fact* not fantasy, so you must *use* the information given to you together with your own knowledge from the work done before the examination.

CHAPTER 4

AGRICULTURAL PROGRESS AND PROBLEMS SINCE 1870

SOURCES

THE GREAT DEPRESSION

THE EFFECTS OF WORLD WAR I

THE EFFECTS OF WORLD WAR II

POST-WAR BRITAIN

GETTING STARTED

The main issues that have interested historians about agriculture since 1870 are not those of *progress*, as in the eighteenth and early nineteenth centuries, but the *problems* farmers have faced in meeting massive foreign competition. Farmers have been caught between *violent swings* in the economy, from prosperity to depression and back again. The whole period from 1870 has also been one of almost *continuous technical change* as new and improved labour saving machines replaced manual labour and farmers introduced new scientific methods. Farming changed from being a simple way of life to being similar to any other industrial business.

Farmers have also organised themselves into an effective *political lobby*. The demand for governments to intervene to protect farmers from foreign competition in the national interest, was finally conceded during World War I, but was only partially accepted during the inter-war period. It was, however, the experience of World War II that finally convinced governments that *strategic needs* meant that farmers *had* to receive subsidies and price guarantees, if Britain was not to be unacceptably dependent upon foreign producers. Just as the huge costs of this policy were beginning to lead to changes in outlook, so British entry to the EEC (Common Market) in 1973 and the acceptance of the Common Agricultural Policy (CAP) provided an even more protective framework for some groups of farmers. During the last ten years the costs of protecting European farmers have become so great that even the CAP is now being severely pruned and farmers are once more facing the prospect of extensive competition from overseas.

Students should be able to:

■ Explain why the 'mid Victorian boom' or Golden Age of farming came to an end after 1870.

■ Describe how farmers tried to adapt to the new circumstances.

■ Describe the effects of changes in government policy upon agricultural prosperity from about 1914 to the 1970s.

■ Describe the main features of the Common Market agricultural policies and how these policies have affected farmers and consumers.

ESSENTIAL PRINCIPLES

1 > SOURCES

The major problem for the historian is the enormous increase in the quantity of material available. Much of the material arises from the increased activity of government interest and/or intervention. There were major enquiries into agricultural problems with large Royal Commissions during 1879–82 and 1894–7; the volume of material from successive government reports and enquiries is even greater during the twentieth century.

2 > THE GREAT DEPRESSION

The period from the 1870s to almost 1914 has been described by historians as one of *depression*. Certainly many farmers in the last quarter of the nineteenth century thought it a period of depression. They pointed to a tremendous fall in prices, lower output and greatly reduced profits. The evidence of large scale cereal farmers to Royal Commissions on Agricultural Depression gave ample evidence of distress since the prices of imported cereals were lower than their own *costs of production*. Low prices forced many farmers into bankruptcy and even landlords were ruined as the value of farm property fell. There was a tremendous flight from the land as rural workers tried to find employment in the cities.

THE CAUSES OF THE DEPRESSION

The causes of this gloomy picture are not hard to find. There was a massive expansion of the *area of land under cultivation* throughout the world during the 1860s and 70s. World supply of cereals in particular rose faster than demand, and at the same time there were tremendous *reductions in transport costs*. The building of railroads and improved methods of handling bulk cargoes meant lower costs for land transport and the larger, faster steamships greatly reduced trans-atlantic shipping costs. Since Britain no longer had any restrictions on imports (see Chapter 3), there was a massive increase in imports of cereals and livestock products from North and South America, Europe, and Australasia.

The world had become a *single market for cereals* and transport costs were only a very small part of total costs. The development of the international telegraph system allowed buyers to keep in touch with markets throughout the world. Improvements in the grading and description of cereals allowed them to buy cereals in whichever market had the lowest prices.

THE WIND OF CHANGE

British cereal producers in the heavy clay lands who had not already changed to pastoral production could not compete with such low prices. Yet many tried to continue, in the belief that the poor harvests at home and the low prices were only temporary. In the long run, only the most efficient large scale farmers on light, sandy soils, and who had adopted the latest machinery, could continue to make a profit. There was a massive change in the *structure* of British farming. Farmers had to shift production into products such as dairy farming, horticulture and fruit production, where foreign competition could not yet overcome the problems of perishability and the other advantages given by closeness to the markets for local British farmers.

Changes in British farming

Until the development of efficient refrigeration in the 1880s, British *meat producers* did quite well. The lower cost of animal feeding stuffs, and the increase in meat-prices due to increased domestic demand as the real incomes of most labourers rose, meant bigger profits. When canned, chilled and refrigerated, meat from North and South America or Australasia *did* become available (the first cargo of frozen meat from Australia was in 1880 on the SS Strathleven), it was of poorer quality than British meat and was really only bought by people on lower incomes. The same was true of dairy and cooked meat products, such as bacon and ham from Europe; they allowed poorer people to increase the range of foodstuffs bought rather than providing direct competition with fresh home produced products.

Farmers who were willing to change, had suitable land, and could acquire both the capital and the appropriate new skills, now shifted to the growth areas of dairy, vegetable or fruit products. Some did very well. Urban markets were growing rapidly as consumers' incomes increased and transport services allowed ready access to towns. Today, we believe that farmers probably shifted into these new markets about as quickly as they could reasonably be expected to. Although *total* farm incomes might not have increased very much, there was a tremendous change in land use and in the pattern of production, and therefore in the *distribution* of total farm income.

For the first time the value of total British farm output came to a standstill. There was a massive flight from the land as farm labourers left the arable areas for better paid jobs in industry. This was in fact just at the time when the wages of farm labourers were rising most rapidly. Relatively high farm wages, together with labour shortage in many regions, led farmers to adopt the latest labour saving equipment in an effort to cut costs and maintain production. Many arable farmers could not survive and as they left the industry so vast acreages of land changed over to pasture (see Figure 4.1). Landowners often had to reduce rents and by the end of the century many large landowners were forced to break up their large estates and sell them to pay off their debts.

	WHEAT (arable)	OTHER CORNS (arable)	FALLOW, GRASS AND PASTURE	MARKET GARDENS
1867	3,368	5,916	15,062	64
1872	3,599	5,975	17,737	232
1895	1,417	5,983	21,816	352
1913	1,756	5,166	21,933	365

Fig. 4.1 Changes in the acreage used for different farm products (in thousand acres)

3 ▷ **THE EFFECTS OF WORLD WAR I**

Although there was some recovery in prices from about 1896, it was not until World War I that farmers began to make good profits once more. Throughout Europe, World War I led to a massive diversion of labour into the armed forces. Perhaps even more important was the requisitioning of horses and carts for transportation. As the war dragged on, so European production of foodstuffs fell dramatically. In England, once it was realised that the war would not be 'over by Christmas', frantic efforts were made to increase production in agriculture as well as industry.

At the outbreak of war Britain depended largely upon cheap foreign foodstuffs. About 80% of the cereals, 40% of meat, 75% of fruit, and all of the sugar came from overseas, together with an enormous range of other foodstuffs and agricultural raw materials. Apart from the establishment of County Agricultural Committees to organise the local supply of labour, fertiliser, machinery and feeding stuffs for animals, almost nothing was done before 1916 to boost domestic production or to organise the distribution of food to consumers.

So long as Britain could get supplies from America there was no problem; but as the German navy developed the use of U-boats and succeeded in sinking merchant ships, so the supply of food began to run low. At the same time the American harvest was poor and the government found that, besides the enormous *cost* of importing food, there was a *shortage of shipping space* to bring in food, munitions and raw materials for industry.

In September 1917, the government finally began to *control prices* for consumers and also introduced *rationing* on basic foods such as bread, sugar and other essentials. By December 1917, shortages of meat, butter, tea and margarine eventually meant that these were rationed too. A proper, well organised rationing system had however really only begun to be organised in the winter of 1918–19, just as the war was coming to an end. The problem of shortages did not end with the war and rationing continued well into 1920.

Attempts to *increase home production* were eventually begun in the autumn of 1917; but it was not really until 1918, when grasslands were ploughed up (and used for corn, barley and potatoes), that there was any significant increase in home production. This of course meant that there was less milk and meat.

The other big changes were on the farms themselves. The Board of Agriculture now organised an army of part-time workers. The *Women's Land Army* was formed in 1917 and included many who had never worked on farms before; even prisoners of war were used The ministry also gave help on the use of fertilisers and on new methods of production and there was a big increase in the use of petrol and diesel tractors. The *Corn Production Act of 1917* gave farmers *guaranteed prices* which it was hoped would encourage them to grow more corn.

GOVERNMENT HELP

The war time shortages and high prices meant that, in general terms, farmers did quite well. The Corn Production Act was an attempt by the government to ensure *stable prices* in order to keep home production at a basic strategic level. Farmers were also encouraged by the *Agriculture Act of 1920*, which gave them minimum prices for cereals, protection for tenant farmers, and an official system for fixing farm labourers' wages. Yet within a year this protective policy was abandoned. The growth of farming production in America and in countries not directly involved in the war produced a massive glut, especially as European farming gradually returned to normal. World prices for foodstuffs and raw materials fell dramatically; wheat fell from 86s–4d (£4.31½p) a quarter in 1920 to 40s–9d (£2.03½p) in 1922. The cost of the price guarantees to farmers was now too high for the government, which repealed its protective legislation in 1921.

During the 1920s and 30s, the government had no consistent or carefully thought out policy towards agriculture. Farmers were generally left to fend for themselves against foreign competition. This meant that even meat and dairy farmers found that they could barely make a living as new technology made it possible for cheap foreign butter, cheese, eggs and meat to be imported at low prices. Some help was given to small-scale farmers in the form of the government providing subsidies to County Councils to rent small farms at lower cost; help was also given in 1928 when rates were no longer needed to be paid on farms and farm buildings. Farmers could also get cheap mortgages to buy and improve property, though few took up the offer. From 1925, the government also subsidised the production of sugar beet. This was quite successful but as a result of the high cost of the subsidy the government subsequently reorganised the industry in 1936. It amalgamated all 18 factories into the British Sugar Corporation and reduced the subsidy.

Other government activities included help for *agricultural research* and attempts to get farmers to organise *co-operative marketing arrangements* similar to those that operated on the continent. The big change in policy came with the general adoption of a *protective tariff policy* after the Great Depression of 1929–33.

 Greater government intervention in agriculture

As a result of three Acts, the *Agricultural Marketing Act 1931*, the *Import Duties Act 1932*, and the *Wheat Act 1932*, farming became a *highly protected and subsidised sector*. Farmers received guaranteed prices for their produce and the government paid the *difference* between the market price and the higher guaranteed price. A *limit* was set on the total amount payable, in an attempt to prevent overproduction. The *Agricultural Marketing Act 1933* set up marketing boards in potatoes, and later in milk and bacon. These bodies regulated the production of farmers and their sales to retailers. They were effectively *government-organised monopolies* that arranged orderly marketing. Despite these attempts to give the British farmer a bigger share of the home market, the decline of rural employment continued. Conditions for rural workers were still much worse than in urban areas, despite attempts to improve both wage rates and the living and working conditions in rural areas.

4 ▷ THE EFFECTS OF WORLD WAR II

The value of these protective measures was to some extent revealed during World War II, when Germany sought to disrupt Britain's international trade and food supplies from America. Some of the lessons from World War I had been learned and although the first two years of World War II were chaotic as the government tried to organise itself, by about 1942 an effective system for planning war time production and the distribution of all agricultural products had been established. Eventually, the government produced an overall plan for *managing the whole economy*, industry as well as agriculture.

During the war period, imports of food were cut back and home production increased by 70% in terms of the calorific value. People did not have much choice, but strict rationing ensured that what they did consume was possibly of more nutritional value than before. The government not only told farmers *what* to produce, it also gave them specific advice and instructions on *how* to produce it. Inefficient farmers could even have their land taken away and given to someone else to farm. Once more, women and children took the place of men, and there was an enormous increase in the use of fertilisers and powered machinery. The number of tractors increased from 56,000 to 203,000 between 1939 and 1946. Farmers not only received guaranteed prices, they also were given large subsidies and financial inducements to encourage them to boost production. The *'Dig for Victory'* campaign also encouraged people to grow their own food in gardens and allotments.

Though wages increased, it is quite clear that farm prices increased much faster than costs or prices in general. Farmers did very well as a result of the war, they not only raised their incomes, they also modernised their farms and equipment at a low cost to themselves.

5 ⟩ POST-WAR BRITAIN

This encouragement to farmers continued *after* the war, as governments sought to boost industrial exports and reduce imports of food and raw materials. The *1947 Agriculture Act* introduced a system of *annual price reviews* which gave farmers guaranteed prices and markets. The government also established a number of *advisory services* for farmers that were designed to help them improve efficiency by increasing output and lowering costs. The immediate post-war years certainly saw a rapid increase in farm production.

Much of the increase in farm production has been the result of *rapid technical changes* and the development of very *intensive factory farming techniques*. British farmers have achieved very high yields, but at a 'price'. The conditions of battery hens and other animals which now spend all their lives in cramped sheds never seeing a field and the pollution caused to rivers by the excessive use of fertilisers which have leached into the rivers, seems to many people a 'high price' to pay in terms of animal welfare and a destruction of the traditional landscape. Indeed the taxpayer has contributed substantially to farm incomes since world prices for most agricultural products have been very low. The *Wildlife and Countryside Act of 1981* now allows farmers to be paid a subsidy for leaving land as it was.

THE COMMON MARKET

Britain's membership of the Common Market has, in many ways, made the problem of protection to farmers even worse. Most European countries have a much larger proportion of their population employed in agriculture and the Common Market governments were anxious to protect so important a sector of their economies. The Common Market Agricultural Policy (CAP) was designed to ensure that Europe had a guaranteed supply of foodstuffs and that farmers received a fair income to keep them on the land. The difficulty has been that the level of subsidy, and a system in which guaranteed prices were set *without any limits on production*, have led to massive butter and beef 'mountains', and wine and milk 'lakes', as farmers increased production and therefore income. The British government has encouraged the setting of limits on the total level of subsidy, but political pressure from countries with large numbers of farmers has made this almost impossible to agree. Slowly, however, schemes *are* being adopted to impose *quotas* on individual farmers for milk and other products, at the same time paying them for preserving the traditional landscape and the natural habitats of wild animals, birds and flowers.

EXAMINATION QUESTIONS

QUESTION

a) Describe the policies of the government towards agriculture:
   either   between 1914 and 1939;
   or   between 1919 and 1954.   *(6)*

b) Explain why the government decided upon these policies.   *(14)*
                                                                          (SEG; 1988)

TUTOR'S ADVICE

a) Whichever period is chosen, you must give a *description* of the policies towards agriculture pursued by the government of the time. In the 1914–39 period, there was considerable protection of British farmers for strategic reasons in the years of the 1st World War, and immediately afterwards. However, these policies soon ceased and farmers were generally left to fend for themselves agains foreign competition. After the Great Depression of 1929–33 the government again started to intervene to protect British farmers. You can *briefly* outline some of the *Acts* passed by governments to help protection. If you took the *longer* period 1919–1954 you miss out the World War I period but include the even stronger protectionist policies of World War II. This time the protectionist policies *continued* after the war.

b) It is important to have read the *whole* question before starting to answer part a). You can see that part b) has 14 out of 20 marks and asks you to explain *why* the government decided upon these policies. So part a) is a *brief* description of *what* happened and part b) is a more detailed account of *why* the government acted as it did. The desire to encourage domestic production so that we would not depend upon foreign supplies in times of war can be mentioned – i.e. 'strategic reasons'. So too can the desire to cut down food imports to help the balance of payments, and so on.

A TUTOR'S ANSWER

QUESTION

Study the Sources A, B and C then answer the questions a) to d) which follow.

Source A (Adapted from Report of a Royal Commission 1879):

> There is agreement as to the extent of the distress which has fallen upon the agricultural community; owners and occupiers have alike suffered from it. All without distinction have been involved in a general calamity.
>
> The two most prominent causes are bad seasons and foreign competitions, made worse by the increased cost of production and the heavy losses of livestock. . . . Labour has been more costly, so that the average labour bill of an arable farm is at least twenty five per cent higher than it was twenty five years ago.

Source B:

	Average annual prices (1867–1877 = 100)				
	WHEAT	BARLEY	OATS	BEEF	MUTTON
1870–74	101	99	97	102	102
1885–89	58	69	70	81	92
1900–04	50	62	69	85	91

Source C (A Punch cartoon of 1876):

Source D:

	1870	1890	1914
Total area of permanent pasture in acres	11,107,860	14,792,439	16,115,750
Total area of arable land in acres	14,849,175	13,079,869	10,998,345

a) Study Source A
   i) What evidence is there in Source A which helps to explain why the government set up a Royal Commission for agriculture in 1879?   *(2)*
   ii) What evidence in Source A helps to explain the increasing cost of production (line 5)?   *(1)*
   iii) Why are reports of Royal Commissions such as this valuable as historical resources?   *(3)*

b) Study Source B
   i) Between which years did prices for agricultural goods decline the most?   *(1)*
   ii) What evidence is there in Source A which helps to explain these price changes?   *(2)*

c)   Study Source C
     i) What does the cartoonist suggest was one cause of the problems faced by British
         farmers?   (2)
     ii) What technological developments outside of Britain contributed to the problems
         faced by British farmers in Source C?   (2)

d)   Study Source D
     i) What change in British farming between 1870 and 1914 is shown in Source D?
                                                                                               (1)
     ii) What evidence in Source B would help to explain the changes shown in Source D?
                                                                                               (2)
     iii) In what other ways did farmers respond to the problems they faced during the
          years 1870–1914?   (4)

**TUTOR'S
ANSWER**

a)   i)   The words 'distress' and 'calamity' certainly suggest a serious situation that needs
          some remedy and government help. Bad harvests, foreign competition, increased
          costs of production and losses of livestock (perhaps through disease or cold!) are
          all mentioned.
     ii) Labour is mentioned as being 'more costly' (in fact 25% higher than 25 years
          previously) and wages are an important part of total costs.
     iii) You could mention that such Reports provide *facts*, given as evidence, that are
          often not available from any other source. 'Witnesses' were often called, giving
          evidence from *different points of view*, e.g. landlords, tenant farmers, labourers,
          etc.

b)   i)   Source B uses *index numbers* for prices, with 1867–1877 as the *base year* (= 100).
          Average prices were *lowest* in the years 1900–04 for all the products (except beef)
          as compared with 1867–77 average prices.
     ii) *Increased production overseas*, leading to foreign competition, will have reduced
          prices on world markets and in Britain. This factor must have been the *most
          important* factor, since bad harvests in Britain would tend to *raise* prices (by
          reducing supply) as would higher labour costs. These factors must have been
          swamped by the great increase in supply from overseas countries forcing prices
          down.

c)   i)   British arable farmers (e.g. cereals) were being displaced by meat and dairy
          farmers who received much higher prices.
     ii) Much cheaper tranport costs, via developments in railways, roads and shipping,
          meant foreign arable farmers could now compete effectively in Britain.

d)   i)   More acres used for permanent pasture and less acres used for arable farming.
     ii) The absolute fall in prices between the period 1867–77 and 1900–04 was greatest
          for *arable* crops such as wheat, barley and oats. Although the price of beef and
          mutton fell, it fell by much less than for arable crops. Therefore farmers had an
          incentive to switch from arable land to pasture land.
     iii) Many farmers tried to *increase the size* of their farms and to use the *latest
          machinery and methods*. So even though there was less total acreage in arable land,
          what remained was often in larger units using more modern methods. There was
          also a switch towards horticulture and fruit production in which British farmers
          could more easily compete with foreign suppliers (perishability, etc). Most of all
          there was a switch to meat production, with more favourable prices and cheaper
          animal feeding stuffs. Foreign competition was less severe in meat products,
          which were often of poorer quality, especially with refrigeration in its infancy.

THE INDUSTRIAL REVOLUTION 1700–1870

POPULATION AND OCCUPATION

THE DOMESTIC SYSTEM

THE COTTON TEXTILE INDUSTRY

IRON

STEEL

COAL

GETTING STARTED

In 1850, the economy and society of Britain was clearly very different from that which had existed in 1700 or even in 1790. Most people were better off materially, with more to eat, better clothes, increased leisure and the expectation of a longer life. Society itself was very different, it was an *urban industrial society*, and attitudes, ideas and beliefs had changed. Today, we expect things to change rapidly, but the idea that industrial and social change never stops had only just begun to develop in the mid nineteenth century.

What was *special* about the events which had taken place in Britain during the eighteenth century was that Britain was the *first country* to go through the process of *industrialisation*, with dramatic changes to the whole way of life. This is what historians really mean by the phrase the 'Industrial Revolution'. The problem is to establish when this process took place. Was the basic framework of the new society established in the period 1760–1830 or over an even shorter period; or did it happen gradually, from about 1600 to 1850? Historians also want to know *how* changes in one part of the economy related to the other parts, and more especially how such changes affected *different groups* in society.

Historians have used the term Industrial Revolution in several different ways. Sometimes it describes the changes which took place in *particular industries* when new ideas and methods of production were introduced. It is also used to describe changes to the *whole economy*, including both the economic and social changes that took place. Both uses of the term are perfectly alright; you should, however, always check when you read a book or source *how* the author is using the phrase.

This chapter begins by explaining the changes that took place in the *whole economy*. It goes on to describe and explain when and how technical changes in *particular important industries* took place and how these in turn led to changes in the *location and ownership* of these industries. It will quickly be seen that the pace of change varied from industry to industry, even though many industries were interconnected. Even in 1850, some *parts* of the rapidly changing industries still used what might be called 'old fashioned' methods. Some whole industries and some major areas of employment were *not* in fact radically changed until the late nineteenth and early twentieth centuries.

All Exam Groups expect candidates to be familiar with the major technological developments in a few selected industries (the most common are textiles, coal mining, iron and steel) and the effects of these changes upon the lives and working conditions of the workers.

Candidates should be able to:

- Date and know who developed the new machines or techniques and be able to describe the changes that took place.

- Explain how these changes affected the location of the industry and how organisation and ownership changed as more capital investment was needed.

- Comment on how these changes affected other industries and helped the economy to grow.

ESSENTIAL PRINCIPLES

1 POPULATION AND OCCUPATION

In 1700, the descriptions of travellers like Defoe and the evidence from the parish registers show that most people lived in the countryside (see Chapter 2). However, this does not mean that they were all farmers. A very large proportion of the population were employed in *several activities*, mixing farming with working part-time in textiles, or as a coal miner or stone mason, and so on. Recent researchers using the parish registers have shown that the guesses by *Gregory King* about the occupations of the population in 1688 are probably wrong in some important ways (see Figure 5.1).

GREGORY KING			MODERN HISTORIAN	
Commerce and Industry				
Merchants & Traders by sea	(greater)	2,000	All Commerce	135,000
Merchants & Traders by sea	(lesser)	8,000	Manufacturing	180,000
Shopkeepers & Tradesmen		40,000	Mining	15,000
Artisans & Handicrafts		60,000	Building trades	77,000
Total in trade and industry		110,000		407,000*
Agriculture				
Freeholders (greater)		40,000	All Agriculture	241,000*
Freeholders (lesser)		140,000		
Farmers		150,000		
Total in agriculture		330,000		
* excludes ordinary labourers				

Fig. 5.1 Occupations in England about 1700

It seems possible that only about 35–40% of the population were employed in agriculture. If our information from the parish registers *is* correct, then England in 1700 probably had a larger proportion of her population in trade and industry than most underdeveloped countries today. England was *already* quite an advanced country. Nevertheless, as information from the Census indicates, the changes that took place over the next 200 years are still quite remarkable.

EXERCISE 1

This exercise tests your comprehension of source material.

Using Figure 5.2, describe the main changes in employment in England and Wales in the nineteenth century.

	1801	1821	1841	1851	1861	1881	1901
Agriculture, forestry, fishing	35.9	28.4	22.2	21.7	18.7	12.5	8.7
Manufacturing and mining	29.7	38.4	40.5	42.9	43.6	43.5	46.3
Trade and transport	11.2	12.1	14.2	15.8	16.6	21.3	21.4
Domestic and personal	11.5	12.7	14.5	13.0	14.3	15.4	14.1
Public and professional	11.8	8.5	8.5	6.7	6.9	7.3	9.6
Total labour force (millions)	4.8	6.2	8.5	9.7	10.8	13.1	16.7

Fig. 5.2 Distribution of the Labour Force (percentages)

TUTOR'S ADVICE

The question is quite straightforward. All you have to do is to learn to read a rather large table and to describe the main trends in your own words. It should be easy to pick up marks on these questions. Often in the examination the tables will not be as large as this and you may simply be asked to pick out one or two important features. The important thing is to *scan the table as a whole* and then to try to note the *really important changes*, rather than trying to describe everything. You can usually get some idea of how much detail is needed by the marks awarded. The Tutor's answer below gives a very full answer.

TUTOR'S ANSWER

Between 1801 and 1901, the total size of the labour force increased by about 3½ times. Employment did not increase in *all* industries at the same rate, so that there were big changes in the *distribution* of the workforce. The *percentage* of people employed in *agriculture* fell gradually between 1801 and 1851, but then very rapidly after 1861. The *actual numbers* of people employed in agriculture *increased* up to 1851 (since total labour force was rising rapidly) and only fell after 1851; but even in 1901 agriculture was still one of the largest single industries.

The big change is the *percentage of people employed in industry and mining*. This rose very rapidly from about 30% in 1801 to nearly 44% in 1861. Though it continued to increase after 1861, industrial employment was expanding less rapidly than before. As industry increased, so did the need for all the *services* such as transport and banking. The growth in numbers employed in *trade and transport* was especially rapid after 1851, and by 1881 more people were employed in trade and transport than in agriculture. The same pattern is true for *domestic and personal services*. The last quarter of the nineteenth century also saw a rapid increase in *public and professional* employment.

Changes in economic structure

These changes in how people worked show how the economy was changing from an agricultural to an industrial one. This change was accompanied by an increase in *total production*. We think that between about 1700 and 1800 *total* production in agriculture and industry increased by about 150%. The increase by 1750 was about 50% and the remaining 100% over the next fifty years. The production from *industry and commerce* increased still faster, by almost 300% over the same period, with about 200% of this taking place after 1760. Some of this increase in production was the result of population having increased, so that there were more workers; but production increased about 50% *faster than* the number of workers, so ways had been found to make workers much more efficient. It is *how* this was done that really makes the changes in industry so important. The increase in production was largely due to *technical changes*.

2 > THE DOMESTIC SYSTEM

In 1700, almost all industrial production was done by *groups of workers in their own homes* using fairly simple hand tools and machines. Some industries, such as ship manufacture, were done in special yards where hundreds of craftsmen worked on a single project, but this was rare. Some industries, such as brewing, glass making and the iron industries, had already begun to use water wheels and large furnaces of coal, coke or charcoal, but again these were unusual. Wind and water wheels were also used in flour milling and in parts of the woollen cloth industry.

The largest single industry was the manufacture of woollen cloth. This was made in many parts of the country, but mainly in E. Anglia, the ridings of Yorkshire and the West country. Most industries were located near to the supplies of raw material. This was especially the case for heavy bulky products (such as iron) which were difficult to transport (see Chapter 8).

3 > THE COTTON TEXTILE INDUSTRY

Industrial growth rates 1785–1830: average annual percentage

INDUSTRY	% growth
Leather	0.75
Beer	0.50
Candles	1.75
Soap	2.50
Paper	2.50
Glass	2.00
Bricks	1.75
Cotton	6.25
Pig iron	5.50
Coal	2.25

Fig. 5.3 Growth of various industries, 1785–1830

By 1800, although all industries had expanded, a few industries had grown very much faster than others. The most noticeable was *cotton textiles* (see Figure 5.3). In 1700 this industry was located around London and used imported spun cotton from India, which was then mixed with other fibres such as linen or flax and woven into a light, but coarse, cloth. A great deal of finished cotton cloth, such as calicoes and muslins, were imported directly from India. By 1800, England was not only a *major producer* of finished cotton goods but was also the largest *exporter* of cotton cloth (Figure 5.4). This was made possible by the development of new machines which made it very much quicker to process raw cotton and then to spin it into yarn which was then woven into cloth. See Figure 5.5 for an outline of the steps involved in the preparation of cloth manufactures.

Some idea of industrial growth is given by the import figures in Figure 5.4. England could *not* produce raw cotton, so it all had to be imported. We do not know precisely *how much* cotton cloth was produced, but we can *estimate* this from the import of raw cotton. We *do* know how much was exported, so we can also *estimate* how much was consumed at home for domestic clothing. This can be worked out from Figure 5.4.

What these figures show is that England had rapidly developed an export trade in cotton goods but, perhaps surprisingly, the major source of growth in the period 1760 to about 1815 was not really exports, but the *home market*. Look carefully at Figure 5.4 and see if you can *explain* why this is so. The answer is in the *proportion* exported. After 1760, the proportion exported falls, so the home market must have been growing *faster* than exports. Exports do not begin to grow faster than the home market until the 1790s and do not regain the 50% level of total production until about 1815. For the rest of the century, the proportion of exports grows rapidly and it is *export sales* which really decide the growth of the cotton industry. Did you reach this same conclusion?

YEAR	IMPORTS (mill lbs)	VALUE OF PRODUCTION £ (m)	% EXPORTED
1700	1.1		
1760	3.4	0.6	50
1780	6.6	4.0	30
1790	31	7.0	23
1800	42	11.1	46
1815	100	30.0	58
1820	141	29.4	53
1830	249	32.1	56
1840	452	46.7	50
1850	621	45.7	61
1860	1,050	77.0	64
1870	1,155	104.9	67
1880	1,386	94.5	74
1890	1,684	101.2	72
1900	1,510	89.2	79

Fig. 5.4 Imports of Raw Cotton and Cloth Exports

STAGE 1	Preparation	sort out fleeces/unpack cotton bales remove dirt/rubbish by hand clean with soap or alkali beat to open up fibres
STAGE 2	Carding/combing	using carding combs – later carding machines – untangle fibres into parallel lines 'draw' fibres into a continuous 'roving' – a continuous sliver of parallel fibres and wound onto cops
STAGE 3	Spinning	fibres are pulled and twisted into a long, thin continous thread (yarn) and wound onto bobbins
STAGE 4	Weaving	yarn of different strengths/thicknesses woven into cloth on a loom – often mixture of linen/wool or linen/cotton used to give different types of cloth

Fig. 5.5 Stages in the production of cloth

THE DEVELOPMENT OF MACHINES

The next problem is what made this expansion possible? The key factor was the *development of machines* which allowed cotton to be spun and woven by powered machinery and allowed Britain to produce cotton more cheaply than any other country. This continued to be the case until the late nineteenth century (see Chapter 6). Before 1770, the growth of the industry was prevented by an inadequate supply of yarn. This was especially so from about 1750, when weavers (woollen and cotton) began to adopt the *fly shuttle* developed by John Kay about 1733. This device (see Figure 5.6), allowed weavers to work faster and produce wider cloths; it added a spring to the side of the loom, and rollers to the shuttle.

SPINNING

The problem was how to speed up the *spinning* of wool and cotton yarn to keep pace with the demands of the weavers. The spinning wheels used to spin yarn are shown in Figure 5.7; look at this figure and *describe* the machine used. Comment upon its size, the materials it was made of, and the people who appear to be using the machine. You should note that it is quite small, is made out of wood and that the spinners are women.

The Spinning Jenny

An attempt to improve the speed of spinning was the machine developed by Wyatt and Paul in 1738. But the first effective spinning device to spin *more than one thread at a time* was made by James Hargreaves, with the *spinning jenny*. This was developed about 1764 and

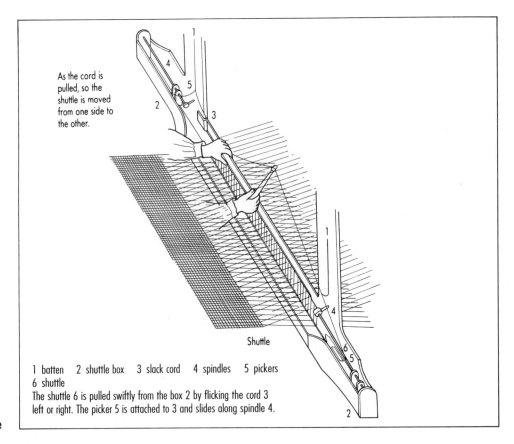

As the cord is pulled, so the shuttle is moved from one side to the other.

Shuttle

1 batten   2 shuttle box   3 slack cord   4 spindles   5 pickers
6 shuttle
The shuttle 6 is pulled swiftly from the box 2 by flicking the cord 3 left or right. The picker 5 is attached to 3 and slides along spindle 4.

Fig. 5.6 Kay's Fly Shuttle

Fig. 5.7 a) The Spinning Wheel

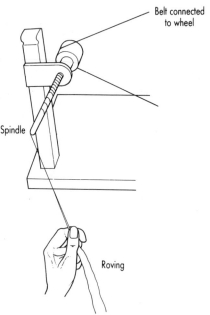

Belt connected to wheel

Spindle

Roving

Fig. 5.7 b) The moving parts

HOW THE SPINNING WHEEL WORKS

1) *The spinster ties a piece of roving to the spindle holding the roving in her left hand.*

2) *With the right hand, the big wheel is turned slowly. This causes the belt to turn the spindle.*

3) *As the spindle is turned, so the spinster draws out the roving pulling it gently and steadily to an arms length. At the same time the thread is twisted between the fingers and thumb to bind the fibres together.*

4) *The thread or yarn is now wound onto the spindle by turning the big wheel.*

was patented in 1770. It was a relatively simple machine made out of wood and powered by hand, but it was soon altered so that it was easier to use. The normal type of jenny found in most cottages was similar to that shown in Figure 5.8. Figure 5.9 is a diagram that explains how it worked.

This machine could be made by any able village blacksmith and carpenter. It was not large and could be used in the home. In many parts of northern towns and villages, terraces of cottages with long rows of windows to let in the light can still be seen today. Other spinners were afraid that Hargreaves' invention would put them out of business and they attacked his home in Blackburn. He eventually set up in business in Nottingham. Hargreaves' patent was contested and, although others copied his machine, he received no royalties.

By 1788 there were about 20,000 jennies in use, some of them able to spin 80 threads. The jenny only produced a rather weak thread that was not suitable for the *warp* (that is threads which go up and down the loom). So the thread of the jenny was used as the *weft* thread (threads which go across the loom) with linen as the warp, to make a coarse fustian.

Fig. 5.8 Spinning Jenny from Edward Baines, History of the Cotton Manufacture in Great Britain 1835

N.B. Hargreaves' original jenny had the handle for turning the bobbins horizontal but this was modified to make it easier for the operator to both turn the handle and draw the thread backwards along the frame.

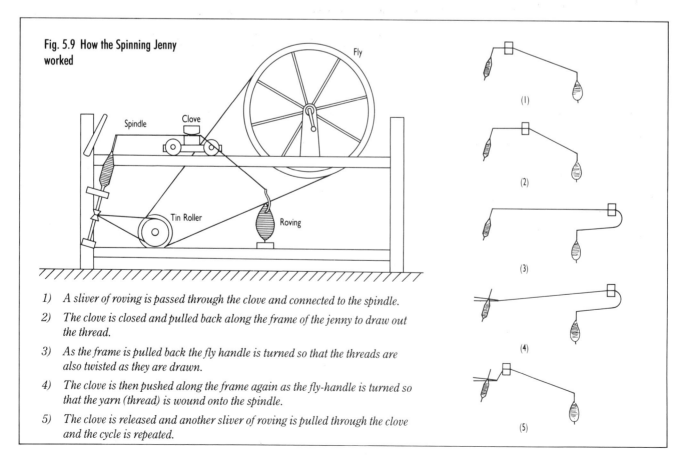

Fig. 5.9 How the Spinning Jenny worked

1) A sliver of roving is passed through the clove and connected to the spindle.

2) The clove is closed and pulled back along the frame of the jenny to draw out the thread.

3) As the frame is pulled back the fly handle is turned so that the threads are also twisted as they are drawn.

4) The clove is then pushed along the frame again as the fly-handle is turned so that the yarn (thread) is wound onto the spindle.

5) The clove is released and another sliver of roving is pulled through the clove and the cycle is repeated.

The Water Frame

This problem of weak threads was solved by the *water frame* (see Figure 5.10), a machine which used the roller spinning principle of Wyatt and Paul. Though patented by Richard Arkwright in 1769, it seems likely that Arkwright actually used ideas taken from a device of Thomas Highs of Leigh. In 1771, Arkwright, in partnership with Jedediah Strutt, set up the first water-powered spinning mill at Cromford (Derbyshire) which was very much like the silk spinning mill of Lombe's nearby. Then, in partnership with David Dale, he built mills at New Lanark (Scotland), at Belper and Derby and then in Marple (Cheshire) with Samuel Oldknow. He took out numerous patents for other devices that prepared the cotton for spinning, but these were disallowed in 1785 and this gave others the opportunity to enter the trade. Partly because Arkwright refused to licence any use of his ideas unless the machine had at least 1,000 spindles from the very beginning, water frames were only used in *large* water-powered factories. This made it easier for Arkwright to collect his royalties. It also meant that only manufacturers who could afford to rent or build large factories could use his machine. This required a considerable investment, not only in machinery and buildings, but also in working capital for raw materials and wages, and to cover the waiting period until the yarn had been sold.

Fig. 5.10 Arkwright's 'Water Frame'. It was so-called because it could be driven continuously by a waterwheel

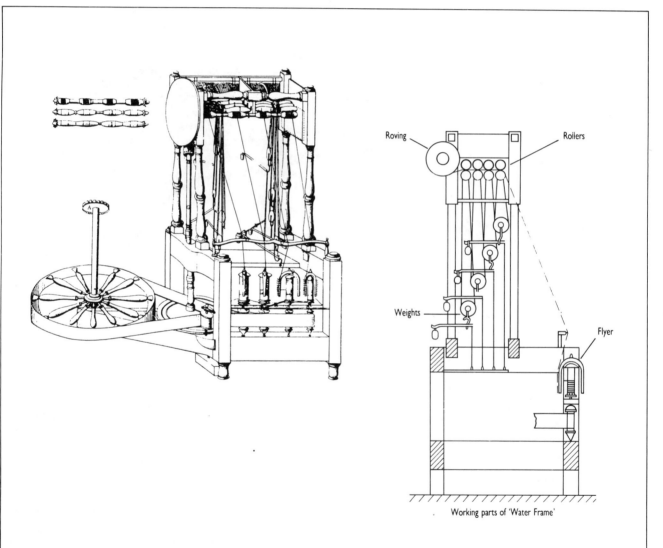

Roving

Rollers

Weights

Flyer

Working parts of 'Water Frame'

Arkwright's water frame works in the following way:

1) *The roving is pulled through a series of rollers which are kept together by a series of weights. These move at different speeds and draw out the roving.*

2) *The twist is given to the thread by the flyer which turns round the bobbin onto which the yarn is wound.*

3) *The rollers and flyers are turned by a belt which is connected to the large wheel at the side which is itself connected by rods and cogs to a water wheel which meant the process was continuous.*

The Mule

Arkwright's machine produced a new type of yarn that was good enough for making calicoes; fine muslins needed a finer, stronger yarn and this only became possible when Samuel Crompton of Bolton combined the roller twist principle of Arkwright with the drawing principle of Hargreaves' jenny. Like the jenny, the *mule* was a simple machine that could have been used in the home; but Arkwright used his patents to block the introduction of the mule until 1790, by which time large mules powered first by water and then by steam engines could be used. By 1792, large cast and wrought iron-framed mules were being made that ran the whole length of a spinning shed. These machines could only be used in *factories*. In factories, almost all the highly skilled machine operators were men, whereas the work on spinning wheels used at home was in the hands of women.

Automation

The next major development was to make the mules more reliable and easier to use. This was done with the introduction of *automatic self acting mules*, such as that developed by Richard Roberts in 1825. These machines allowed manufacturers to replace the more expensive skilled men with cheaper and less skilled women operatives. Men were now generally used only as *overseers* and *mechanics* who set up the machines.

Although the simple *hand machine* greatly increased the amount of yarn that could be spun, the introduction of *water powered machines* improved productivity tremendously. With the new lower costs, competition among manufacturers led to lower prices, *despite* the fact that *raw cotton prices* increased for most of the period to about 1810. This was because the demand for cotton increased faster than planters could produce it.

COTTON SUPPLIES

At first, cotton came from India, Egypt or West Africa, but at least 50% came from the Caribbean by the late eighteenth century. In the 1770s, after the War of Independence, cotton began to be grown on the islands off the coast of Carolina. The type of cotton grown at this time was sea island cotton, so called because it would only grow near the sea. There were other cottons, but they had large seeds which were difficult to remove. This problem was solved in 1793 by Eli Whitney's *cotton gin*. At first British manufacturers were unwilling to use these other cottons because they did not spin well on their machines. However, as their machines improved and these cottons became cheaper than sea island cotton, so manufacturers became more willing to use them. By 1815 at least 20% of imported cotton came from America. By the 1830s this had risen to about 80%. During the American Civil War in 1862–65, imports of cotton from America fell to almost nothing, but by 1871 were back to their previous levels.

REGIONAL DEVELOPMENT

The *cotton spinning industry* rapidly became a *factory industry* which at first was located wherever there were good supplies of *clean water*, both to wash the cotton and to power the machinery. Most factories were in isolated *rural areas* so that manufacturers often had to build village communities almost from nothing. As the industry grew, getting both skilled and unskilled labour became a problem. This was partially solved as machines became easier to operate. Men were gradually replaced by women and children, who could be paid much less. Women and children had usually worked alongside husbands or relatives in the rural mills, doing jobs such as carding or piecing (repairing the threads as they broke), which men could not do easily.

❝❝Location in the North West❞❞

Labour became more readily available when the use of *steam engines* from the 1790s, allowed new factories to be built in *towns*. During the 1790s the industry began to become concentrated in the Manchester region, and in the nearby towns of Cheshire and Lancashire. This was because the area had an ample supply of labour, access to cheap coal from local coal mines, and a good transport network (see Chapter 6). The rather damper or more humid climate of the river valleys also meant that less time was spent on repairing breakages of thread. However, the real advantage that Lancashire developed over other regions was that the latest technologies were adopted very quickly by local manufacturers, with the result that the region built up a large pool of highly skilled workers in a variety of closely connected trades. There were not only spinners and weavers but dyers, manufacturers of machinery, and banks and markets which specialised in the cotton trades. Merchants found that in and around Manchester they had access to a very wide network of specialist traders and services which they could not easily find elsewhere.

THE LOOM

Until the 1820s, *cotton weaving* remained a *handicraft trade* carried on in the home, and skilled weavers were the aristocrats of the trade, earning very high wages. In 1784, The Rev. Edmund Cartwright had invented a practical *power loom*, but it was not generally adopted until the 1820s when Sharp and Roberts improved it considerably. In some branches of the industry, high quality handloom weaving continued until the 1860s, because the power loom could not produce the fancy weaving that was often required. Many manufacturers used *both* power looms and handloom weavers because this gave them a reserve of handloom weavers to be used when demand was high. Gradually the intense competition for work amongst handloom weavers forced wages down to impossibly low levels; even the Irish migrants, and women and children who had become part-time weavers, found the wages too low.

YEAR	POWER LOOMS	HANDLOOM WEAVERS
1795		75,000
1813	2,000	212,000
1820	14,000	240,000
1829	55,000	225,000
1833	100,000	213,000
1835	109,000	188,000
1845	225,000	60,000
1850	250,000	43,000
1861	400,000	7,000

Fig. 5.11 The numbers of Power Looms and Hand Loom Weavers

N.B. These figures are really only the best estimates from various sources.

OTHER TEXTILE INDUSTRIES

Other textile industries found it difficult to adopt the various new machines as quickly as cotton spinners and weavers. In some cases differences in the fibres made it difficult to use these new machines, but in others, resistance from well-established craftsmen and conservative merchants slowed innovation. In the case of *wool*, there were also difficulties about increasing production until new sources of supply became available from America and Australasia in the nineteenth century. Growth was steady, but not spectacular, and the main change was the *shift in location* from the south west and East Anglia to Yorkshire. It should be remembered, however, that the total value of cotton production did not exceed wool until about 1815. Since most of the wool used at this time was *locally produced*, the woollen industry made a rather more significant contribution to the local economy. There was also considerable employment in other industries, such as silk, linen and jute.

4 ▷   IRON

The manufacture of *iron* is really a chemical process, and one that was not understood until about the 1860s. However, practical ironmasters had, by experiment and experience, found the best combinations of raw materials, heat and time, to produce different types of iron (see Figure 5.12).

CAST IRON

Cast iron, is made in a blast furnace (see Figure 5.14 below) and is strong but brittle. It is used whilst still molten and poured directly into moulds to make castings such as pots. Some cast iron is poured into moulds called *pigs* and allowed to cool; this is then called *pig* or *bar iron*. When it is reheated in a charcoal furnace and beaten with hammers, it is changed into *wrought iron*. Wrought iron is *not* brittle and can be shaped even when cold (but often whilst still hot) by rolling and slitting into nails, metal tools, farm implements etc.

The geographical distribution of iron production is shown in Figure 5.13. Until the 1750s this pattern was unchanged. The sudden increase in demand for iron in the 1750s and 60s, both for domestic and military use, meant that it now became worthwhile to make greater use of *coke smelting*. The use of coke as an alternative to charcoal had been developed by Abraham Darby of Coalbrookdale in about 1709. He used his iron to manufacture cast iron pots, fire-backs, pipes and cylinders, and all kinds of fancy shapes. The reason for this was

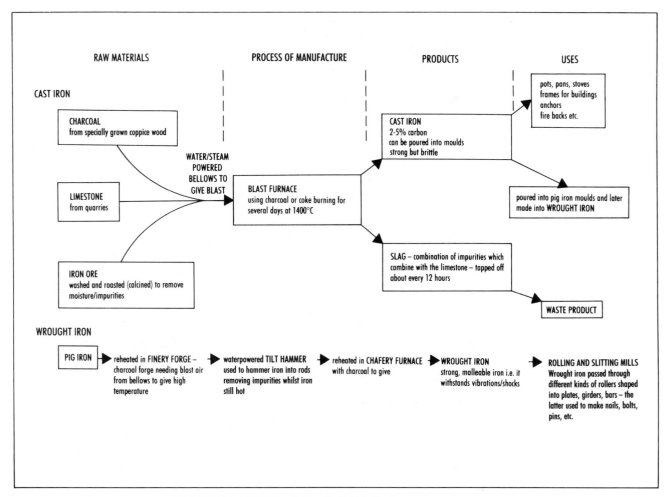

Fig. 5.12 The smelting of iron ore in the eighteenth century

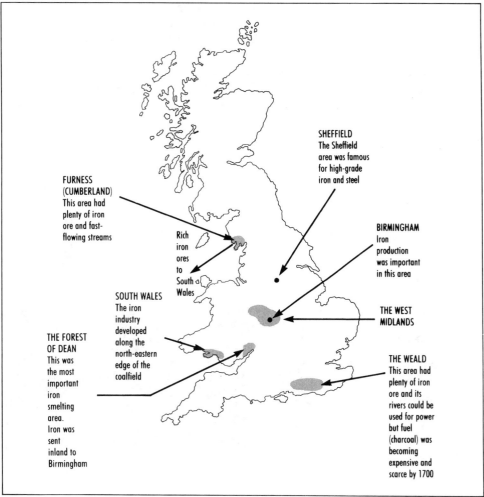

Fig. 5.13 The iron industry in 1750

that *coke smelted iron* had a high *silicon* content; this made it more difficult to reheat in the forge to make wrought iron. However, the silicon also meant that the cast iron ran very smoothly, and Darby developed a special method of using sand to make his casting moulds. It was this process that he patented; he also tried to keep the art of doing it from being used by other iron masters. His apprentices had to sign an agreement that they would not reveal his methods or cast iron pots to anyone else.

The combination of his cast iron and his special moulding process allowed Abraham Darby to make very thin walled castings. This was very economical with iron, and especially useful when it was necessary to keep the weight of the casting to the minimum, as in a cooking pot or steam engine cylinder. Darby's superior technology in moulding allowed him to develop a special relationship with *steam engine manufacturers*, such as Newcomen and later Boulton and Watt, for whom he made piston cylinders and other parts. Darby did not patent his coke making process, even sharing it with other local iron masters, but it was not widely adopted before 1750. Darby had no need to patent the method because other iron masters did not *want* to use it; the forge masters who made wrought iron preferred charcoal-made cast iron, even if it was imported. It was only when the cost of imported bar iron and charcoal became expensive that it became worthwhile to use the coke method more generally.

FURNACE DEVELOPMENT

As demand for iron grew, so did the number of furnaces; after 1750 most of the new furnaces used coke. In 1760, there were only 14 coke furnaces and 61 charcoal furnaces, but by 1790 there were 86 coke and only 14 charcoal furnaces.

The blast furnace

Improvements to *blast* furnaces, especially the use of water powered bellows to increase the air blown into the furnace, allowed the *size* of furnaces to increase considerably. By 1742 the Darby's used a Newcomen steam engine to pump water up the hill to the water wheel, which then powered the furnace bellows. By 1775, over half the coke furnaces used steam engines since this allowed them to get a better blast of air and therefore to achieve higher temperatures in the furnace. It also meant that the furnace no longer had a problem of water supply during the summer months, so that *coke furnaces with steam engines* were able to work about 47 weeks a year instead of the normal 30 weeks for a *charcoal water powered furnace*.

By 1815, the improvements in blast furnaces meant that enormous furnaces with a capacity of 1,000 tons were now possible, with many furnace sites having two or three such furnaces. It was now vitally important for furnaces to be sited where vast quantities of

Fig. 5.14 a) Blast Furnace, about 1650

Fig. 5.14 b) Earl Granville's Shelton Furnaces and Collieries, about 1873

(a)

(b)

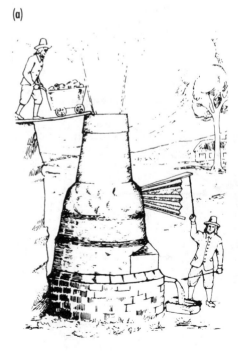

From Griffiths Guide to the Iron Trade of Great Britain 1873

coal and limestone could be brought in, and the cast iron *transported* to other sites. There was a major problem of handling raw materials and molten metal. Blast furnace sites had to be close to canals, and later railways, and most of them had extensive trackways and lifts to carry raw materials about the site. The differences can easily be seen by comparing Figure 5.14(a) with Figure 5.14(b).

Other improvements to furnaces included the use of *pre-heated air* by James Neilson in 1828. This saved about 30% on fuel consumption; by 1840, Welsh iron masters had found ways to recycle the heat from the furnace to feed both the blast and the steam engine, making still more fuel savings. By 1830, improvements in furnace design meant that the average furnace produced about 2,500 tons a year; by 1870, this had risen to 9,000 tons a year.

The reverberatory furnace

The other big change was in the *production of wrought iron*. Various ways were developed before the 1780s to use coal instead of charcoal. One way was to reheat cast iron in a forge to remove the silicon, to break the cast iron up into pieces and then put it into clay pots and reheat it in a coal *reverberatory furnace*. This was known as the *Staffordshire method* and was developed by the Wood brothers in the 1760s. In 1783 and 1784, Henry Cort took out patents for using coke in a reverberatory furnace, and his method is shown in Figures 5.15(a) and 5.15(b). The iron never came into direct contact with the coal, and the gases which contained the sulphur were led off through the chimney. Cort himself was never able to get his idea to work properly and it was Richard Crawshay at the Cyfarrthia works who finally made the method practicable.

Fig. 5.15 a) Henry Cort's
Reverberatory Furnace

Fig. 5.15 b) Cort's Pudding and
Rolling Mill

Both figs from C. Tomlinson,
'The Useful Arts and Manufactures
of Great Britain', 1848

Puddling

The *puddling method* was a major breakthrough since it combined all the processes into a much shorter and continuous process. The iron was heated in the furnace and was constantly stirred to keep the iron in contact with the heat so that all the slag and impurities were burnt off. It could then be taken in hot molten balls and, after cooling, be rolled into bars. Instead of taking several weeks, the process now only took a couple of days and the savings were enormous. In the 1830s the process was improved by Joseph Hall who found that by mixing furnace cinder into the molten cast iron, the process of conversion to wrought iron became even quicker, with the amount of pig iron needed to make a ton of wrought iron reduced from 40 to 21 cwt.

TECHNOLOGICAL CHANGE

As in the textile industries, *technical progress* greatly improved efficiency and lowered costs of production. Iron became much cheaper and was now available for many more uses than before. The most spectacular use was probably in construction. The Darby's built the first iron bridge at Coalbrookdale (1780). Following the great floods of 1795, when the only bridge not damaged was the Coalbrookdale iron bridge, there was a rush to build new iron bridges. Iron was also used in aqueducts, the most spectacular being Telford's at Pont Cysyllte on the canal to Llangollen (see Chapter 7). Many cotton mills used an iron girder framework in what were called fireproof buildings, and Brunel made great use of iron in his steam ships. Many items of everyday life in the 1850s such as cheap tools, cooking stoves, gas and water pipes, would have been impossible without the technical changes that had brought a reduction in the cost of iron and an improvement in its quality. Above all, the railway system would not have been practicable without these developments in iron. Perhaps even more than cotton, the Industrial Revolution was the 'age of iron'.

The new technologies were based upon *coal*, so ironworks had to be sited near or on the coalfields. Fortunately in many cases *iron ores* were also found in the coal seams, and so the location of the industry changed from being in isolated rural furnaces, in woods and close to streams (Figure 5.13 above), to being in the coal fields of Shropshire, Staffordshire and South Wales. By 1806, 70% of pig iron was produced in these areas and altogether, 87% of production was on the coalfields.

Iron works became huge places, with vast quantities of raw materials stored on site and with great quantities of metal being produced. They had to be located where there were good *transport links*. As the size of the blast furnaces got bigger, so iron masters invested large sums of money in equipment. The Coalbrookdale Company had a capital investment of £166,000 in 1809; by 1851 it had risen to £366,000. Other companies, like Crawshays, were about the same size. By the 1830s the largest iron works employed several thousand men and the companies had not only iron works, but coal mines and engineering works as well. They had become very big businesses, and to be run efficiently they needed book-keepers and salesmen, as well as engineers and iron masters.

YEAR	TOTAL (000 tons)
1720	25
1788	68
1796	125
1806	245
1823	455
1830	677
1840	1,396
1843	1,215
1847	1,200
1852	2,701

Fig. 5.16 Pig iron production (1720–1852)

5 >   STEEL

The first half of the nineteenth century was the age of cast and wrought iron, but the second half was the age of *steel*. This was the result of *three* developments. *Henry Bessemer's converter* developed in 1856; the *open-hearth process* developed by William Siemens in 1860, but later improved by Henry Martin in France; and the Sidney Gilchrist Thomas and Percy Gilchrist *basic method* developed in 1878. These developments transformed iron and steel making from an art into a carefully controlled scientific process in which steels of particular types were produced for particular purposes. By the last quarter of the century, an understanding of the chemistry of steel making was an essential feature of successful production.

STEEL PRODUCTION

Steel is an *alloy* of iron and carbon (cast iron has a great deal of carbon, wrought iron has almost none); the problem is to get *the right amount* of carbon. Before the 1850s, the reheating of wrought iron for several days in a clay container with pieces of charcoal (which is a pure form of carbon) produced a form of steel known as blister steel. If this is reheated and hammered, an even better quality steel is produced, namely *sheer steel*. This process was greatly improved by Benjamin Huntsmen who in 1740 developed the *crucible* or *pot furnace* (see Figure 5.17). This is the type of furnace which survives at the Abbeydale

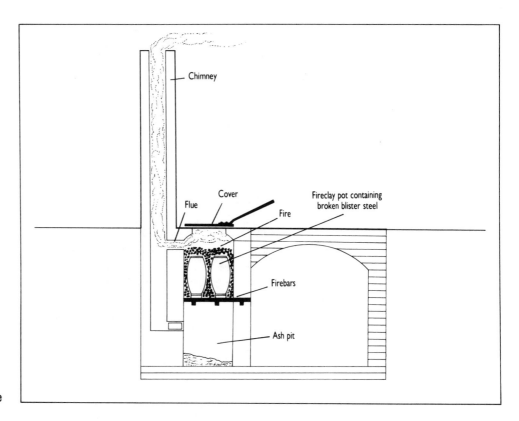

Fig. 5.17 Crucible or Pot Furnace

Industrial Hamlet museum outside Sheffield. In this furnace, small pieces of sheer steel and charcoal are carefully weighed and put into crucible fireclay pots. These are then heated in a coke furnace to an intense heat, so that the steel melts; after several days the pots are removed and the molten steel poured into moulds. This process gave a very high quality steel, but it was very expensive to make and was only used for the highest quality cutting tools.

The Bessemer Process

Steel making in bulk begins with the *Bessemer process* (see Figure 5.18). This process is quite different from Huntsmen's. It uses a large metal converter to change wrought iron into steel, by blowing cold air into molten iron. At first nobody believed Bessemer when his ideas were published in 1856, especially when a demonstration of his process failed to work properly. In fact the process works very well, because the oxygen in the air causes a chemical reaction to take place that creates its own heat. Chemists call this an *exothermic reaction*. To work properly to make steel, the process needed to use coal with a low sulphur content and non-phosphoric iron ores. At first the steel was rather brittle, but this was solved by adding manganese (discovered by Robert Mushet). It took Bessemer nearly three years to sort out these 'teething' problems, but when this had been done, the process worked and manufacturers began to adopt it.

A   *the converter at rest*
B   *the converter tilted and molten iron poured in*
C   *the converter blowing – with cold air through the tubes*
D   *steel is poured into the ladle*

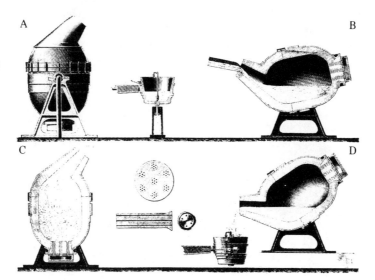

Fig. 5.18 The Bessemer Process. Diagrams from Henry Bessemer's 'An Autobiography', 1905

The Bessemer process was very quick. A *puddling furnace* made about 5 cwt (250 kg) of wrought iron in 2 hours. The *Bessemer converter* made what was called *malleable iron* (but today we call it mild steel) in about 20 minutes. When the teething problems had been overcome and the process scaled up to full commercial size, several tons could be made in less than half an hour. Costs fell dramatically, and as the price of steel fell, so demand increased. Production of Bessemer steel had risen to about 1.3m tons in 1880, 3.6m tons by 1890 and 7.6m tons by 1913.

The Siemens Open-Hearth Process

The Bessemer process is a *batch process*; the converter has to be loaded and emptied at intervals. The Open-Hearth process developed by William Siemens, although it also needed non phosphoric ores and was slower, was *continuous* and more easily controlled. The steel produced was of a much better quality. First the carbon had to be removed from the pig iron by heating in a gas furnace; then scrap iron or ore could be added, followed by other chemicals (Figure 5.19). The first Siemens steel plant was built at Landore near Swansea, and was producing a thousand tons a week by the later 1860s. But the process was slow to be taken up, possibly because many manufacturers had already invested heavily in Bessemer converters.

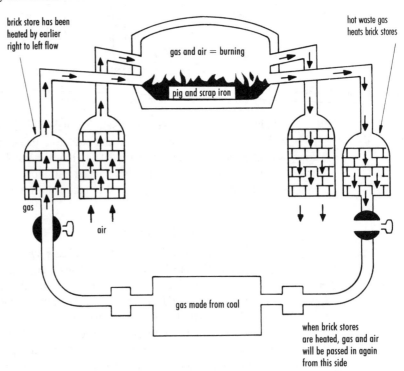

Fig. 5.19 The Siemens (Open-Hearth) Furnace

Both the Bessemer and Siemens methods had to use *non-phosphoric ore*. In England, such ore is found in Cumberland but the rapid growth of the industry meant that vast quantities of ore had to be imported from Spain and Sweden. This problem was overcome by the *basic process* patented by Sidney Gilchrist-Thomas in 1879. This process removed the phosphorus chemically by adding a *limestone lining* instead of silica (or acid fireclay) lining to the furnace. Limestone was also added at the same time as pig iron to the furnace. This method also worked on open hearth furnaces.

| YEAR | BESSEMER | | OPEN-HEARTH | | TOTAL |
	Acid	Basic	Acid	Basic	
1870		329			329
1875		620		88	708
1890	1,613	402	1,463	101	3,579
1900	1,254	491	2,863	283	4,901
1913	1,049	552	3,811	2,252	7,664

Fig. 5.20 U.K. Steel production (thousands of tons)

Source: Mitchell and Deane, *Abstract of British Historical Statistics*, p. 136.

6 〉 COAL

Date	Output (millions of tons)
1700	2.5
1800	11.0
1810	14.3
1820	17.4
1830	22.4
1840	33.7
1850	49.4
1860	80.0
1870	110.4
1880	146.8
1890	181.6
1900	225.3

Fig. 5.21 Coal output 1700–1900

The use of *coal* in Britain goes back to antiquity, but like iron and steel, coal was one of the basic pillars of industry in the nineteenth century. It was not only a major industry (employing over a million people in 1913), it also became the principal source of power, and without it the expansion of other industries would have been severely limited.

Before 1800, coal output was quite small and coal was mostly used as a domestic fuel (Figure 5.21). In the towns coal was the major fuel and source of heat, even during the seventeenth century. In 1661 John Evelyn, a noted diarist, commented on the need to get rid of that 'hellish and dismall cloude of sea coale'. He suggested that a number of industries such as brewing, soap and salt boiling and dying should be removed from London. Coal fields (such as those around Newcastle) where coal was near the surface and close to water transport, expanded considerably because of this domestic demand. The growth of urban areas and the use of coke in iron making (see above) massively increased the demand for coal, and this led to the rapid growth of coal output in Lancashire, Staffordshire, Cumberland as well as in the north-east of England.

COAL MINING DEVELOPMENTS

To obtain increased supplies, landowners not only had to sink new mines but to take their shafts much deeper than was possible with *adit mines* or *bell pits* (see Figure 5.22). In Staffordshire during the eighteenth century, most pits were shallow, being no more than 60 feet deep; but during the 1760s, John Roebuck had sunk pits to 420 feet in Scotland, and even 450 feet was not unusual in the north-eastern pits or Cumberland in 1730. By 1793, the deepest pit, the Howgill colliery at Whitehaven, reached a depth of 993 feet; by the 1830s, the deepest pits were in the north-eastern coalfield at over 1500 feet deep.

As pits became deeper, so the problems of drainage and ventilation became worse. This was of course a common problem to all mines, including lead, tin and copper. Deep pits also increased the problem of getting men and equipment down the pit shaft.

Drainage pumps

Adit mines could be *drained* naturally, but where this was not possible, pumps had to be used. At first these were simple rag pumps, but during the eighteenth century, Newcomen engines came into widespread use to lift water to the surface. Some 78 Newcomen pumps were in use by 1733, and at least 321 by 1775. In some mines several engines were in use, lifting the water to the surface in stages. From 1775, Watt's improved pumping engine became available and it was widely used after 1800 when the patent expired. Engines became more readily available and cheaper. As pit shafts went deeper, they needed to become wider; in 1793, John Buddle was already using sections of cast iron, bolted together to form a tube, if there was a danger of walls collapsing.

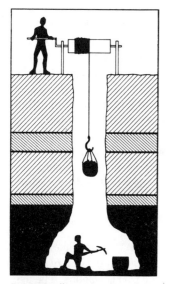

Fig. 5.22 Bell pits which have fallen in can be found all over the coalfields of Britain

Ventilation pumps

Steam engines also helped to overcome the problem of *ventilation* by pumping air through a system of shafts and tunnels. Before steam engines, the problem had been overcome by trying to create a natural convection draught, using furnaces in one or more shafts (see Figure 5.23). This was extremely dangerous, since in most mines methane gas (fire damp) collects underground and when mixed with air it explodes. In 1765, Sir John Lowther even offered to light the streets of Whitehaven with gas piped from his mines. One way to get

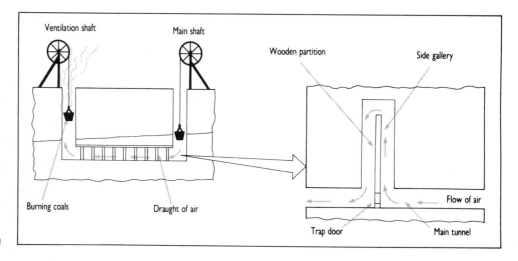

Fig. 5.23 Mine Ventilation

rid of gas was for firemen to try and ignite it underground *before* it reached too high a concentration. The other dangerous gas was choke damp (carbonic acid gas) which collected in pockets and meant there was no air or oxygen. During the 1760s, James Spedding invented the technique known as 'coursing the air'. Trapdoors were built underground in the roadways so that the air was forced to circulate the pit in a particular way, depending on which coal face was being worked. John Buddle improved on this by 'splitting the air'. He divided the workings up into separate routes of about four miles in length and used by-pass tunnels so that there was a free flow of air, and no concentrations of gas were possible. Of course this method now meant that there was a need for 'trappers' to work long shifts underground just to open and close the doorways as the wagons (known as corves) went along the roadways. Effective fan ventilators were not developed until the 1840s as steam engines became more powerful, and even then were not widely used till the 1860s.

Lighting

Lighting was the third major problem underground. Until the development of safety lamps, miners generally used ordinary candles. These were dangerous and did not give off much light. *Safety lamps* were developed by William Clanny, a Sunderland doctor, in 1811. He filtered the air through water, but the candle then gave off such a dim light that it was rarely used. In 1815, after discussions with John Buddle and William Clanny, Sir Humphrey Davy experimented with various ways to protect the flame of the candle. He used a wire gauze that prevented the explosive gas getting to the candle flame but allowed oxygen through. The first prototypes were in use by 1816 and improved ones, with a reflector, a little later. At the same time, George Stephenson produced a number of lamps using the same principle. Whose lamp was developed first is difficult to say, but it seems likely that Davy had perfected the wire gauze principle a couple of weeks before Stephenson. Further improvements during the nineteenth century meant that lamps became even safer and gave off a much better light. Nevertheless, in many mines safety lamps were *not* used and it could even be argued that because safety lamps allowed miners to go into deeper and more dangerous mines, they led to more accidents. Safety lamps were still in general use in many mines into the twentieth century when they were finally replaced by battery lamps.

Transport systems

Other improvements in the mines included *better underground railways*, using wheeled iron trucks rolled on rails instead of sledges. The use of gunpowder also allowed *wider roadways* to be built so that on the main tunnels pit ponies could now be used to pull wagons. The use of *steam engines* made it possible to haul coal wagons directly up the shaft to the surface. It seems possible from illustrations that this was being done even as early as the middle of the eighteenth century. Certainly we have as evidence both illustrations and the remains of horse whimsey gins that were used to haul up coal (see Figure 5.24).

Fig. 5.24 Whimsey Gin used to haul coal to the surface

From W.H.Pyne, Microcosm, 1803

The practical use of steam engines as *winding gear* came with Pickards development of the crank (1780) and Watt's sun and planet gear (1782), which converted the up and down motion of the piston and beam of a steam engine into a rotating movement. It was however only with the lapse of Watt's and Pickard's patents in 1790 and 1791 that steam engines were widely used to move coal or to lower people down the shafts. Flat rope which easily wound onto a drum was invented by John Curr in 1798, and double link iron chains were in use by 1810. Accidents with men riding on corves hooked onto ropes or chains were not unusual and cages for men and wagons were developed by J. Hall in 1834, though it was not till the 1840s that they were made safe by the addition of rails that guided the cage up the shaft between rails. In the 1840s, the use of wire rope (developed in 1834) was gradually being adopted.

Many of these new techniques and ideas were very costly to put into effect, and the existence of many small pits meant that old fashioned and unsafe practices continued for many years, despite the work of mines inspectors in the 1840s and 50s. Even with these improvements, work underground was an extremely dangerous and back-breaking job. Practically all the work underground was heavy manual labour in appalling conditions. Coal was dug using hand picks, often in narrow shafts, and wagons and sledges were pushed and hauled to the roadways by hand (see Figure 5.25). Accidents involving hundreds of deaths by explosions or drowning were not unusual, and 'minor' accidents where the roof caved in, or a wagon came off the rails were commonplace.

Fig. 5.25 Hauling coal by hand

Children's Employment Commission, 1842

EXAMINATION QUESTIONS

QUESTION 1   Study Sources A, B, and C below then answer the questions which follow.

Source A Taken from an engraving of the *Severn Gorge at Coalbrookdale*, 1788:

Source B (Adapted from Arthur Young's *Annals of Agriculture*, 1785):

Crossing the ferry where Mr Darby has undertaken to build a bridge of one arch of 37
metres of cast iron, I passed to his works by Coalbrookdale. The waggon ways that lead
down to the river are laid with cast iron instead of wood; and those made for limestone
waggons on the steep hills are so designed that the loaded waggon winds up the empty
one on a different road. . . . These works are supposed to be the greatest in England.
The whole process here is gone through from digging the limestone to making it into
cannon, pipes, etc. etc. All iron is raised in the neighbouring hills, and the coal dug
likewise, which is charred * – an invention which must have been of the greatest
importance after the quantity of cordwood in the Kingdom declined.
(* = turned into coke)

Source C:

To *IRONMASTERS, and Manufacturers of Steam-Engines, Boilers, Castings, Rails, Bar Iron, &c., &c.*

MILTON IRON WORKS.

TO BE LET, for a term of 21 Years, and may be entered upon the First of October next, all those Old-established Iron-Works, called "THE MILTON IRON-WORKS," situate near to the Elsecar Coal-Field and the Tankersley Park Ironstone Grounds, and at a convenient distance from the Manufacturing Towns of Sheffield, Rotherham, and Barnsley, in the County of York. The Works consist of—

TWO BLAST FURNACES, with every requisite Appendage:—

line 14   FORGE and MILL, with Puddling and other Furnaces, Chafery for Drawing Uses, Rolling and Slitting Mills, &c., capable of Manufacturing from 90 to 100 Tons of Finished Iron per Week :—

FOUNDRY, with Pits, Drying Stoves, and every requisite Apparatus for making Engine Work, and Castings of every description, to the extent of 100 Tons per Week :—

ENGINE-FITTING SHOPS, with Lathes, Boring and Planing Machines, Boiler Makers' and Smiths' Shops, and every requisite for carrying on Engine and Railway Work to a large extent:—

Together with an ample supply of ELSECAR COALS, and TANKERSLEY PARK and SWALLOW-WOOD IRON-STONE, on terms to be agreed upon.

The Works possess at present excellent Canal and River Communication, and will shortly have the advantage of the South Yorkshire Railway.

N.B.—Although the Owner of the Works would not absolutely restrain the Lessees from making and Manufac-

line 33   turing Hot Blast Iron, yet he would prefer treating with parties who would undertake to make and manufacture Cold Blast Iron only.

For further Particulars, apply to **Mr. NEWMAN**, of Darley Hall, near Barnsley; or Mr. WOODHOUSE, of Overseal, near Ashby-de-la-Zouch.

Darley Hall, near Barnsley,

a) Study Sources A and B.

   i) Explain why Coalbrookdale was a good place for iron production in the late eigtheenth century. *(4)*

   ii) What evidence is there to suggest that transport was difficult in Coalbrookdale?

   (2)

   iii) Explain why the *invention* referred to in Source B (line 8) was so important to the development of the iron industry. *(3)*

   iv) Name **two** uses for iron which were new at the time, as indicated in Source B.

   (2)

b) Study Source C.

   i) Give **two** pieces of evidence in Source C which suggest that this source is of a later date than Source A or B. *(2)*

   ii) Explain the importance of *puddling* (line 14) and *hot blast iron* (line 33) in the development of the iron industry. *(2)*

c) Sources A, B, and C are different types of historical evidence. How useful is each to someone studying this period and topic? *(5)*

(LEAG; 1988)

QUESTION 2   A structured essay.

a) How did the major technological developments of 1780–1850 in the iron industry affect both the location and scale of production in this industry?

b) Describe the importance of each of the following developments in the manufacture of steel:

   the Bessemer converter; the open-hearth process: the basic method.

QUESTION 3   Look carefully at the sketch map opposite of the Coalbrookdale Industrial Site, and then answer the questions which follow.

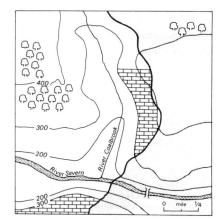

Key
- Limestone
- Heavily wooded areas
- Coal and iron field

a) i) Who built an ironworks on this site in the early eighteenth century? *(1)*

   ii) Why was the heavily wooded area important to the early iron industry? *(3)*

b) Why did Coalbrookdale become so important in the development of the iron industry?

   (6)

c) 'The wars in the eighteenth and early nineteenth centuries were the main reason for the expansion of the iron industry before 1815.' Do you agree with this statement? Explain your answer fully. *(10)*

(MEG; 1988)

A STUDENT'S ANSWER WITH EXAMINER'S COMMENTS

QUESTION   Structured essay questions give you the opportunity to show that you know what happened and that you can explain why certain events or people were particularly important or significant in history.

a) Briefly describe the domestic system of manufacture in the textile industries about 1700.

b) Describe the main inventions adopted between about 1760 and 1800 and explain how these affected the location and organisation of the cotton industry.

a)   The domestic system was when yarn and cloth were
     made in the workers own home. A clothier would
     bring the raw wool or cotton round to peoples homes
     and the wife and children would first card it then
     spin it into yarn using a spinning wheel. Later the
     yarn would be woven into cloth by the husband and
     either the cloth would be collected by the clothier
     or be sold in a local cloth market.

66 Shows good basic knowledge of facts. Might have explained that often several spinners worked for a single weaver and that work could be done in the home because the machines were reasonably cheap and did not need mechanical power. Might have explained the processes done in the home in more detail. 99

b)   The first changes in cotton affected the spinning
     part of the industry. About 1765, James Hargreaves
     invented the spinning jenny. This was a machine
     that could instead of spinning only one thread like
     a spinning wheel, it could spin between 12 and 28.
     This meant that more yarn at cheaper prices could
     be provided for the weaver. This machine was small
     and hand powered so that it could be used in the
     weavers or spinners own home. Later in 1770,
     Richard Arkwright invented the water frame. This
     used a different way to spin yarn but more
     importantly, Arkwright would only allow people to
     use his invention if they built large machines that
     need water power to drive them. This was so that it
     was eaiser to collect the royalties for his patent.
     But it did mean that only people who could afford
     to build a large machine and provide the water
     power could use it. Slowly all spinning came to be
     done in factories which had to be built near a good
     supply of water. This was so that there was plenty
     of water to drive the wheel and also to clean and
     wash all the cotton. In the 1780s the difficulty of
     finding sites for water powered spinning mills that
     were close to good transport such as canals or
     where the manufacturer could get cheap labour meant
     that new factories were built near to towns. This
     became possible because now steam engines were able
     to drive the machinery. Canals could not only bring
     in the cotton but also they made the cost of coal
     much less, and there were a lot of people living in
     towns who needed work. At first, only spinning was
     done in the factory, weaving was still done on hand
     looms in peoples houses and spinners could earn
     very high wages, but in 1785, James Cartwright
     invented a power loom. This did not work very well
     so hand loom weavers were not affected very much.
     It was only during the 1820s that power looms began
     to be good enough to replace hand loom weavers.

66 Quite a well informed account that keeps to the point. Explains clearly the advantages of the jenny, but does not mention that spinning now became a man's job. Makes very good point about Arkwright's water frame and why it needed to go into a factory, but forgets to mention Crompton's mule, 1779. Makes good point about the change from rural to town mills, but forgets to mention that the centre of industry was changing to the north-west, the area around Manchester. Other good points include comments on transport and on the slow use of power weaving looms. 99

THE TRANSPORT REVOLUTION

SOURCES

TRANSPORT IN THE EIGHTEENTH CENTURY

ROADS

INLAND WATERWAYS

RAILWAYS

GETTING STARTED

The basic problems concern the links between industrial development and the rate at which transport services hindered or encouraged the growth of the economy. In the early eighteenth century it is widely believed that existing transport services could not cope with the growth in demand as agriculture and industry expanded. This encouraged an expansion of *existing* transport services and a search for *other methods of transport* that were cheaper and more reliable. Better transport services led to lower costs and gave industry access to more customers. The building of new transport facilities also increased employment and the growth of the economy.

In the nineteenth century, it seems that technical developments in engineering took place *faster* than the demand for improved transport services. New technologies, such as steam, petrol and diesel engines, provided the possibility of alternative transport systems. As these new technologies became cheaper and more reliable, so they gradually *displaced* the older methods of transport. Often this was because they were also more convenient. These newer methods of transport usually *linked together* many different sections of the engineering and construction industries, and required enormous investment, for example in railway track or roads. They had a big impact upon the whole economy by increasing employment and reducing transport costs. They led to major changes in the structure and character of industry and major changes in the way people lived, thought and behaved.

Candidates should be able to:

- Explain the need for transport improvements in the eighteenth century.

- Describe how roads and canals were built in the eighteenth century, with some knowledge of the role of particular engineers.

- Explain how transport improvements contributed to the development of the economy and helped the growth of particular industries.

- Describe the technical developments that made the development of railways possible.

- Describe and explain the effects of railroad developments upon the growth of industry, trade, and the social effects upon people's lives, with particular attention to towns.

ESSENTIAL PRINCIPLES

There are many different sources used by transport historians but, as with agriculture, the problem for the eighteenth and early nineteenth centuries is that much of the material refers to a *particular* road, canal or region. It is therefore difficult to generalise about the country as a whole. The descriptions by travellers can be invaluable in outlining the conditions they found at a particular time, and we even have travel guides and timetables for the seventeenth as well as the eighteenth centuries. As usual, however, it is often unwise to rely upon a *single* source for information. Today, historians have been able to piece together the records for transport services in many regions. We now have quite good estimates for the road and canal mileage open at different times, the journey times between towns, the costs of travel and the goods carried. We also have lots of contemporary illustrations of coaches and the like.

For the nineteenth and twentieth centuries the range of available sources increases substantially. There is an enormous quantity of official government material on the building of particular canals and railway lines, with reports and enquiries into almost every aspect of transportation, giving invaluable information on the costs of construction, the goods carried, costs of travel and problems of safety. Not only are there hundreds of photographs, but in many parts of the country there are also museums concerned with waterways, docks and locomotives. A quick check with the local tourist information office will tell you which of these are nearby. It is well worth a visit just to get some idea of how a canal lock worked, or what it was like to have lived on a canal barge or worked as an engine driver or porter.

Much of the evidence of transport developments is still around us, to be seen even in the streets of modern cities and towns, demonstrating just how much transport improvements have helped to change the physical environment in which people lived.

Many textbooks suggest that in the eighteenth century, England's transport services were very poor. Certainly in comparison with today, travel by road was slow, expensive and uncomfortable, but in most ways it was *adequate* for the needs of industry and commerce of the time. Most people did not need to travel very often or far from the village or town in which they lived. Industries supplied *local markets* and used *local raw materials*. It was the growth of population and the manufacture of goods for sale in other parts of the country, or even for export overseas, that led to problems. Even before 1700, the growth of trade and traffic, especially that going to London or to one of the other major ports, had led to some improvements in both road, river and coastal shipping. But these were piecemeal and often not very effective. Unfortunately, central government would not be responsible for the upkeep of the basic road system.

The road system built by the Romans still existed, with a network of well-built and regularly maintained roads linking London with the major towns in the provinces, but it was not in a good state of repair (if travellers' tales are any guide). Roads were the responsibility of local parishes and although the *Highways Act of 1555* said that each parish was to appoint a surveyor to maintain the roads throughout the parish, this was rarely done properly. Up until 1835, the surveyor could require the parishioners to work for up to six days on road repair (*statute duties*) but few surveyors had any technical qualifications and local residents often refused to do their duty, despite the possibility of a fine.

THE HIGHWAYS ACTS

In 1662, the *Highways Act* banned wagons pulled by more than seven horses or with wagon wheels less than four inches wide. The idea was to limit the size of the wagons and the weights they carried and to try and prevent the roads being rutted by narrow wheels. This, and similar Acts, were not successful in preventing the steady increase in traffic, especially that going into London.

In 1767, the first *General Highway Act* tried to give clear guidelines about the size of roads into market towns and in 1773 the Act was made clearer with detailed regulations on the sizes of wheels and the limits to be placed on the numbers of horses that could be used with wheels of different sizes. The responsibility for roads was given to the *Quarter Session Courts*, and they were allowed to abandon little used roads in order to improve the main roads. The statute duty of parishioners to repair the roads was also altered. In fact this legislation was not really effective and in 1835 *all* the regulations trying to control wheel sizes and the weights of wagons were abandoned. Instead, parishes were amalgamated into *highway districts* which were given clear powers and responsibilities. They were allowed to employ professional engineers and to pay for the upkeep of the roads with a local rate.

TOLLS

These problems led local J.Ps. in Hertfordshire, who were supposed to have overall responsibility for the Great North Road (nowadays the A1), to ask Parliament in 1663 for permission to bring back the ancient custom of *paveage*. This allowed them to charge *tolls* for the use of a particular road and to use this money to keep the road in good repair. This was also tried in several parts of Essex, Norfolk, Sussex and Gloucestershire, but was only partially successful. In 1706, the first two private *Turnpike Acts* allowed groups of local trustees, usually local business men and J.Ps., to be responsible for different parts of the London to Holyhead Road. By 1720, this system was proving to be so successful that it was adopted in many parts of the country (see Figure 6.1). At first, these *Turnpike Trusts* as they were called, were only for a period of 21 years, but very soon they were given almost unlimited powers to borrow money to build and repair the road, to decide on the level of tolls and to collect these in whatever way they decided.

By 1770, about 15,000 miles of road were turnpiked; by 1830 this had risen to 22,000 miles. Expenditure by Turnpike Trusts on improving and maintaining roads was about £60,000 in 1750; by the 1770s it had risen to about £200,000, and by 1800 to about £500,000; in 1820 it was over £1 million. It was only in 1820 that annual expenditure on turnpikes was actually greater than that on parish roads.

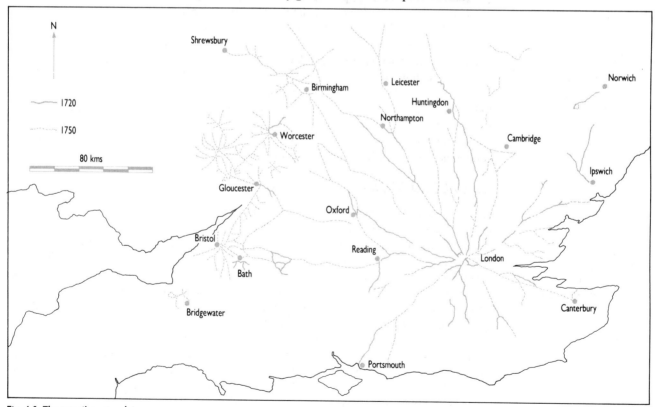

Fig. 6.1 The turnpike network in Southern England around 1750

ROAD BUILDERS

The turnpike roads may have been quite expensive to build and maintain but they did lead to the development of effective methods of road building that were cost effective. They also led to the first proper road engineers, men such as John Metcalf (1717–1810) (often known as 'Blind Jack of Knaresborough'), Thomas Telford (1757–1834) and John Loudan McAdam (1756–1836). It was Metcalf who established the basic principles of road building

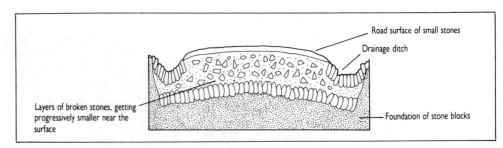

Fig. 6.2 Cross-section of Metcalf's
road

in the 180 miles or so of turnpike roads he built in Yorkshire and Lancashire between 1765 and 1792. He ensured that the road had a good foundation of stones. He then built up a smooth convex surface using *progressively smaller stones* for each layer so that water would readily run off into ditches beside the road which were lower than the foundations (see Figure 6.2).

Methods of road building

McAdam's methods were similar, but he gave even more attention to the problem of *drainage*. He showed that if this was done, a foundation of large stones was unnecessary and could even lead to a lesser likelihood of potholes. His roads were also made up of layers of progressively smaller stones but he allowed the traffic to compact each layer and did *not* put a convex curve or *camber* on the road. He was perhaps the most successful road contractor of his day and organised his gangs of workers into specialist teams, each with a particular job. His methods were quick and cheap. He was responsible for about 700 miles of road in 15 counties and he gave evidence on many occasions on how to build roads to Parliamentary select committees and improvement commissioners. He built up a successful construction company and his work and ideas were continued by his sons. McAdam's methods led to a new word entering the language – to *macadamize* – to build up a road using layers of stone of the same size. Later, in 1882, when rubber-wheeled vehicles became common, it was reported that broken stone or iron stone, when mixed with tar or pitch and creosote, made a smooth waterproof surface. Indeed, a surface from which rubber tyres did not pick up stones. McAdam himself never used tar; metal rimmed or wooden wheeled vehicles, he maintained, did not need it.

Telford's methods were much more expensive than those of either Metcalf or McAdam because his roads were built to a much higher standard. He used broken stones of different sizes in several thick layers. Each layer was heavily compacted so that the stones were solidly bound together. His roads were built to last much longer before being repaired and could carry much heavier traffic loads. Some stretches of the A5 north of Shrewsbury are today still basically in the form engineered by Telford. More than any of the others, Telford was a civil engineer who built not only roads but also hundreds of bridges and aqueducts out of both stone and cast or wrought iron. Even today the milestones and plaques which commemorate his work can be seen on many roads in the north and midlands.

ROAD CONDITIONS

How effective the Turnpike Trusts were, is a difficult question to answer because the evidence is so conflicting. Arthur Young was often complaining about the poor condition of the roads, even at the end of the eighteenth century, and Dickens, in the Pickwick novels, gives descriptions of horrendous journeys especially during winter time. In Arthur Young's case, despite his complaints about the terrible roads of Sussex, he still travelled over 100 miles per week in a light chaise. In 1768, during a tour of the northern counties covering 1460 miles, about 930 miles was on turnpikes. He described about half of the roads as 'good' and this even included some parish roads. About half of the remaining turnpikes were 'middling' and the remaining quarter, 'bad'. His later tour, in 1813, noted 'great improvements' even in the roads of Sussex, especially the road from London to Horsham. Other travellers also noted the improvement and many of them were less critical than Young. Foreign travellers or Englishmen who travelled abroad almost always said how much better and easier it was to travel in England.

Travellers' tales of British roads

Henry Homer, in his *Enquiry into the Means of Preserving and Improving the Publick Roads (1767)*, stated that:

'There was never a more astonishing revolution accomplished in the internal system of any country. The carriage of grain, coals, merchandise, etc. is in general conducted with little more than half the number of horses which it formerly was. . . . Everything wears the face of dispatch and the hinge which has guided all these movements, and upon which they turn, is the reformation which has been made on our public roads.'

ROAD NETWORKS

Some indication of the improvements brought by turnpikes is the reduction in travel times and the availability of services from London to other major towns. By the 1770s, all of the major towns and cities were provided by a network of good roads that linked them both to one another and to other towns in their region. This led to tremendous improvements in coaching services and in the transport of passengers and mail, or light manufactured goods. In 1740, there had only been one coach per week between London and Birmingham; by 1783 it had risen to 30 and by 1829 it was 34 a day. The same pattern was true for connections between London and other cities (see Figure 6.3).

There were considerable improvements in the quality and cost of travel arising from competition between companies. In the 1830s Chaplin and Company of London, was the largest coach company; it had 64 coaches, 1,500 horses and an annual tunrover of about £500,000. It is reckoned that by 1830 there were about 4,500 departures from London weekly, giving a possible 58,000 passengers.

Customers nevertheless complained bitterly about both the costs and discomfort of travel. This was especially true of local residents who found that they had to stop at toll gates and pay for travelling along the road. Such complaints were often exaggerated and the increase in long distance traffic usually meant that short, local travel was effectively subsidised by the long distance traveller. More reasonable was the complaint that trustees did not always maintain the roads as well as they should and kept too much of the profits. The turnpike roads were not planned as part of an *overall* system and even in the 1820s some lengths of turnpike were too short and were not connected up to form proper through routes. This same criticism is often made of modern motorways.

	To Bath		To Manchester		To Edinburgh
1740	35 hours	1740	72 hours	1740	170 hours
1760	29 hours	1760	58 hours	1760	160 hours
1780	15 hours	1780	31 hours	1780	80 hours
1800	14 hours	1800	28 hours	1800	65 hours
1820	12 hours	1820	28 hours	1820	55 hours

Fig. 6.3 Travel times for coaches from London 1740–1820

4 › INLAND WATERWAYS

In fact roads could really only cope with part of the increased demands for better transport in the eighteenth century. They were hopeless for the carriage of heavy, bulky or low value goods. Wagons were too slow and could not carry goods economically over any distance. Such goods could only be carried by rivers and sea. Even in 1700 it seems that practically all Britain's major towns were less than 15 miles from navigable rivers. Many of the rivers could be improved by dredging, the removal of obstructions such as dams or weirs and the building of proper locks to regulate the flow of water and to provide a guaranteed depth of water for cargo vessels.

There was a considerable improvement in these services at about the same time that turnpikes developed and the same basic procedure was adopted. A group of local businessmen would apply to Parliament for a private Act to establish a river improvement company and to charge tolls for building locks, etc. The first improvements were on rivers which had a heavy volume of traffic or the potential for heavy traffic, such as those that connected ports with inland areas. Other 'attractive' rivers were those where bulky, heavy raw materials such as coal, limestone or stone were found nearby.

CANAL SYSTEMS

In the early eighteenth century, proposals for *canals* were made by several people, but the engineering problems were too difficult. However on the Wey and Irwell (in the 1720s), new channels were cut and the rivers locked in such a way that they had effectively become canals. Engineers such as Thomas Steers learned to deal with complex engineering problems. Steers built new docks in Liverpool and London, improved the River Douglas at Wigan and finally built the first proper canal between 1730 and 1742 in Newry in Ireland. This gave access to coal in Tyrone.

Steers had also been involved in proposals for improving the links between Liverpool and the inland towns by improvements on the Mersey-Irwell. The *Sankey Brook Navigation* finally first opened in 1737, and five years later was extended to the Mersey. This can be considered the first English canal, although the work was not completed until 1740.

Improvements to the other main tributary, the Weaver, despite being considered in 1663, were not begun till 1728 and only completed in 1734. This series of improvements allowed large 35-ton sailing barges to carry coal and salt between the salt-whiches in Cheshire, the coal fields of Lancashire and the port of Liverpool.

The one town that was *not* properly connected with Liverpool, despite its extensive trade, was Manchester. Attempts were made to overcome this problem when the first Duke of Bridgewater obtained an Act in 1737 for the *Worsley Brook Navigation*; but this proposal was abandoned because the Duke could not come to an agreement with the Old Quay Company who ran the Irwell Navigation. The problem of flooding in the Dukes mines at Worsley finally became so serious that in 1757 Francis, the third Duke of Bridgewater, asked his estate manager John Gilbert to plan a way to drain the mine. Gilbert did the early work on surveying the route and the underground workings but the work on the canal proper was done by James Brindley. In 1759 and 1760, a series of Acts were granted and work begun on a canal. The first canal was only ten miles long and, by following the contours, Brindley did not have to build any locks. He did, however, have to overcome a wide range of engineering problems such as crossing the boggy Trafford Moss, building embankments, tunnelling and finally building a bridge or aqueduct to cross the River Irwell at Barton.

In 1761, the first cargo of coal was unloaded at the quayside at Stretford and finally, in 1765, the canal was completed at the huge Castlefields basin almost in the centre of Manchester. It was now possible for a single horse to bring 50 tons of coal at a steady 4 miles per hour from the Worsley mines, through a series of underground tunnels and lifts, to the surface canal and then directly in to Manchester. After the canal was fully opened to Manchester, the price of coal in Manchester fell from 7d (3p) to 3½d.

In 1767, after another fight with the Old Quay Company who opposed his private members bill in 1766, Brindley extended the canal 10 miles westwards to Runcorn to link up with the Mersey. This effectively destroyed the Old Quay Company's monopoly on the

❝The Bridgewater Canal ❞

1 Bridgewater
2 Trent & Mersey (Grand Trunk)
3 Oxford
4 Thames & Severn
5 Staffordshire & Worcester
6 Coventry
7 Forth & Clyde
8 Leeds & Liverpool
9 Lancaster
10 Huddersfield
11 Grand Junction
12 Kennet & Avon

——— navigable rivers

——— canals

Fig. 6.4 Map of canals about 1820

river trade between Manchester and Liverpool and the carriage of freight fell from 123,917 tons in 1776–7 to 5,284 tons in 1779–80.

At Runcorn a flight of 10 locks allowed barges to bridge the 24 foot difference between the height of the canal and that of the River Mersey. These were finally replaced in 1875 by the massive Anderton steam lift. By 1782, Bridgewater had also built a new dock to handle the increased volume of traffic along the canal together with a canal complex at Castlefields basin almost in the heart of Manchester.

Between 1766 and 1772 there was a rash of canal promotions with a second period of 'canal mania' during the 1790s. Brindley himself was responsible for building about 365 miles of canal when he died in 1772, the most important being the Grand Trunk built between 1766–1778. This was like a central spine from the north to the south and linked the Mersey and Bridgewater canal with the River Trent and the Staffordshire potteries (Figure 6.4).

EFFECTS OF CANALS

Canals were never a transport system as such. There was no overall planning and they developed wherever local businessmen believed there was a local need and could raise the capital. They were all shapes and sizes, although the typical Brindley narrow canal was able to take barges of 72 feet by 7 feet, carrying about 25 to 30 tons; others, such as the Erewash, could take boats 78 feet by 14 feet. On the Droitwich canal, the locks were only 64 feet long, so even Brindley-type narrow boats would not fit. Nevertheless, in 1800 it was possible to travel to most towns north and south and east and west, using a combination of canals and river navigations. Canals did *reduce the costs of transport considerably*, and by 1813, even the most expensive canals were less than 50% of the cost of travel by road over long distances. On the Grand Trunk, the cost of freight from Manchester to Lichfield fell from £4 to £1 per ton. The journey of pottery from Wedgewood's Etruria to Manchester was £2.75 per ton by road, and £0.75 per ton by canal.

Canals *lowered costs of production for industry* by bringing cheaper raw materials and providing access to wider and more distant markets. This encouraged industry to increase its *scale of production* and in some cases this led to a searching for new and cheaper methods of production. The most important commodities carried on canals were the heavy, bulky, raw materials, such as coal, iron ore, stone, marl and even groceries; but in many areas agricultural products such as wheat, corn, malt, beans and wool were carried to distant markets. Thus canals helped to even out regional price differences, and probably to reduce prices generally, in the first half of the nineteenth century.

Canals encouraged the development of civil engineering, because almost all canals not only required extensive dock facilities but cuttings, bridges, aqueducts and locks. Telford's Pont-y-Cysyllte aqueduct carried the canal in a cast iron trough for 1007 feet at a height of 127 feet above the river Dee on slender stone pillars and is still a marvel to look at today. Engineers learned *how to construct* and also *how to administer and organise* large teams of workers or 'navvies'. As with the textile, iron and coal industries, canal construction was big business that needed capital and organisation.

5 ▷ RAILWAYS

Railways were probably the most important single factor in the growth of national economies. Their combination with ocean-going steam shipping after 1850, was probably the most important factor in the opening up of the international economy. Railways affected almost every aspect of economic and social life.

The earliest railway was the Stockton to Darlington in 1825, but this development was the result of many years experience in the use of wooden and metal trackways in coal mines and iron works over the previous 50 years. In many areas horses pulled wagons on tramways. In Derbyshire the Peak Forest Railway used the natural gradient to allow convoys of wagons carrying stone to link the quarries at Chapel-en-le-Frith with the canal at Bugsworth. To be effective, tramways needed an independent source of power and this was provided by the steam engine.

STEAM LOCOMOTIVES

The problem was to make a steam locomotive that was powerful enough to pull an economic load and light enough not to break the cast iron rails. Trevithick's high pressure engine of 1804 was not really sufficiently powerful or reliable to do the job, and it was not until 1825 that George Stephenson's '*Locomotion*' was used successfully on the Stockton to Darlington line. Even then the line also used stationary engines on some steep gradients and at first allowed horse-drawn vehicles to use the line. The company operated almost like a canal or turnpike, allowing anyone to use the line with their own wagons on payment of a toll.

RAILWAY COMPANIES AND NETWORKS

The first modern railway was the Liverpool to Manchester Railway opened in 1830. This used Stephenson's new engine, the '*Rocket*', which had won the trials the previous year at Rainhill. The line adopted Stephenson's standard gauge of 4 feet 8½ inches (copied from the gauge used in the Newcastle collieries) and set the pattern for later railways in other ways. The company owned all the rolling stock and ran the whole business itself, without sub-contracting out to anyone else. From the very beginning, passengers were catered for and, initially at least, this provided more than half its total revenue.

There were still a great many technical problems to overcome to make the railways an effective competitor with the canals on long distance bulk freight. However towards the end of the 1830s, other railways were being planned to link the major cities with one another. As with canals and turnpike trusts these were all joint stock companies which needed a private Act of Parliament to obtain limited liability. The cost of building a railway was immense and railway *companies* began to issue shares in relatively small sizes to obtain capital from small local businessmen and landowners as well as the extremely wealthy.

As Figure 6.5 shows, the growth of railway lines was fairly rapid and occurred in three main periods. The first, in the years 1835–7, the second 1844–6, and the third in the mid 1860s. This phased activity reflects the problem that railways were a very speculative venture; they took a long time to build and therefore to earn any profit and it was not always certain that they would be able to compete with existing canals. Once they *had* demonstrated that they were profitable and that there was enough traffic for both canals and railways, so new lines were quickly promoted. By 1850, the basic outline of the mainline network had been laid. In later years it was merely a question of filling in the gaps and of building the suburban lines from the cities. The big development in the 1860s was the replacement of iron rails with new steel track and the conversion of single lines into double track.

Years	Mileage sanctioned	Miles open	Capital authorised £m	Actual expenditure	
				total £m	per annum £m
1800–20	–	190	–	1.5	–
1821–25	62	27			
1826–30	287	71	4.0	1.0	0.2
1831–37	2,120	443	51.4	11.5	1.6
1838–41	104	957	11.0	27.4	9.1
1841–43	160	546	12.6	14.9	5.0
1844–46	8,043	1,048	207.0	50.2	16.7

Fig. 6.5 Railway mileage and capital investment (1800–46)

RAILWAY CONSTRUCTION

Railway construction not only required enormous capital (Figures 6.5 and 6.6); like the canals it also needed constructional engineers. The scale of the operation was larger and the nature of the engineering still more complex than for the canals. This led to the development of large companies *specialising* in railway engineering. Amongst the most famous are, Peto and Betts, Jacksons and Firbanks and Thomas Brassey. In 1850, Peto was employing 14,000 men and Peto and Brassey both undertook contracting jobs overseas. Many of the navvies employed on construction were Irish and were often disliked by locals in the places they were working because of their unruly and ill-disciplined nature. It seems, however, that complaints of their rowdiness were often exaggerated. The labourers were often victims of the contractor's desire to keep costs as low as possible by only providing very poor accommodation and by running a 'tommy' or 'truck' shop on the site and compelling the navvies to spend part of their wages at his shop. Labourers had also to put up with terrible working conditions and the frequency of accidents when driving tunnels or building bridges was comparable to that in the mines.

Year	CONSTRUCTION ACTIVITY			OPERATING ACTIVITY		
	Mileage under construction	*Numbers employed (000)*	*Capital investment £m*	*Mileage open*	*Numbers employed (000)*	*Traffic receipts £m*
1845	–	–	13.0	–	–	6.2
1846	–	–	30.2	–	–	7.6
1847	6,477	257	43.9	3,252	47	8.5
1848	2,958	188	33.1	4,252	53	9.9
1849	1,504	104	24.9	5,477	56	11.9
1850	864	59	13.1	6,308	60	13.2
1851	734	43	9.9	6,698	64	15.0
1852	738	36	9.7	7,076	68	15.7
1853	682	38	10.2	7,512	80	18.0
1854	889	45	12.7	7,803	90	20.2
1855	880	39	11.3	8,116	98	21.5
1856	963	36	9.0	8,506	102	23.2
1857	1,004	44	9.6	8,942	110	34.2
1858	1,014	38	9.3	9,324	109	24.0
1859	993	40	9.9	8,796	116	25.7
1860	1,051	54	11.0	10,201	127	27.8

Fig. 6.6 The Growth of the Railway Industry (1845–60)

THE SOCIAL AND ECONOMIC EFFECTS OF RAILWAYS

Railways affected almost every aspect of social and economic life. In economic terms they created a tremendous demand for all kinds of goods and services.

Technical effects

Railways obviously needed *railway track*. It would seem to be a simple matter to calculate how many miles of track were built and therefore how much extra iron was needed. However, iron rails had to be designed to withstand the weight of the wagons and ways had to be found to stop them bouncing about as the engine went over them. This meant the development of 'sleepers' and of various ways to fix the track. These were complex engineering problems and, once overcome, led to the production of nails, nuts and bolts on an enormous scale. Locomotive engineering was in many ways the equivalent of space engineering today. It was the *lead* in new engineering technology. The railway companies had to plan, design and usually build all their own engines and of course had to train their own engineers and craftsmen to do this. Even in building the lines, the quantity of *stone and brick* for the track, bridges and eventually stations was probably even greater than the amount of iron. The same is true for *wooden sleepers*.

How did the manufacturers of these products cope with the increased demand. In many cases they had to expand production and this often meant investment in new plant and equipment. To some extent the increase in production was less than might be expected. Although railways were *planned* when the economy was booming, very often by the time the route had been agreed, Parliamentary permission obtained and the capital collected from shareholders, the economy was no longer growing so fast. However, the building of the planned railway usually continued, in this way helping to boost the economy and to prevent the depression being greater than it might have been.

Employment

The construction of railways gave employment to thousands of labourers at a time, often when many would otherwise be out of work. This meant that they had incomes to spend on basic food and clothing, so that the *consumer* industries were stimulated by higher demand. This construction phase did not last very long (see Figure 6.6), and by 1850 more people were employed in *running* the railways than in building them. Although many people in the railways were relatively unskilled, running the railways also required a whole host of more numerate, literate and mechanically skilled workers. Think for example how many stations there were and the need for people to keep records of how many tickets were issued and to keep account books. The maintenance of the railway rolling stock and track also required an immense number of engineers, as did the development of signalling equipment and the use of the electric telegraph, not to mention the engine drivers and guardsmen.

Railways were big business and they not only faced problems with engineering, but also with the running of a big business so that all the different parts operated smoothly. Railway companies were pioneers in business administration and labour relations. They were a model that many other businesses were to follow.

Communications

The effects on other business, once the railways lines had been built, are equally obvious. Railways *widened the market* for businessmen and gave *quicker communications*. They were not *initially* cheaper than canals, which continued to expand their carriage of low value heavy bulky freight right up to the 1860s. However the railways opened up new opportunities to passenger traffic and to the transport of perishable goods. When the system had been fully developed by the later 1860s, railways could also offer a quicker and cheaper service than canals. In these ways the railways helped to reduce costs and to improve efficiency throughout the economy.

Environmental effects

Perhaps the most obvious effect of railways is still with us today – their *physical impact upon the environment*. Railways changed the face of cities, with the massive new stations and marshalling yards built on the fringe of the city centre. Many of the major stations are interesting for the way they used standardised cast and wrought iron parts and glass to create massive, yet light, buildings. The building of such stations and railway track meant demolishing large numbers of cheap housing and building bridges (viaducts) that went right over the top of houses. This created a level of noise and pollution from the steam engines at least as bad as petrol and diesel engines.

Railways changed people's lives (see Figure 6.7). The general introduction of 'railway time' or Greenwich Mean Time throughout the country signalled a new clock watching attitude. With the introduction of new ideas and their mass communication via newspapers, and with national advertising and sales, the pattern of local customs and regional attitudes was gradually broken down. England became not only a *national economy* but a *national society*. The opportunity to travel to the Great Exhibition of 1851 was only possible because of the railway. Railways had not yet developed suburban and commuter lines but they had made possible the development of excursions and holidays on a scale that had never been possible before. In 1851, these opportunities were restricted to the well to do; but by the 1890s there had been an enormous growth of seaside and holiday resorts such as Blackpool, Southend and Weston Super Mare.

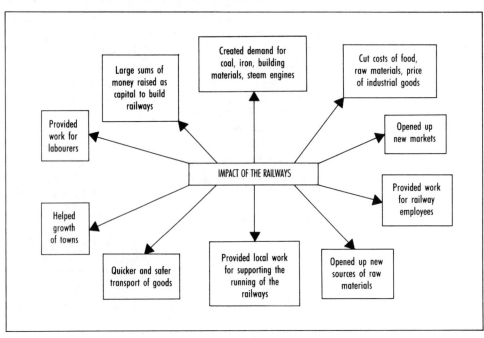

Fig. 6.7 Social and economic effects of railways

E X A M I N A T I O N   Q U E S T I O N S

QUESTION 1

This question is of the structured-essay type.

a) When and why did the Duke of Bridgewater decide to build a canal?
b) Who was the engineer responsible for building the Bridgewater Canal? Describe how he overcame the special problems of building this canal.
c) What were the economic effects of building canals?

TUTOR'S ADVICE

In a) and b), candidates would need to know the basic facts about the building of the Bridgewater Canal, by James Brindley. How it not only drained the Duke's mines at Worsley but eventually allowed barges to go right into the workings making it easier to get the coal out. You could mention the problems of high charges for shipping coal on the river, Brindley's aqueduct across the river, how to keep the canal on the same level without too many locks, how he used puddled clay to line the canal to stop water from draining away. In c), candidates should know that the cost of transporting coal to Manchester was about halved (i.e. not the cost of coal only the cost of *shipping* it!). Lower prices helped the Duke to sell more coal. Eventually, the canal became part of a national network connecting Manchester to all the major ports and cities. There developed a big canal complex of warehouses etc. in Manchester as the volume and value of transported goods such as coal, lime, building stone, cotton etc. increased. Many factories were built on the side of canals and some had special unloading bays that took barges right into the factory. Canals stimulated trade, lowered transport costs, and provided and enormous number of new jobs.

QUESTION 2

This question tests comprehension and your ability to make use of sources.

Source A: A foreigner's view of travel by stage coach from Leicester to London in 1782.

'The getting up onto a seat on the top of the coach was at the risk of one's life and, when I was up, I was obliged to sit just at the corner of the coach with nothing to hold on to but a sort of little handle fastened on the side. . . . The coach proceeded at a rapid rate down the hill. Then all the boxes, iron nailed and copper fastened, began, as it were, to dance around me; they all appeared to be alive, and every moment I received such violent blows that I thought my last hour had come . . . I was obliged to suffer torture for an hour . . . At last we came to another hill, when I crept back to the top of the coach . . . It rained incessantly, and as before had been covered with dust, so now we were soaked in rain.'

Adapted from comments made by Charles Moritz in 1782.

Source B: A famous agricultural journalist's view of the roads.

Wigan. I measured ruts four feet deep, floating with mud from a wet summer day; what must it have been like after a winter? The only mending it receives is the tumbling in of some stones.
Kendal to Windermere. Turnpike. What is finished is as good, firm, and level a road as any in the world.
Driffield. Most excellent. Firmly made of good gravel; free from ruts and loose stones, and of a proper breadth.
Sudbury. Ponds of liquid dirt and a scattering of loose flints, sufficient to lame every horse that moves near them.

Comments made by Arthur Young in about 1770.

Source C: Stage-coach services from Edinburgh, 1763–1815.

In 1763 there were two stage-coaches with three horses, a coachmen, and postillion to each coach, which went north to the port of Leith (a mile and a half distant) every hour from eight in the morning till eight at night, and they took a full hour upon the road.
There were no other stage-coaches in Scotland except one, which set out once a month for London, it took from twelve to sixteen days for the journey.

In 1783, there were five or six coaches to Leith every half-hour, which ran it in fifteen minutes. There were stage-coaches to every considerable town in Scotland, and to many of them two, three, four, or five. To London there were no less than sixty stage-coaches monthly, or fifteen every week, and they reached the capital in four days . . .

A person may now [in 1815] set out on Sunday afternoon from Edinburgh to London, may stay a whole day in London and be back again in Edinburgh on Saturday at six in the morning! The distance from Edinburgh to London is 400 miles.

Forty years ago it was common for people to make their will before setting out on a London journey.

Adapted from *Fugitive Pieces*, (1815) by W. Creech.

Source D: A stage-coach in London in 1812.

(SEG; 1988)

Source E: Turnpike Trusts.

In 1706 Parliament created the first Turnpike Trust. This was a scheme whereby local leading citizens could set up toll gates and maintain the roads with the money received. Charges varied but were usually ½p for a horse, 2½p for a coach or waggon, 2½p for a score of cattle and 1p for a score of pigs; foot travellers did not pay.

Toll gates and turnpikes flourished throughout the eighteenth century and did not begin to die out until the coming of the railways.

Turnpikes were often unpopular. Local people objected to paying tolls and farmers did their best to avoid the gate keepers. The Welsh drovers often avoided the turnpike and cut through the fields, whilst young 'bucks' amused themselves by leaping their horses over the gate. At times, riots broke out, gates were torn down and gate keepers assaulted. Perhaps the most famous of these were the Rebecca Riots, when a party of rioters disguised as women, attacked the toll gates in the South Wales area.

Despite the opposition the number of turnpike roads continued to grow and by 1830 there were about 35,200 km of them, about one half of which were said to be fairly good.

from *Machines, Men and Money*, (1969) by D. P. Titley

Study Sources A to E and then attempt all parts of the question. When referring to the Sources in your answers, you should identify them by letter.

a) Explain why Charles Moritz's journey (Source A) was so uncomfortable and dangerous.

(5)

b) "Source B is more useful than Source A in a study of road transport in the late eighteenth century". Do you agree or disagree with this statement? Give reasons for your answer. (6)

c) Could the stage-coach which Charles Moritz used in 1782 (Source A) have been like the one in Source D? Explain your answer. (5)

d) "Travel by road improved between 1763 and 1815." Explain whether or not the evidence in Sources A to E supports this statement. (8)

a) In 1782 roads were still the responsibility of local parishes. The Highways Act of 1555 said that each parish was to appoint a surveyor to maintain roads in the parish, but this was often neglected. You could describe the 'Statute duties' of six days road repair per year by each parishioner – and how this was often ignored. Although Turnpike roads were established at this time, they were to grow still faster *after* this time. Also the benefits to the road surfaces of the work of Metcalf, Telford and Macadam were only in their infancy at this time.

b) Source B gives *specific* examples from first hand experience. The account provides important detail, showing that Arthur Young was an observant 'witness'. Source A also is the account of first hand experience. It is however a rather more general and entertaining account, giving less specific detail. It also refers to a *single* journey, whereas Source B provides data for useful *comparisons* of roads, giving a rather more rounded view.

c) By 1812 (Source D) there had been tremendous improvements in both road conditions and the quality of coaches used in passenger transport. The 1812 stage-coach had passengers *inside*, unlike the 1782 stage-coach of Charles Moritz. He sat on top of the coach, hanging on to small handles and at the mercy of dust and rain. Improved design and greater competition between coach operators had, by 1812, led to better quality stage-coaches.

d) Source C provides useful data for this comparison. In 1763 there were only three stage-coaches in the whole of Scotland, the two mentioned plus the one setting out each month to London. By 1783 there were *numerous* stage-coaches 'to every considerable town in Scotland' and sixty stage-coaches each month to London.

In 1763 it took from twelve to sixteen days to reach London; by 1815 the travelling time was only some three days.

Source E mentions the growth of turnpike roads to 1830, with some 35,200 km of them, around half being 'fairly good'. So from 1763 to 1815 we can suppose that there was a continued rise in the number of turnpike roads, likely to be better quality than the roads they replaced.

Source D provides an illustration of a stage-coach in London in 1812 which would appear likely to give a much more comfortable ride than that described on a stage-coach in 1782 (Source A).

A STUDENT'S ANSWER WITH EXAMINER'S COMMENTS

QUESTION

A short answer/structured essay question.

a) What were the major problems when travelling on an unimproved road in the 18th century?

b) How did turnpike roads help to overcome these problems?

c) Explain how a turnpike trust was organised and operated.

---

a) Travel in the eighteenth century was very difficult, roads were in a bad condition. They were dirt tracks full of pot holes. In winter when it rained or snowed they were impassable and pictures show that stage-coaches got stuck and had to be dug out. Journeys took a long time and were expensive because people had to stay overnight at coaching inns. The stage coaches were often held up by highwaymen. Goods were usually sent by pack horse trains or wagon. These were very slow and could not carry heavy or bulky goods. Coal or heavy machinery usually went by ship around the coast or by river boat if possible.

b) Turnpike roads were companies of local businessmen who got together and paid an engineer like Macadam or Telford to rebuild a road using a proper stone surface. Both men used layers of stones of different sizes to make a good hard surface so that the water drained off the sides into ditches. The businessmen then charged tolls for people to use the road so that they made a profit. Many people did not like to pay the tolls at the toll gate especially when the roads were not kept in good repair.

c) Turnpike Trusts were organised by groups of businessmen who got permission from Parliament to take-over the roads and to keep them in good repair. Travellers who used the road had to stop at the toll gate and pay a toll before they were allowed to use the road.

Examiner's comments:

Despite the exaggeration, this could have been a very good answer since there is a lot of accurate and relevant information. Unfortunately much of it is in the wrong place. Apart from part a), the candidate rarely answers the question set and puts in lots of accurate *but irrelevant* information that gains no marks. It seems the candidate cannot choose the right information to answer the question, e.g. in b) there is no need to make the comments about *who formed* Turnpike Trusts, this is only relevant to c). Comments on: how the work of the engineers made turnpike roads better than other roads; how they speeded up travel times and made travel more comfortable, in better types of coaches; etc., would all have been much more valuable. There should have been comments in part b) on the turnpike system as a whole. The problems of high tolls and the short lengths of unconnected highway leading into towns would have shown a real appreciation of both the value and limitations of the turnpike system. In part c) there could be more detail on how turnpike trusts were formed, and on the problems of operating the system; the answer could include details about how tolls were collected, what they were supposed to be used for, and the problems of bad management.

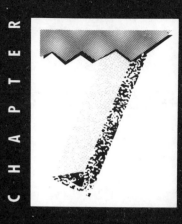
TRANSPORT DEVELOPMENTS IN MODERN TIMES

SEA TRAVEL

MOTOR VEHICLES

RAILWAYS

AIR TRANSPORT

SOCIAL AND ECONOMIC EFFECTS OF TRANSPORT DEVELOPMENT

GETTING STARTED

The development of new methods of transportation since 1850 has not only made travel quicker and more comfortable, it has created a mass market for leisure travel on an international scale. Changes in the methods of travel and communications have been the result of applying advanced technology to a number of different fields. This has led both to the invention of new products and also to improved methods of manufacture. The period since 1945 has seen rapid developments in the means of communications. These are perhaps as great as those which took place in the nineteenth century and are having similarly important economic and social effects.

Candidates should be able to:

- Describe the major developments since the 1890s concerning international transport by sea and air and the development of motor vehicles.

- Describe and explain how transport developments since the 1890s have affected everyday life.

As with other topics, precisely which of these issues is likely to appear on a *particular* examination paper depends on the syllabus studied. Always check and remember that it is not normally advisable to try and revise topics that have not been covered by your teacher. If you study the material in this chapter carefully, you should find that it is possible to explain the need for, and the results of, *any* transport development, at least in a general way.

ESSENTIAL PRINCIPLES

1 > SEA TRAVEL

In 1850, an extensive framework of international trade already existed. It was however much smaller than today, and the movement of goods and people across seas and oceans was an expensive and extremely hazardous affair. By the 1890s, not only had the cost of international travel fallen considerably, but the development of steam-engined ships with steel hulls had also made it possible for both passengers and goods to be carried in bulk.

STEAMSHIPS

The development of steamships, able to steam across the Atlantic and, eventually, to Asia and Australasia, depended upon developments in a whole host of connected industries. Engineers had to learn to make much more powerful, reliable and economical engines. Iron masters had to find ways of producing large sheets of metal that would not corrode in salt water and ways of fitting them together so that they did not come apart. Above all, ways had to be found to propel and steer the ship efficiently.

Paddle boats

Steam barges and steamboats had been used on canals, rivers and the coastal trade from the early nineteenth century, even before steam engines were used in locomotives. Many of these used *paddle wheels* to push them through the water. The big advantage of these vessels was that they gave the opportunity to have *regular services*, more or less independent of the tide and current, unlike a sailing ship. Such paddle steamers were first used as ferries and as mail boats, where regular services were important. These steam boats were generally made out of wood and used so much coal that they could not make long trips without refuelling.

By the 1840s larger paddle wheeled steam ships did offer a regular service across the Atlantic, but they were much more expensive than sailing ships to operate. These paddle steamers were still built primarily out of wood, and often used sails in combination with their paddle wheels when possible. On the first Cunard steamer, the Britannia, of its total capacity of 865 tons, 640 were needed for coal.

> Brunel and the development of steam ships

The pioneer in the development of large steam ships was I. K. Brunel. In 1838 his paddle steamer, the 1500 tons *Great Western*, did the journey from Bristol to New York in 14 days. On this journey, the *Great Western* almost caught up with the steamship *Sirius* which had left Dublin three days earlier and only got to New York a couple of hours before the *Great Western*. When the *Sirius* ran out of coal, she could only keep her engines running by burning part of her cargo. Despite Brunel's success he only had one ship, and so the contract for the transatlantic mail service went to Samuel Cunard, a Canadian, who built four new steamships that operated from Liverpool.

By 1845, Brunel had a much larger steamship, the *Great Britain*. This was the first ship to be made of iron and to use the *screw propeller* developed in 1838 by Francis Pettit-Smith. Without the large paddle wheels on the side, the *SS Great Britain* was much faster than other steamships. By 1858, Brunel had built the massive Great Eastern, a ship of 20,000 tons which used paddles, sails and propellers. Despite using 300 tons of coal a day, this vessel could carry 4,000 passengers and 5,000 tons of cargo across the Atlantic in 11 days. A bigger ship was not built until 1901, and the Great Eastern ought to have been successful. Unfortunately, on her maiden voyage five people were killed and people said the ship was jinxed. The ship was never commercially successful and she finally ended up as a cable layer.

Iron-hulled steamships were not particularly successful until the late nineteenth century. They were expensive to operate as they used too much fuel, which also left little cargo space, and the maintenance costs were very high. The period from 1850–1900 is really the era of the *sailing ship* and in particular of the *clipper ships*. Improvements in hull design, the development of better rigging, and the use of small steam engines on some sailing ships to handle the sails, meant that the productivity of sailing ships more than kept pace with steam. Sail captains were also helped by the publication of very much better charts of ocean currents and winds by the United States navy, leading to faster sailings. Gradually, however, the improvement in steam engines and the development of steel provided steam boats with the improved performance they needed to compete with sail on the shorter transatlantic cargo routes.

ENGINE DEVELOPMENT

The main development in *engines* was the use of *compound engines*. Though patented in 1804 it had not been adopted because the technology of the day was inadequate to make safe high pressure boilers that did not explode. By the 1860s the use of steel boilers and the general improvements in engineering meant that this was no longer a problem. By the 1870s the use of such engines had reduced coal consumption by more than half the level of the 1850s. The possibilities of the new technology were shown in 1865 when a voyage was made non-stop from Liverpool to Mauritius (in the Indian Ocean), a distance of 8,500 miles. The opening of the Suez Canal in 1869 cut out the need to sail round Africa and greatly reduced the sailing distance from Europe to Asia.

By the 1870s, most of the trade between Britain and India was by steamships. In 1883, there was a greater tonnage of steamships than sailing ships in use, but sailing ships continued to be built and were still widely used on the very long *bulk* cargo routes to China and Australasia. Many sailing ships were used to carry coal from England to other countries which had not developed their coal industries, such as Africa and India, in order to supply steamships with sufficient fuel. Sailing ships were cheaper than steamships and were used when speed was not essential, as with non-perishable cargoes such as wool. Even in 1900 almost a quarter of all ships registered in Britain were still sailing ships.

The turbine engine

The final developments came with the application of what were called *triple expansion boilers* and the *Parsons turbine engine* (Figure 7.1). These used very high pressure steam at over 150 lbs per square inch and needed very strong steel boilers. Improvements by 1890 meant that this had risen to 200 lbs per square inch, and fuel costs were cut by a further 50%. The development of the Parsons turbine engine (patented 1884) again cut down fuel costs and greatly increased the speed of ships. Parsons showed the value of his new engine and impressed the Royal Navy when he turned up as an uninvited guest at the Spithead naval review in 1896 in his steam yacht the *Turbania*. This was so fast that she could not be caught by any of the naval destroyers. From 1905 all new naval vessels used this new type of engine, and the Cunard shipping line used it in their new passenger ships, the *Lusitania* and *Mauretania*, built in 1907. Although experiments with diesel engines were being tried, by 1913 they only accounted for about 3% of the world's shipping.

Fig. 7.1 Parsons Turbine Engine

THE EFFECTS ON TRADE AND INDUSTRY

The effects of these technical developments upon ship design, efficiency and speed is indicated in Figure 7.2. There were also major effects on the British shipbuilding industry and trade. The most obvious benefits were in *trade*. Ocean freight rates tumbled. In 1863 it cost 8 shillings (40p) to transport a quarter of wheat across the Atlantic; by 1901 it cost 1s–3d (6p) (see also Chapter 3). It became possible to send bulk cargoes over enormous distances, and as prices fell so demand increased.

Year	1838	1871	1907
Name of ship	*Sirius*	*Oceania*	*Mauretania*
Length (feet)	208	420	762
Gross tonnage	700	3 808	31 938
Horsepower	320	3 000	70 000
Speed (knots)	7.5	14.75	25.0
Material	wood	iron	steel
Engines	paddle	compound screw	turbines
			quadruple screw
Time to cross Atlantic	16 days	9 days 10 hours	4 days 10 hours

Fig. 7.2 The impact of technology upon shipping

Passenger fares did not fall, except on sailing ships, but the rise in fare prices was less than wages and the passengers preferred the extra comfort and safety of the steamships. During the last quarter of the nineteenth century there was an enormous increase in the numbers of immigrants using steamships (see Chapter 12). Even great luxury liners relied upon the large number of immigrants to make them profitable.

The massive expansion of trade in the nineteenth century was accompanied by an equally large development of ports, docks and harbours. London, Liverpool, Birkenhead and Glasgow all built new docks and cargo handling facilities. There was an even greater expansion of the British shipbuilding industry.

The shipbuilding industry

Britain gains from changes in the type of ship

So long as shipping was dominated by sailing ships, so England was at a big disadvantage over American shipbuilders who had access to very good quality, cheap timber and to other shipbuilding materials. Once ships began to use *steam engines* and *metal hulls*, this advantage was reversed. Britain's lead in iron and steel production and the vast size of her engineering industries meant costs of production lower than those of any other nation, even where these nations had the necessary expertise. An enormous growth of *shipbuilding* occurred in places where there were deep estuaries, large open spaces for ship yards and a ready availability of both skilled labour and iron. This meant that shipbuilding came to be concentrated upon the Mersey, Clydeside and the Tees-Tyneside regions. Although London and other ports remained important as repair yards until the early twentieth century, the major building of ships was in the three northern regions.

By 1871, the British shipbuilding industry produced more than 382,500 tons annually; by 1911 it had risen to 999,000 tons, and almost 95% of these ships were produced on the Clyde and the north-east coast. Before 1914, the vast bulk of the world's merchant marine was built in British shipyards and the British merchant fleet was the carrier of the world's commerce.

2 ⟩ MOTOR VEHICLES

The *motor industry* was one area of manufacture where Britain could not claim to be a pioneer in the nineteenth century. It was not really until after 1920, when British manufacturers began to adopt the mass production methods developed by American industry, that a large scale motor industry developed in Britain. Motor cars as a mass consumer product and the major form of travel did not develop in Britain until the 1950s.

'HORSELESS CARRIAGES'

The early technology of motor vehicles was developed by the French and Germans. In 1860, in France, Etienne Lenoir fitted a gas engine into a car and this was improved upon by others in the 1870s. It was not until 1878 that Karl Benz developed the first petrol driven vehicle; by the later 1880s, 'horseless carriages' were being made in several countries. At first these 'cars' were really carriages without horses, hence the name 'horseless carriage' given to the early vehicles. They were noisy, uncomfortable to ride in and not very reliable. It was not until 1894 that Rene Panhard and Emile Levassor produced what would be recogised as a proper motor car. The first British motor car was made by John Henry Knight of Farnham, Kent, in 1895.

Motor car development in America

The most rapid development of the motor car was in America. The enormous size of the American market, and the much higher general level of incomes, meant the possibility of *large scale demand*. American engineering companies had already developed what was known as *standardised parts* for a whole range of consumer goods that were made in bulk, and this technology was now applied to the motor car. The rapid development of a cheap, mass produced product also encouraged technical developments in engineering and design which made the American motor car very cheap and fairly reliable. By 1913 about 30% of all American cars were sold at below £200. Production of motor cars in America rose from 4,192 in 1900 to 548,139 in 1914, and to 1,525,578 in 1916. Even before 1914 the industry was dominated by a relatively small number of manufacturers.

Motor car development in Britain

In Britain, by comparison, the industry was little more than a cottage industry. In 1905 there were 197 companies, and even in 1914 there were still 113 companies producing very small numbers of almost hand-produced vehicles. Some of these companies had developed from bicycle or motor cycle manufacturers. In 1904, there were only 8,000 cars registered for use, and even in 1914 there were only 132,000 with most of these being imported from Europe.

 **Reasons for slow growth of car industry in Britain**

The main reason for the slow growth of the British industry seems to have been the *unreliability of the product* and its *high cost* rather than the restrictions imposed by legislation. The 1865 Locomotive Act, the 'Red Flag Act' had imposed a speed limit of 4 mph on all 'road locomotives' in country districts and 2 mph in towns. Also a man had to walk 60 yards in front to warn other road users. This Act was amended in 1878 so that a red flag did *not* have to be carried by the safety man, who now had to walk only 20 yards in front of the vehicle. In 1895 the act was finally repealed, though speed limits were imposed.

The motor car was really only just becoming a practical vehicle mechanically and the terrible state of the roads (see below) was a greater hindrance than the Red Flag Act. Enforcement of the speed limits of 14 mph (later 12 mph) was not a serious problem at first, since few cars could maintain this speed for any length of time. The *reliability* of the car was a major problem. This is clearly indicated by the fact that 23 out of the 33 cars that began the 'Emancipation' run from London to Brighton to celebrate the abolition of the 'Red Flag Act' in 1896, failed to complete the journey.

LARGE SCALE PRODUCTION

Although a number of British motor companies, such as Morris, Humber, Rover and Rolls Royce, had been begun before World War I, it was not until the 1920s that they began to develop as large scale producers. The war had led to all kinds of developments in engineering, and the shortage of horses for transport had increased the demand for both motor cars and larger lorries. The protection of the McKenna import duties also helped to protect the industry from imports, although Henry Ford, who had developed the mass produced Model T in 1908 in America, had already begun to assemble cars at a factory in Manchester in 1911. In 1921, economic difficulties led to a slump which resulted in a considerable number of bankruptcies, amalgamations and mergers between motor firms who had set up to meet the new demand for cars.

The most significant change, however, was introduced by Morris. In 1921 he adopted an aggressive policy of substantial price reductions on his cars to encourage sales. In 1921 he reduced prices from £465 to £375, and by 1922 the same car was selling for £225. Surprisingly, Morris began to make profits instead of his earlier losses, since sales picked up so quickly that he was able to expand production and to introduce still more efficient methods of production. In 1922, he designed the first Austin Seven which, like Henry Ford's Model T, was intended for quantity production.

Assembly line techniques

Flow line production techniques had been developed by Henry Ford. Here the car moved along an 'assembly line' and, at different stages, workers specialised in fitting on a particular part. Flow line techniques were copied by all the producers of mass production cars. It meant that manufacturers now relied upon the ready availability of cheap, mass produced *components* from other manufacturers. Motor car companies such as Morris did not produce very much of the car themselves. They designed the car and made some parts, usually the engine and possibly parts of the body, but most of the rest was 'bought in' from other specialist suppliers. What the motor car companies did was to *assemble* parts produced to their specification by other companies.

The *scale of production*, and therefore the cost at which cars were made, was determined by the potential *size of the market*. A large market enabled the producer to adopt large scale methods of production, leading to lower costs. The key to demand was *consumers' incomes*. During the inter-war years the number of people who could *afford* to buy a motor car was limited, so by comparison with other countries, the growth of the British motor industry was sluggish.

THE GROWTH OF THE INDUSTRY

The industry nevertheless did grow considerably (see Figure 7.3) and the number of cars in use had risen to just over a million in 1930. By 1938, there were almost 2 million cars in use. Britain had also built up a substantial export trade. In 1924, only about 15,000 vehicles had been exported, but by 1929 this had risen to 40,000. Although exports fell during the depression of 1929–33, by 1937 they had reached almost 100,000 vehicles. Most of these vehicles went to Commonwealth countries which had protected trade links with Britain, but these figures do indicate the potential for growth.

Date	Cars (private)	Total (all vehicles)
1904	8,465	8,465
1910	53,196	143,177
1914	132,110	388,860
1918	77,707	229,428
1921	242,500	845,709
1929	980,886	2,181,831
1932	1,127,681	2,227,099
1938	1,944,394	3,084,896
1946	1,769,952	3,106,810
1959	4,965,774	8,661,980
1969	11,227,900	14,751,900
1985	16,453,000	21,166,000

Fig. 7.3 Motor vehicles in use 1904–85

The motor car as a mass consumer product in Britain is, however, a development of the years since 1950. Much of the growth of the motor car industry is the result of applying mechanisation and mass production techniques in order to reduce the costs of manufacture. During the 1950s and 60s, the automation of the production process had greatly increased *output per man* and *reduced costs*. This meant that the big rises in incomes that were now taking place allowed more and more people to afford a motor car. The number of vehicles on the road increased from about 2 million in 1950 to 5 million in 1960, rising to over 21 million in 1985. Besides being a major industry, both as employer and exporter, the motor car also began to create all kinds of changes and problems in the way people lived (see below).

3 > RAILWAYS

The development of alternative forms of inland transportation eventually had a major impact upon the *railways*, but the decline of the railways really only began to occur after the 1920s, and more especially since the 1950s. During the later nineteenth century railways continued to expand as new lines were built out into the rural areas and, in the 1890s, into the suburbs of towns and cities. In London there was the progressive expansion of the underground and, up to the 1930s, the development of electrified services to the outer London districts where considerable new housing development had taken place. During the First World War, when the government had effectively nationalised the railway companies, a considerable degree of rationalisation had taken place. The question was, should the government continue to run the railways?

THE RAILWAY COMPANIES

After considerable discussion the government decided they should not. Instead, they were to be returned to private enterprise but *reorganised*, so as to encourage greater efficiency, and more *carefully controlled*, so as to prevent the abuse of monopoly power. The *Railways Act of 1921* organised four main groups: the London, the London and North Western, the London and North Eastern, the Southern and Great Western. The Act also outlined some detailed and complicated rules for setting passenger and freight rates, and a system for regulating the companies. In other words, the new Act was a sort of halfway house between public ownership and private enterprise. As such, it had the weaknesses of both. Railway companies found it very difficult to respond quickly to competition, whether for suburban passengers (where they faced competition from the new 'omnibus' companies) or for local and medium-distance freight (where lorries provided competition). Most railway companies now began to develop their own bus passenger services and all had a fleet of lorries to transport goods directly to customers' doors from the railway.

There was a general stagnation of industry during the inter-war period. This meant that there was not the expansion in traffic needed to provide the increased income for the railways to modernise their equipment and services. Railways had largely ceased to be the profit making ventures that they had been in the nineteenth century. At the same time, many socialists argued that they were too important to the economy as a whole to be left to private enterprise. As a *natural monopoly* they needed to be regulated and, for the sake of efficiency, transport as a whole needed to be co-ordinated.

RAILWAY NATIONALISATION

When the Labour party was returned to office in 1945 after the war, the railways had experienced a further period of effective war-time nationalisation. The benefits of an *integrated* system of transport were preferred by many to competition and in any case the Labour party was committed to government control of key parts of British industry. Its proposals had been outlined in various papers written before the war by Herbert Morrison and were included in the election manifesto. The plan was for an integrated public transport service. The *Transport Act of 1947* to some extent put this into effect. The Act nationalised *all* transport services, including the road haulage and bus passenger services that had been built up by the railways in the inter-war period. A controlling body, the *British Transport Commission* (BTC), was established with overall authority. There were to be four major separate Executives, for Railways, London Transport, Hotels and Road Transport (later Road Haulage and Passengers), and for Docks and Inland Waterways.

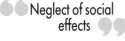
Public service or commercial profit

What was *not* clear in the Act was to what extent the BTC was supposed to run a *public service* which was to provide a cheap and subsidised service, and to what extent it was expected to operate on *commercial lines*. The change of government in 1951 eventually led to the *Transport Act of 1953* and to the denationalisation of most of the road services, leaving the government owning what was in effect a major loss-making industry. Without massive investment in new equipment and a careful rationalisation of services, there was little that could be done to make the railways pay. By 1962, the annual operating loss had risen to over £100m. There had been a 25% loss in passenger travel between 1938 and 1962 and, after a considerable rise in goods traffic in the 1950s, a steady reduction in goods traffic.

THE BEECHING REPORT

An attempt was made to revitalise the railways and to reorganise public transport in general. This was the aim of the *Transport Act of 1962*. It reorganised the railways and other transport services into 5 separate organisations, each directly responsible to the Minister for Transport. The person responsible for the British Railways Board had already been appointed; he was Dr Richard Beeching, a former director of ICI. In 1963, the *Beeching Report* 'Reshaping the Railways' was published. This quickly became known as the 'Beeching Axe'. He proposed to close over 5,000 miles of unprofitable railway lines, together with 2,363 stations. A whole host of services would be rationalised and the activities of the railway streamlined. At the same time a very large programme of modernisation was to be undertaken. This report ignored the *social effects* that such a programme of cuts would have upon rural areas, with no alternative transport service. It also ignored the effects of changing the transport network upon the *economy as a whole*. The aim was to make the railways commercial and to cut losses, not to judge any reduction in overall social benefits through the loss of railways as an amenity for rural areas. Nor was it to judge any increased costs borne by society as a whole from increased road congestion, pollution or the need to build more roads. The report *did* recognise that 'It might pay to run railways at a loss in order to prevent the incidence of an even greater cost than might arise elsewhere if the railway were closed.' Despite considerable debate on the report in Parliament and the press, the government went ahead with the recommendations.

Neglect of social effects

By 1967 most of the cuts in lines and services had been undertaken and much of the new

Date	Miles open	Passengers carried (million)
1845	2,441	30.4
1900	18,680	1,114.6
1945	19,863	1,055.7
1960	18,369	721.3
1965	14,920	580.5
1985	10,410	697.4

Fig. 7.4 Railway mileage and passengers carried 1845–1985

rolling stock and lines brought into use. Between 1963 and 1970, the overall deficit of £135m had become a surplus of almost £10m, but it had taken seven years and a surplus had only been achieved in the last two. The problem that remains to be answered is was it all worth it? Has the better commercial performance of the railways been worth the *social cost* of closing stations and shifting a great deal of freight traffic on to the roads. This is a problem to which we will return.

4 › AIR TRANSPORT

The development of *air transport* services in many ways follows a similar pattern to that of steamships. The basic invention was there, but it took a long time before it became a commercial proposition on a large scale. The earliest flights were in balloons, filled with hydrogen gas which was lighter than air. Despite being used for entertainment and military reconnaissance during the American Civil War and the Franco-Prussian War, they had little practical use as transport.

AIRSHIPS

Before 1914, the main development was in Germany, where large, light, metal-framed airships were developed. By 1912, Ferdinand von Zeppelin had managed to use a petrol engine to drive propellers which allowed the airship, or dirigible as it was known, to be steered. These enormous light metal-framed cigar shaped balloons, or 'Zeppelins' as they were called, caused panic when they were used for bombing raids over Britain, but they were of little practical use, except as reconnaissance.

The development of airships continued after the war and several huge ones were used for long distance commercial flights across Europe and the Atlantic. The size of the airframe allowed the cabin space to be quite luxurious, but the danger of accidents and the crash of the R101 in 1930 when 40 people were killed meant that their use was generally abandoned. Today, however, modern technology and the availability of gases which do not burn, have encouraged several companies to begin building them once more for commercial use, transporting heavy loads over long distances in regions such as Africa and India where airfields for modern aircraft are not available.

FIXED-WING AIRCRAFT

The major development in aerial flight has been *fixed-wing aircraft*. The first proper flight was in 1900, when Wilbur and Orville Wright, two bicycle mechanics, managed to fly for 12 seconds at Kitty Hawk in Carolina, America. By 1908 this flight had been extended to 75 minutes, and by 1909 Louis Bleriot had flown across the English Channel. Like the early motor cars, aircraft were curiosities with little practical use until a whole host of technical problems had been overcome. But the military potential of such a flying machine encouraged governments to spend a great deal of money in research, to develop more powerful engines and better airframes. By the end of World War I, aircraft had developed tremendously and in 1919 the flight by two RAF pilots, Alcock and Brown, across the Atlantic showed the progress that had been made.

AIR ROUTES

During the 1920s, attempts were made to develop commercial *air routes*. From 1921, the government subsidised several companies to operate routes to Europe. In 1924, following an official enquiry, the government agreed to continue this subsidy but only if the companies merged to form a single organisation. This company was called *Imperial Airways*. It offered four routes to major European capitals and received further income from the mail service.

During the inter-war years, improvements in aircraft design and in the performance of engines made it possible to fly around the world (1924 by three American pilots) and eventually to develop long distance routes to Africa, India and Australia. All of these were heavily subsidised by the government, which thought it necessary to develop such links with the Empire (as it was then known). During the 1930s several companies developed internal routes in the UK; most of these were operated by Imperial Airways for the railway companies, but in 1934, the post office even began to use aircraft for mail services. In 1938, after complaints about inefficiencies in the air services offered by Imperial Airways, a government enquiry recommended reorganisation of the company and an increased level of subsidy to promote the development of the British aircraft industry. The existing private companies were merged and a new company *British Airways* was formed. The government arranged that British Airways and Imperial Airways should share the subsidy and be the only licensed companies, sharing the air routes between them. In 1938, Sir John Reith who had organised the development of the BBC, was appointed Chairman of Imperial Airways. Between 1938 and 1940, he organised the merger of Imperial Airways with British Airways.

AIRCRAFT DEVELOPMENT

> Defence spending helps technical development

Commercial air travel came to an end with the war but, as in World War I, it was war which provided the basis for future commercial development. Governments spent vast sums in producing new engines and aircraft capable of travelling long distances and of carrying heavy bomb loads. They also spent vast sums on research into navigation aids, including radar and communications, and on the development of efficient ways of manufacturing aircraft cheaply and in quantity. It was these developments which laid the basis for commercial civilian aircraft in the 1950s and which pushed forward the production of larger aircraft that could become commercially successful.

In many ways the same is still true today. The large American, British and European aircraft manufacturing companies rely upon government sponsored research for defence contracts to provide the *development costs* of new engines and aircraft frames that will eventually be developed into civilian commercial aeroplanes. For reasons of military strategy, as well as commercial considerations, all the major industrial nations have subsidised the development of commercial aircraft and airline services. Projects such as Concorde, the first supersonic commercial aircraft which was developed jointly between France and Britain and which began flying in 1976, would never have been undertaken by private companies. Such ventures are too risky and the prospects of future profits are so slim that the investment could hardly be justified commercially. Modern aircraft developments are so expensive that it has often been necessary for the European nations to combine together to share the risks.

The development of large aircraft and the application of jet engines to civilian aircraft in the BOAC Comet of 1952, led to the emergence of a totally new transport industry. The continuous development of aircraft design has created machines capable of carrying hundreds of people thousands of miles without stopping. Smaller aircraft can even land in the centre of cities such as London on special short runways, less than a mile from the city centre. Millions of people now expect to go on an aircraft every year for their foreign holidays. Research is currently in hand to develop HOTOL (horizontal take off and landing) spaceships which can fly from London to Australia in a matter of hours by going out of the earth's atmosphere. Such 'progress' would have been undreamed of even 50 years ago, but may become a commercial reality within twenty years. Developments in air transport have had a major impact upon the economy and upon many aspects of how we live, perhaps not always to our benefit. These are discussed in the next section.

5 ▷ SOCIAL AND ECONOMIC EFFECTS OF TRANSPORT DEVELOPMENT

The analysis in Chapter 6 of the economic effects of railways is equally useful for discussing the effects of any transport innovation. However this section will concentrate upon the social effects of 'progress' in transport. By reducing both the cost and time taken to travel, transport improvements have given people *more choice* about where to live, where to visit, etc., undreamed of in the nineteenth century. The development of new methods of road transport has created new opportunities for leisure, but has also created or made worse problems of congestion and pollution. This has generally led governments to intervene in several ways.

They have been forced to improve the quality and character of the roads, by developing better road surfaces, improved street lighting and drainage. The development of decent roads both within, and on the outskirts of, towns and cities allowed the development of horse drawn carriages for the well-to-do and eventually of horse drawn buses for the ordinary workers. By the 1890s there were also horse-drawn trams, and later electric trams and trolley buses.

CONGESTION

The addition of motor cars and lorries in the twentieth century has only made a bad congestion problem even worse. It was complaints about the noise and dust made by motor cars that led to the adoption of tarmac and to its general use as a road material after 1890. It was the problem of speeding motor cars and fears about safety that led to speed limits, to regulations about lights and brakes on motor cars and eventually to the development of traffic lights and pedestrian crossings.

Transport developments have changed the *physical character of our cities*. Cities have had to adapt their roads to cater for the changing methods of transport. The cities of the nineteenth century were not built to handle today's traffic and so we have had to knock down houses and to rebuild or redevelop city and town centres. The dual carriageways and arterial roads built in the inter-war years have become unable to cope with the volume of modern traffic. So in the 1950s we began to build motorways such as the M1 (opened 1959) and today we have a substantial network of three-laned highways connecting most cities. Now, we are beginning to find that even *these* are inadquate and there are demands for even larger four- and five-laned routes on the busy sections, such as the M25 and M1.

In the cities, the problems caused by street parking eventually led to restrictions such as the use of parking meters and the introduction of traffic wardens to enforce the law. Many towns have tried to discourage the private motorist, not only by restrictions but also by improvements to public transport systems, such as cheap buses, park-and-ride schemes and special bus lanes at peak periods. Some have even now begun to build inner city motorways and ring roads to try and divert through traffic away from city centres.

A few *new towns* built since the 1950s tried to *anticipate* the problems of the motor car. Apart from ensuring that all houses had garages, they also built subways and bridges for pedestrians to cross busy roads. They even provided pedestrians and cyclists with special routes that were separate from motor vehicles. Many towns now try to ban the motor car from the centre completely, with pedestrian-only zones.

POLLUTION

We have also become increasingly aware of the problem of *pollution*, especially the effects of lead in petrol and the long term consequences of allowing petrol and diesel engined cars and lorries to empty their exhaust fumes into the atmosphere. The government has issued new regulations that greatly reduce the amount of waste gases that can be allowed to escape from a petrol engine. These problems are not in fact new; consider for example how much manure must have been produced by all the thousands of horse drawn carts and taxis that used London's streets in 1900. Where did it all go? Who arranged for its removal?

Of course there are many positive benefits of transport developments. Many of us can now live in quiet rural and suburban areas. We can afford to own a car and to travel where we want to, when we want to. Millions of us travel abroad both by car, ferry and aeroplane, and soon by Channel tunnel. The vast majority of people now go shopping in their own car, often to large superstores on the edge of towns. The problem is what are the social costs compared to the social benefits of introducing *new* ideas and developments? What is going to be done to solve those problems which we have *inherited* from the past? What are we going to do about preventing similar problems developing in the future?

EXAMINATION QUESTIONS

QUESTION

a)   Describe the major developments which have taken place in road transport since the 1890s.
b)   How has the development of the motor car affected other forms of transport?
c)   What have been *either* the social or the economic effects of motor cars upon British society since 1900?

TUTOR'S ADVICE

Part a) is a straightforward description. You can outline some of the *key facts* mentioned earlier in this chapter. Part b) requires some *analysis*. You have to look at the advantages and disadvantages of motor transport as compared to *other types* of transport, particularly railways. Again *analysis* is required in part c). Remember to look at *either* social *or* economic effects. The *social* effects have more to do with people's way of life, work and leisure patterns, the environment, etc. The *economic* effects have more to do with the output of different industries and of the nation as a whole. It also involves things such as the distribution of goods and people, the pattern of employment, the balance of payments and so on. You could, for instance, mention how motor cars have led to the rise of a major industry supporting many component industries, especially in the Midlands. You could touch on the more efficient means now available of transporting goods throughout the UK, and to ports and airports. Lower transport costs reduce prices and help British goods to be competitive. Of course many cars are *imported*, more than are exported, giving balance of payments problems; and so on.

A TUTOR'S ANSWER

QUESTION

Study Sources A, B, C and D below and then answer the questions a) to c) which follow.

Source A (Taken from Berget's *Conquest of the Air*, 1909):

When it is necessary to travel very quickly one will need to use the aeroplane, and without doubt we shall soon see 'aeroplane liners' of huge dimensions carrying numerous passengers. Perhaps they will be built for transatlantic passages . . . One would travel from Europe to the United States of America in a single day. But when speed is unnecessary the airship, even if it travels at less speed, has the advantage. Not only is it safer but an airship can carry more passengers in greater comfort. Its career is far from ended; it has no more than begun but it will develop side by side with the aeroplane.

Source B (The burnt out wreckage of the R101, October 4 1930):

Source C (From Captain J. H. Lock's *Log of a Merchant Airman*, 1941):

Freight helps to reduce the running costs: the bigger the aircraft the more economical it is to run, because it produces a large income yield. I have carried incredible varieties of freight, particularly goods urgently needed – motor car parts, swarms of bees – yes!, tropical fish, films, cameras, furs, skins, Old Masters, gramophone records, bullion . . . A contrast between 1924 (opening of Imperial Airways) and 1938 (when the British government took control of Imperial Airways, which became BOAC): in 1924, 3 tons of mail was carried in a year; in 1938, 40 tons a week.

Source D (A Boeing 747 taking off from Heathrow):

a) Study Source A
   i) What advantages does the author of Source A say airships have over aeroplanes?
                                                                                              (2)
   ii) Why might Berget's view of the future development of the aeroplane have seemed
       unrealistic to many people in 1909?   *(2)*

b) Study Source B.
   i) What does Source B reveal about the construction methods used in building the
      R101?   *(2)*
   ii) What effects did the incident shown in Source B have on the development of air
       travel?   *(2)*

c) Study Source C.
   i) With reference to Source C explain the increasing importance of air freight
      transportation in the period 1934–38.   *(3)*
   ii) Source C is taken from an autobiography. How useful is such a source to someone
       studying the development of air transport?   *(3)*

d) What evidence in Source C would explain the development of aeroplanes such as the
   Boeing 747 shown in Source D?   *(2)*

e) To what extent does the evidence in Source B, C and D support the predictions made
   by Berget in Source A?   *(4)*

                                                                                    (LEAG; 1988)

a) i) Safety and comfort. Can carry a greater number of passengers
   ii) 1909 was only 9 years after the first proper flight of fixed wing aircraft by the
       Wright brothers in 1900. The longest flight time was only around 75 minutes and it
       was only in that year that Louis Bleriot first flew across the English Channel.

b) i) That the materials and gases used in airships too easily caught fire and were unable
      to withstand accidents.
   ii) The use of airships was largely abandoned. It meant that more resources were put
       into improved fixed wing aircraft. The recent revival of airships for cargo transport
       is based largely on the availability of gases which do not burn, and other technical
       and design improvements.

c) i) Air freight transport becomes more economical the bigger the aircraft. Since
      aircraft *were* getting bigger over this period, this meant that more income could be
      received from using aeroplanes for freight. In addition, the British government was
      encouraging an increased use of aircraft for *mail* deliveries, giving further income
      and encouragement to air freight traffic. Large aeroplanes are able to transport all
      types and sizes of cargo.
   ii) An autobiography is a personal account. It helps us to see one person's view.
       There is always the possibility of bias of course. It will help therefore to consider
       facts and figures, as well as other people's views, in order to get a more general
       picture.

d) The larger the aeroplane, the more economical it is to run. This applies just as much to
   passenger transport as to freight. The large fuel costs of the aircraft are spread over a
   large number of passengers in the Boeing 747, making *fuel cost per passenger* (part of
   running costs) relatively low.

e) Source B certainly does *not* support Berget's confidence that airships are safer than
   aeroplanes and that they would continue to develop side by side with the aeroplane.
   They went into rapid decline after 1930.
      Source C partly supports Berget's prediction that we should soon see 'aeroplane
   liners of huge dimensions', though Source C is about freight carriage rather than
   passengers.
      Source D again supports Berget's prediction of huge aircraft, and this time for
   passengers. However it also contradicts his expectation that airships, not aeroplanes,
   would continue to prosper in passenger travel since they could 'carry more passengers
   in greater comfort'. The large bodied aircraft is so economical and relatively comfortable
   that it is now the major means of air travel.

URBANISATION; THE HOUSING PROBLEM

URBAN PROBLEMS IN THE 19th CENTURY

PUBLIC HEALTH ACTS

HOUSING AND TOWN PLANNING

HOUSING PROBLEMS IN THE 20th CENTURY

HOUSING IN THE 1920s AND 1930s

HOUSE BUILDING AND SLUM CLEARANCE

GETTING STARTED

The rapid growth of towns in the eighteenth and early nineteenth century made the existing problems of overcrowding and poor sanitation considerably worse by creating large concentrations of people on a scale never seen before. Such large concentrations of people, especially when they were out of work or complaining about increased prices and low wages, increased government fears about social unrest and revolution (see Chapter 9). However, the main problems in the growth of cities arose from inadequate arrangements for dealing with the vastly increased scale of *housing* which led to overcrowding, pollution and sanitation problems. The rapid growth of new industrial centres also created poor *working conditions* which are dealt with more fully in Chapter 9. In both spheres governments were forced by public pressure to act.

Gradually the responsibilities assumed by central and local government have fundamentally changed our notion of what is right and proper for the government to do. Areas of responsibility which were once exclusively private have now become accepted as public responsibilities because they have consequences for the whole of society. This has created the problem of how best to administer and control large, and sometimes rather faceless, bureaucracies. Students will be expected to:

- Describe the emergence of public health and sanitation as a problem in the ninteteenth century.

- Describe and explain how governments were forced into action to solve the public health and housing problem.

- Comment upon the effectiveness of government policies in solving these problems.

- Offer critical comments about the progress of town planning and the changing pattern of city life styles.

E S S E N T I A L   P R I N C I P L E S

1 > URBAN PROBLEMS IN THE 19th CENTURY

The problems of ill health arising from overcrowding and poor sanitation were nothing new. Even in the eighteenth century, people such as Howard and Jeremy Bentham had pointed out the connection between outbreaks of 'gaol fever' in prisons and the insanitary conditions. They suggested model prisons which were well ventilated and with proper 'privies' (toilets) in each cell. Since little was done in prisons, action on general public health was even less likely. Improved conditions throughout the major cities would require public intervention on an unprecedented scale and a major reform of local government. Effective sewerage, drainage and anti-pollution actions needed to be tied-in with town planning and with the regulation of house building. Such intervention was regarded as unacceptable because of the interference with private property rights and the accepted role of the state.

In the early nineteenth century, existing vested interest groups of local politicians and businessmen would have regarded any direct intervention by Parliament and the central government as undemocratic. It was not until the problems became so bad and the demand for reform so great, that local, and later central, governments were forced to intervene.

HOUSING DEMAND

Cities grew so fast that builders could not keep pace. Houses became overcrowded and rents increased enormously. The demand for housing encouraged speculative building of houses for rent. To keep costs low, houses were built to poor standards. There was no attempt to plan new developments as part of an overall plan of houses, shops and general facilities for the public. Often houses were built on any vacant space. Houses rarely had proper foundations and builders used poor quality bricks. Inside, large stone paving slabs were put directly on to the earth as the floor. There were no building regulations and no officers to inspect the houses to ensure they were safe as there are today. Such houses were called *jerry-built*, though it was not until 1869 that the word is first used in print (the word jerry was widely used in the 1820s and 30s to describe a person who was mean and a bit of a crook or had a poor reputation). Large numbers of new houses were built around small square courtyards with minimal consideration for basic facilities such as drainage, sewerage, refuse collection or fresh water and light. Where courtyards were not possible, long terraces of back-to-back houses or blocks of tenements were provided. Such places were usually grossly overcrowded and landlords rarely bothered to maintain them in a good state of repair, so that they rapidly degenerated into filthy, disease-ridden slums.

Even in the eighteenth century, London had parts of the city and outer suburbs where the poor became concentrated into slums. The word *slum* was originally slang for a room of low repute; by 1821, it was being used to describe the poorer parts of London riddled by crime. But it was not until the 1860s that the word slums and jerry-built came to mean overcrowded housing of poor quality.

HOUSING CONDITIONS AND PUBLIC HEALTH

In most towns the local authorities lacked the power, or refused to control housing development. In the 1820s and 1830s reform groups and statistical societies in all of the major towns carried out extensive surveys of housing conditions and of the problems of public health. These private surveys and reports were confirmed by reports on living conditions for the Poor Law Commission by doctors, though Southwood-Smith in 1847 complained that during the first half of the century, the medical profession had not done enough to promote sanitary reform.

These reports showed how death rates were higher in towns than in rural areas, and that outbreaks of typhus, smallpox, yellow and scarlet fever, diarrhoea and typhoid were all more common in towns. This is not of course to say that housing conditions were generally very much better in the countryside. The only disease that doctors knew how to deal with was smallpox, which could be prevented by inoculation. In many cities the Poor Law authorities undertook mass inoculation throughout most of the century. As the appalling conditions became more widely known and as wealthier householders became more aware of how their lives could be threatened by diseases starting amongst the poor, so pressure for improvement built up in all the major cities.

Improvement Commissioners

Some towns set up special bodies called 'improvement commissioners' who collected rates to improve roads, pavements and sewerage. These usually only provided a service to the well-to-do, who were able to afford additional rates. It was only after the *Municipal Corporations Act of 1835* that most of the major new industrial towns began to get the kind of general administrative body needed to take action. There were *Poor Law Medical Officers* who described conditions in the poor districts and recommended action; some towns had local boards of health with medical officers on them, but little notice was taken of their proposals. Even crises such as the outbreaks of cholera in 1831–2, 1848–9, 1854 and 1867 did not lead to much effective action by Parliament. However, there was considerable debate and investigation about the *causes* of the spread of disease. Medical knowledge about the causes of disease was very limited. Chadwick, like Southwood-Smith, believed that infections were caused by miasma – or smells – which if condensed and injected into a person would cause death. There were reports of grave diggers and others dying as a result of smelling the contents of coffins which burst open, or after clearing out muck from enclosed places.

Infectious diseases

It was not until 1848 that the organism which carried cholera in water was identified independently by Dr John Snow and Dr William Budd. In 1854 when cholera reoccurred in Bristol, Budd was able to prevent it spreading by disinfecting the sources of the outbreak. Pathologists who knew of Budd's work began to examine the bodies of cholera victims to identify the bacteria causing the infection, and were able to show that the same bacteria were present in the air of cholera wards in hospitals. Many doctors clung to the miasmatic theory however. By the middle 1850s, under the influence of Chadwick, local boards of health in London still emptied practically all the sewers directly into the Thames, which was also the main source of drinking water (see Figure 8.1).

Generally, however, Chadwick's influence in getting streets cleaned and pollution removed had a beneficial effect. Nevertheless another area in which Chadwick was wrong was his failure to recognise that poverty led directly to ill health, because disease was more likely amongst low paid and the unemployed who suffered from an inadequate diet and malnutrition.

a) Cholera Epidemics

Year	Deaths from Cholera
1833	22,000
1848	72,000
1853	20,000
1866	14,500

b) Cholera in a London area

This diagram, from a book by Dr J. Snow, shows deaths from cholera in a small area of London during a period of 11 days in 1854. A mark or bar is placed on the house where deaths from cholera took place. The deaths all centre on the pump in Broad Street.

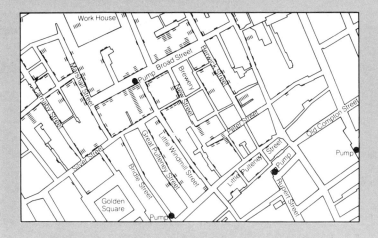

Fig. 8.1 Deaths from Cholera

2 > **PUBLIC HEALTH ACTS**

The campaign for a general public health Act effectively began when Chadwick included in the *1838 Poor Law Annual Report* information from Poor Law medical officers about an outbreak of typhus, following reports from Drs Arnott, Kay (later Kay-Shuttleworth) and Southwood-Smith on contagion in their districts. This led directly to the *1840 House of Commons Select Committee Report* which heard evidence and reported to Parliament on the Health of Towns. In 1842, Chadwick's Report to the Poor Law Commissioners on the *Sanitary Condition of the Labouring Population* contained detailed descriptions of the terrible living conditions amongst the poor, and it was extensively reported. Though the *Nuisances Prevention Act* was passed in 1846, little notice was taken of his proposals for a national body like the Poor Law Commissioners to be responsible for sanitary reforms. Many local politicians were afraid that such a body would become too powerful.

The 1840s saw a steady stream of reports but the first action was taken by the city of Liverpool, which in 1847 appointed the first local medical officer, Dr Henry Duncan, under a private Act, the *Liverpool Sanitary Act*. Similar action was taken in London in 1848 with the appointment of John Simon. Parliament took no general action to remove such nuisances or to prevent them happening, despite a continued propaganda campaign from Chadwick, from the Health of Towns Association (led by Southwood-Smith) and from the doctors' journal *The Lancet*. Sanitary reform did not arouse the same passions and concerns as the abuse of women and children in factories (see Chapter 9).

❝❝ The 1848 Public Health Act ❞❞

In 1848, Parliament finally passed a *Public Health Act* which permitted towns to appoint a local board of health where 10% of the ratepayers asked for it, or where the death rate had reached 23 per thousand. The Act provided genrral regulations for sanitation. All new houses were to have WCs or 'privies' and ashpits. Houses within 100 feet of a public sewer were to be connected to it or to have a cess pit. Cellar dwellings were to have their ceiling at least 3½ feet above street level and a space in front that could be drained. Amongst many powers given to local Boards of Health was the power to approve plans for new roads and the provision of a water supply. They were allowed to widen roads and, if necessary, to buy up premises to do this. They also had powers to regulate all kinds of public nuisances, such as slaughter houses, common lodging house, and graveyards. They could even provide basic public amenities, such as public privies, cemeteries and even public parks.

With the power to raise local rates, borrow money for capital expenditure and pass local bye-laws allowing fines up to £5, local Boards of Health were potentially very powerful agencies for solving sanitation problems. The difficulty was in getting towns to *adopt* the Act. A few towns adopted it and quickly appointed medical officers of health, but it was not until 1872 that local governments were *all* required to do so.

URBAN POLLUTION AND DISEASE

The slowness of action is largely explained by four factors: technical, financial, ideological and political. There were various theories of how diseases were spread. Most, including Chadwick, believed in the *miasmatic theory*, that is that smell spread disease (the *bacteriological theory* was not proved until the last quarter of the century). As we know today, they were wrong, but this did not really matter since the proposals made by Chadwick for the removal of nuisances and the installation of proper sewerage and water facilities were the *right actions*. The real problem was a *technical* one – how to provide an efficient water supply and how to get rid of waste sewerage. The problems of pollution were caused in part by industry. Factories, and later railways, belched out smoke and chemical pollutants into the air and rivers, and people lived very close to the factories. But the biggest problems were the pollution caused by the 'dirty trades' and the waste products of people, not the new industries.

Of course the muck from horses and cows was a problem. Many of these animals were kept in back gardens or sheds, very close to houses and many poor people even kept a pig in the backyard. The increased numbers of people meant an enormous increase in human waste or 'night soil'. The sewers and drains that existed were only intended to drain rainwater from the streets; they could not cope with human waste which was carried away from cess pits and privies by dung carts.

Sewage systems

There were many disagreements as to the best way of solving these problems, partly because the scale of the engineering problems was so vast and the cost enormous, and these caused delay. It had to be proven that John Roe's system of disposing of sewerage, strongly recommended by Chadwick, actually worked, namely that sewerage could be flushed away with water and carried through glazed pipes that did not leak. Engineers had to learn what size of pipes was most effective and what was the best way of constructing sewers with pipes at the correct angles for carrying away the waste. Above all, there had to be an adequate supply of water, not only to carry away the waste but also to provide fresh clean water to every house. Engineers had to build reservoirs, and iron and steel manufacturers had to develop ways of providing cheap pipes and taps so that each house could have its own water supply. Flush toilets had to be invented and ways found to pump the sewerage into the rivers and seas so that it could be disposed of. The problems created by an industrial society could only be dealt with by the technology of an *advanced industrial society*.

Many towns preferred to build new town halls than to improve the town drains. The ratepayers were concerned that rates would rise and that they would end up paying for services to the poor. Many preferred private companies that would charge each person for the service given.

Gradually these problems were overcome, and between 1848 and 1875, considerable progress was made as more local authorities took up the powers permitted by Parliament, usually after outbreaks of cholera. Unfortunately, power was not with a *single body* but with lots of different groups. This led to inefficiency with lots of duplication and confusions over who was responsible. The campaign for reform was also badly hit when Chadwick and Southwood-Smith were forced to resign from the General Board of Health in 1854, accused of being dictatorial in the use of their powers, Shaftesbury was forced to resign as chairman and Sir Benjamin Hall, an opponent of health reform, took his place. In 1858, after further criticisms, the Board was abolished.

THE SANITATION ACT

The question is, was the General Board of Health and the 1848 Act very successful? In some areas the local Boards of Health had worked very effectively, especially in the major cities, but many areas had not adopted the Act. In Leeds, even in 1865, houses could still be built *without* sewers and proper street paving. The *Sanitation Act of 1866* was meant to remedy this problem, since it *required* local authorities to put into effect the duties allowed them under the 1848 Act. They also had the power to *enforce* their decisions upon individuals. In practice the Act did not work very well because it was not clear *which* authorities were responsible for carrying out the Act.

In 1871, after a report by a Royal Sanitary Commission, the *Local Government Board Act* effectively established a government Ministry to regulate the activities of local authorities. Finally, in 1872 the *Public Health Act* established *Sanitary Authorities* throughout the country to be responsible. The 1875 *Public Health Act* brought together, and made clear, the terms and requirements of *all* the different Acts passed in earlier years so that the Sanitary Authorities knew precisely *what* they were required to do.

Though many problems remained about implementing the legislation, by the end of the nineteenth century the two major problems of urban sanitation and the control of epidemics had largely been solved. Reformers could now turn their attention to other related issues, principally housing and town planning.

3 ▶ HOUSING AND TOWN PLANNING

Some of the earliest attempts at planned housing for industrial workers took place during the eighteenth and early nineteenth centuries. Cotton manufacturers, especially those who sited their spinning mills in rural areas because of the availability of clean water, found that existing housing was often inadequate. Some, like the Greggs at Styal Mill, Cheshire, could adapt existing farm buildings, but as their labour force expanded so they had to build new homes. Many of these manufacturers found that it helped to attract and keep skilled workers if they provided what was a model community. Workers rented good quality homes according to their position in the factory and the owners often provided the Church or chapel, a school and probably even a shop. At Styal and at New Lanark, where Robert Owen built a factory (see Figure 8.2), the shop was even run as a co-operative.

HOUSING COMMUNITIES

There are many examples of such communities, not only in the textile trades but also in the iron and coal trades where owners found that it could make good business sense to be philanthropic and provide good living as well as working conditions. One such community,

Fig. 8.2 Robert Owen's New Lanark Mills

Saltaire, just twenty miles from Bradford, was planned from scratch by Titus Salt to house his workers who worked in the woollen mill on the other side of the river. Saltaire and most of the other company towns were employers' towns and often controlled in a way that would not be accepted today. At Saltaire, for example, public houses were not allowed, workers were given particular types of house according to their status, and the houses in each street show clearly these differences in status.

Such schemes were, however, unusual, especially once it became possible for manufacturing industries to develop in existing urban areas. Faced with an ample supply of labour, most manufacturers did not involve themselves actively in developing housing for their workers. It was not however until the 1880s that other manufacturers adopted anything similar to Salt. George Cadbury began Bourneville (near Birmingham) in 1879, but most development took place after 1895. Port Sunlight near Birkenhead was begun by W. H. Lever to house workers from his soap factory in 1888. In some ways Lever was like Owen at New Lanark, since the carefully planned village was part of an elaborate scheme of labour–management relations. Even today, Port Sunlight, with its wide roads, open spaces, parks and public amenities, is very striking. Similarly at Earswick near York, Joseph Rowntree also tried to provide well-built and sanitary houses that were affordable by his workers. However he made little attempt to try to direct the lives of his workers.

'GARDEN CITIES'

In 1898, Ebenezer Howard published a book, 'Tomorrow' (later called *Garden Cities of Tomorrow*) in which he argued that the environment in which people lived could determine the *attitudes* of individuals towards others and how they behaved within the community. Howard argued that towns should not only be on a small scale and have plenty of space, but that residential areas should be clearly separated from factories, workshops and commercial activities. Many of Howard's ideas were taken up by the *Garden City Association*, formed in 1899, and were put into practical effect when work began in 1904 on Letchworth Garden City, using the same architect who had designed New Earswick for Rowntree. This was followed in 1920 by Welwyn Garden City, both towns being on the outskirts of London.

THE URBAN HOUSING CRISIS

The Garden City movement really had little effect on existing towns or on the great mass of the working classes who still lived in appalling conditions in inner city areas. Though the action of local Boards of Health was gradually to improve public health, they did nothing to solve the housing crisis. Conditions in the cities and suburbs were, to some extent, getting worse in the mid-nineteenth century. Developments such as railway stations and new roads led to the demolition of large areas of working class housing, forcing workers into just as overcrowded areas in the suburbs. Improved urban transport facilities, such as horse-drawn trams, suburban railway lines and, from the 1890s, electric trams (and later petrol buses) did mean that the middle classes, and later the better off workers, could move to the suburbs where new housing was being built.

From 1851, Shaftesbury's *Labouring Class Lodging Houses Act* allowed local authorities to build lodging houses; Acts of 1866 and 1868 allowed them to take action to prevent overcrowding and to force landlords to demolish or repair insanitary houses. Little was done in fact and the same applied to the 1875 *Artisans Dwelling Act*, which allowed authorities to redevelop insanitary areas and to build houses for sale. Though the Act was used to redevelop parts of Birmingham, it was expensive, because owners had to be compensated.

Housing for the working classes was helped by the activities of charities such as *The Improved Industrial Dwellings Co.* which, from 1863, built houses to rent for the deserving poor, or the *Peabody Trust*, which built large blocks of cheap tenements for rent in London. The really destitute were to some extent helped by the activities of *Octavia Hill* who purchased older houses to rent at low rates. Even the *Royal Commission on Housing of the Poor 1884–5* did not help very much. Despite all the evidence, the resulting *Housing of the Working Classes Act 1890*, which allowed the new county and borough councils to borrow money to build new houses for rent after demolishing insanitary housing, was only used on any scale by the London County Council (LCC).

4 **HOUSING PROBLEMS IN THE 20th CENTURY**	The major development in housing during the twentieth century was the acceptance by governments in the inter-war years that they had a responsibility to improve housing conditions in the cities. After 1945, the new Labour government accepted that the destruction of the war years, and the poor condition of housing in many rural as well as city centres, required a massive housing programme that was best carried out by local government. Although Conservative governments have put greater emphasis upon private building and home ownership, they too have generally accepted the need for a substantial local authority housing sector. It is only under the various governments of Margaret Thatcher that the government has sought to reduce the size of local authority housing and required councils to sell off their housing stock.
5 **HOUSING IN THE 1920s AND 1930s**	The war period of 1914–18 brought house building to a halt because of the shortage of raw materials and skilled labour. To prevent massive increases in rents, the government was forced to introduce a policy of *rent controls*. When the war ended, the government was faced not only by a massive shortage of housing but also by rents that had been kept low, discouraging landowners to build more houses for rent. The political and social consequences of allowing rents to rise to their full economic level was unthinkable; yet without higher rents how were landowners to be encouraged to build more houses? The government had accepted the need for policies to encourage house building and yet wanted to ensure an increased supply of houses for rent at reasonable prices.

HOUSING POLICIES

The initial housing policy of the government after 1918 benefited the lower middle class and the better off working class. It was only later that it helped the poorer, low paid manual workers. The *1919 Addison Act* meant that local authorities had to provide housing for *general needs* rather than just slum clearance. To help them do this the central government offered subsidies. Local authorities and non-profit making Housing Trusts could claim payments to cover their losses in providing low rented housing.

The absence of strict government controls on the *type* of housing provided meant that many of the houses built were of a high cost variety, with the main gainers being the private builders who tendered for the local authority contracts. To curb the cost of the subsidy, the Addison Act was replaced in 1923 by the *Chamberlain Act*. This laid down *standards* for the type of houses to be built and provided for a *fixed subsidy* of £6 per house for 20 years. This subsidy was available to private builders, and only given to councils if they could show that the private sector could *not* meet their housing needs. Local councils, if they wished, were also allowed to give mortgages to people who wanted to become owner-occupiers.

The Wheatley Act

The first Labour Government of 1924, although it did not have an overall majority, nevertheless passed the fairly radical *Wheatley Act*. This provided a subsidy of £9, for 40 years, to local councils who built houses to be let at controlled rents. Though the Labour government did not survive beyond 1924, Chamberlain on his return to office did *not* alter the Wheatley Act, and there was a substantial expansion of council housing in the major cities such as Manchester, Sheffield and London. Some of the estates built during this period were enormous, especially those built by the London County Council on what was then the outskirts of London. The Becontree estate in Barking and Dagenham, built between 1924 and 1935, had about 350,000 houses, and involved the relocation of almost 750,000 Londoners. The St Helier estate in Mitcham provided houses of an almost identical design, but not on quite such a large scale. Similar estates were built in Manchester and Sheffield.

Though these schemes rehoused many thousands of people, very few of them were in fact slum dwellers. The comments about people using their baths to store the coal were simply not true. In practice most of the houses were still at rents which the poorest families *could not afford*. Also, because many houses were built outside London, workers found that the costs of travelling to work on the underground were very high. Many people from Barking and Dagenham who worked in central London cycled the 12–15 miles to work to save on the bus and tube fares. Slum clearance schemes did not really begin until the 1930s, being the result of policies introduced by the second minority Labour government of 1929.

The Housing Acts

The *1930 Housing Act* introduced by Arthur Greenwood, aimed at knocking down the old insanitary housing in city centres which had survived from the nineteenth century, allowing modern housing to be built in their place. However, the clearance programme had barely begun when the financial crisis of 1931–3 put an end to the scheme. Though the number of houses built by local councils increased, most of the new housing built in the 1930s was by private builders. Between 1929 and 1935, the cost of building materials fell by about 12% and the total cost of building a house by just over 10%. The actual prices of houses often fell by much more than this, and with cheaper and easier mortgages now available, those fortunate enough still to be in work often found that they could now afford to buy a new house (see Figure 8.3).

	1919 TO MARCH 1930	MARCH 1930 TO 1940
By local authorities for		
slum clearance		329 400
other	529 400	304 200
total	529 400	633 600
By private enterprise		
with state subsidies	411 300	21 900
other	530 900	2 062 300
total	947 200	2 084 200
Total houses built	1 476 600	2 717 800

Fig. 8.3 a) Number of houses built in England and Wales 1919–39

		TOTAL	PRIVATE	LOCAL AUTHORITY
Labour	1947–51	185 900	29 900	156 000
Conservatives	1952–54	275 900	62 600	213 300
	1955–64	288 500	155 600	132 900
Labour	1965–70	363 000	198 900	164 100
Conservatives	1971–74	286 400	178 900	107 500

Fig. 8.3 b) Houses built 1947–74

Though subsidies to local authorities were removed in 1933, the *1935 Housing Act* again required councils to submit schemes for slum clearance. However the extent to which these were implemented varied widely. The very poorest sections of society were not helped very much by the inter-war housing programmes. Great care and consideration was at this time being given to the *general* needs of the population and to the planning of public amenities such as shops, schools and leisure facilities, when planning new housing estates. The mistakes which had been made on council estates in the 1920s, when houses were built before the provision of transportation, schools, and health services, had very largely been learned. The *1932 Town and Country Planning Act* gave local authorities powers to plan the use of areas as a whole and to separate out housing from industrial building. In 1939, one of the results of this Act was to create a zone called the 'Green Belt', an area in which new housing was supposed to be banned. Other cities adopted similar ideas.

6

HOUSE BUILDING AND SLUM CLEARANCE

The problems of dealing with slum clearance have only really been dealt with since 1945. In some senses it was the extensive bombing of many industrial cities during World War II which helped to 'solve' the slum clearance problem. Not only did house building come to a halt during the war, but at least half a million houses were destroyed by bombing. This, together with the growth in population, meant that there was a backlog of at least 1¼ million houses in 1945. Indeed the growth of population expected in the post-war period suggested that there was a need to build at least 3 million houses by the early 1950s. The 1945 Labour government was committed to a massive programme of cheap, rented council housing and to the regulation of rents. In 1946 *Rent Tribunals* were allowed to fix rents on furnished properties and the *1949 Landlord and Tenant Act* gave the tribunals powers to control rents on unfurnished houses too. The problem of course with this legislation was that by fixing rents at relatively low levels, there was no encouragement to private landlords to build houses for rent.

TOWN AND COUNTRY PLANNING; 'NEW TOWNS'

The biggest changes however came with the extension of the planning powers of the county councils. As a result of the *1947 Town and Country Planning Act*, they were required to provide long-term development plans for their area. In those 'Development Areas' of high unemployment and declining industry, trading estates were to be established, and 14 'New Towns' were proposed to end the unplanned sprawl of the major cities which had taken place in the inter-war years. These 'New Towns' were to be built by Development Corporations with 14 planned by 1950, and a further 14 in the 1960s. These 'New Towns' were to be new, carefully balanced communities, offering families the chance to settle in a new environment away from the congestion and overcrowding of the old city centres. They were to offer local employment and modern housing in pleasant, semi-rural surroundings of wide open spaces, parkland and carefully planned shopping and leisure areas. In the meantime, the general shortage of building materials forced the government to take emergency short-term measures such as building 'prefabs'. These were small bungalow type buildings, usually made out of asbestos type materials that were bolted together in sections. Though they were not built after 1948, and were only meant to last 10 years, many of them were still in use in the late 1960s and early 70s.

The Labour government's policy emphasised council house building, with generous grants to local councils. The return of the Conservative government in 1951 led to a change in emphasis. Greater encouragement was given to private builders and, especially after 1956, local councils were restricted to slum clearance and replacement housing.

'High rise' developments

In the 1960s, the restrictions by central government on local authority housing led to the adoption of what were supposed to be cheap, *high rise industrial housing*. The massive blocks of flats in London, Manchester and Sheffield, as well as in some of the new town city centre developments such as Basildon, mirrored the skyscraper office blocks that were appearing in the City of London. It is only since the late 1970s that we have become aware of both the social and safety problems caused by such buildings. The free spaces around 'tower blocks' that were meant to be open spaces for car parks and leisure have become playgrounds for vandals; the lifts seem to be permanently out of order and the long, ill-lit corridors and stairs have become vandalised and places to be wary of muggers.

The aim of keeping communities and families together, rather than forcing them to move to remote estates in the new towns, has not succeeded either. Elderly people, or mothers with young children, have found themselves cut off from meeting others and locked up behind their own front doors. Mothers could hardly be expected to look after their preschool children playing on the swings and roundabouts on the ground, when they themselves lived some 20 floors up.

In general, residents tended to dislike tower blocks, preferring their old houses, with small gardens and backyards which gave them space of their own, yet with frequent opportunities to see and meet others. Design and safety weaknesses in high rise housing have become more evident in recent years, such as the rusting of the steel bolts which kept the great slabs of concrete in place. It was however the gas explosion at *Ronan Point* in 1968, when great chunks of the tower block fell away, that led to the abandonment of such schemes. Some councils have already begun a policy of knocking down their tower blocks and most now have a policy of rehousing elderly people and those with young families in low rise buildings.

Inner city re-development

Since the 1960s, architects too have learned their lessons. Less emphasis is now put on building new towns in the green belt, or on tearing down old houses in the inner cities and building new concrete jungles. Instead we have come to recognise that once built on, the countryside cannot be replaced. We have begun to *redevelop* the inner cities by the renovation of older properties wherever possible. Architects are more aware of the need to produce buildings which allow people to maintain a sense of humanity and dignity. The closure of the inner city docks in places such as London and Manchester, and the reclamation of derelict warehouses and mill buildings in many northern cities, are creating opportunities to redevelop and rejuvenate city life. The problem is that many city centre schemes seem only to provide luxury apartments rather than to meet the more basic housing needs of the poorly paid.

EXAMINATION QUESTIONS

QUESTION   This is a structured essay-type question.

a)   Explain why in 1848 Parliament passed the 1848 Public Health Act.
b)   Explain why there was strong opposition to the 1848 Act.
c)   How effectively did this Act solve the public health problems of the major towns?
d)   What other measures were taken to improve public health in towns before 1900?

TUTOR'S ADVICE

Much of this answer is based on a knowledge of the *facts* outlined in this chapter. There is of course an element of *analysis* based on these facts. In part a) *avoid* listing a string of clauses of the 1848 Public Health Act. You are asked *why* Parliament passed that act. You might note that the local boards of health were only appointed where 10% of the ratepayers asked for them, or where the death rate reached 23 per thousand. Clearly the *wishes* of ratepayers were regarded by Parliament as important. The fear of contracting disease, especially at a time of high death rates, as in an epidemic, would give ratepayers (and voters) a desire to improve standards of health in their locality for their own protection.

In part b) you could mention the confusions in the medical profession as to the true causes of disease. Public hygiene was regarded as irrelevant to the spread of disease by many doctors. You could also mention the fear of many people to put too much power into the hands of a public body, such as a local board of health.

In part c) you could discuss the *technical* problems of achieving the desired improvments in health, such as an efficient water supply and sewerage system. You can also touch on the *political unwillingness* of many authorities to put the 'optional' Act into effect, and the *financial inability* of many authorities to do so.

Part d) gives you the chance to bring in facts and issues outside the 1848 Act. You could mention the *Sanitation Act of 1866* which *required* local authorities to implement the 1848 Act. The Local Government Board Act of 1871 established a government ministry to oversee and co-ordinate the activities of individual authorities. A wide range of possible Acts and attitudes can be discussed here.

SOCIAL PROBLEMS IN AN INDUSTRIAL SOCIETY

PROBLEMS OF REAL INCOMES AND STANDARDS OF LIVING

SOURCES AND EVIDENCE

QUANTITATIVE EVIDENCE ON WAGES AND PRICES

WORKING CONDITIONS

FACTORY REFORM

THE PROGRESS OF REFORM

GETTING STARTED

The development of an industrial society between 1700 and 1850 made a whole host of *existing* social problems, such as urban overcrowding and the operation of the Poor Laws, worse. It also created a series of *new* problems such as the need to regulate and control conditions in the new factories. The process of industrialisation changed the structure of society, it created new classes and eventually shifted the basis of political power. Arising out of these changes were new ideas and attitudes towards social and economic problems and new social and political institutions. In particular we can trace the development of ideas concerning how the economy of a nation was best left to the operation of 'natural laws' and how government intervention should be kept to a minimum. This idea is sometimes called 'laissez faire'. The interesting thing to note is that at the very time when the belief that the state should *not* interfere was generally accepted, the state in fact intervened deliberately, purposefully and effectively, in an increasing range of social problems. The question is, how and why did this happen? Also, if industrialisation led to increased wealth and incomes, why does it seem that social distress was on the increase for much of the period between 1790 and 1850?

It is generally expected that candidates should be able to:

- Describe and account for the major developments affecting the real incomes and welfare of labourers.

- Describe how, and explain why, governments intervened in a range of social problems, especially the Poor Laws and factory reform.

- Discuss the role of major social reformers in bringing about changes in public attitudes and the law.

- Discuss and comment upon the effectiveness of government policies in dealing with these problems.

ESSENTIAL PRINCIPLES

1 > **PROBLEMS OF REAL INCOMES AND STANDARDS OF LIVING**

There is no doubt that in the long term, industrialisation created a richer and wealthier society. We are all better off today than even the well-to-do craftsman and his family in the eighteenth century. Such evidence as we have also clearly shows that for much of the eighteenth century, the labouring classes became better off. How else can we explain the increase in population? There is general agreement that the period after the 1850s saw considerable improvements in the incomes of the labouring classes. People clearly became very much better off than their parents or grandparents were in the eighteenth century. The problem period is that from about 1790 to the middle 1840s; this is a period of rapid industrial change but one in which there are numerous complaints about distress and hard times.

Did the social and economic changes that took place 1790–1850 mean that, on average, the labouring and working classes from the countryside and towns became better off or worse off? The real answer of course is that we will never know, because to talk about the average working class person is a nonsense. Today we are aware that there are even considerable differences between families living in the same street, where the parents do similar jobs and earn a similar wage. There are of course still greater differences between different social groups and between different regions, which were probably even greater in the nineteenth century. So increasingly, historians have begun to discuss the impact of change upon *particular occupational groups* in *particular regions*.

A second problem concerns what it is that is actually under discussion. Some historians talk about *standards of living* and others about *social welfare*. What we need to know is, did the *overall well being of families* improve or deteriorate during this period? Although there are many disagreements about basic 'facts', there are also considerable areas of agreement among historians about probable general trends. Most historians today generally accept that, even between 1790 and 1840, on average, most labourers were probably a little better off materially. They had more to eat and drink and lived longer. However, many historians believe that nevertheless the *quality of life* for the urban and rural labouring classes became very much worse. Their conditions of employment, housing, and actual freedom deteriorated. Others do not believe this to be the case. The problem is one where it is possible for everyone to have a reasonable opinion which is *different*, because the nature and character of the evidence which we have is so *conflicting*.

2 > **SOURCES AND EVIDENCE**

As has been suggested before, the problem is not that historians have *too little* evidence. It is that the evidence is not of a type or in a form that allows the historian to make a reliable description of the circumstances, or an analysis and explanation. In general terms we have *two broad categories of evidence*. The first is *quantitative* data. Details of how much people earned, the prices they paid for food, clothing and other goods, and so on. In theory this should allow us to easily calculate how wages changed over a period of time, and whether labourers were able to buy more, or fewer, goods. Unfortunately in practice we cannot always do this.

The second kind of evidence is *qualitative* data. This includes written descriptions or illustrative material describing conditions of work or housing conditions, and perhaps providing comments about health or a general account of particular regions and groups of workers and how their lives have changed over the years. Again, in theory we ought to be able to use this material to describe the kinds of changes that took place, and to suggest whether, on balance, conditions were getting better or not. As with the statistical evidence, we find that we cannot always do this. It is not that the data is unclear or inaccurate or unreliable; it is whether such information is *representative enough* for us to draw general conclusions. There were so many differences between individuals, groups and regions during that period that although we have a great deal of material, it is not possible to make generalisations about the whole country. Whilst some social groups appear to have been doing well, others did badly. So almost any position can be defended.

3 > QUANTITATIVE EVIDENCE ON WAGES AND PRICES

Ideally, what the historians would like to be able to do is what governments do today; i.e. *measure changes in incomes*. We would like to be able to construct a *cost of living index* and to use this to show how the real incomes changed, i.e. what people could actually buy with their wages. To do this we need accurate information on weekly earnings together with regular information on how the prices of food and all the other things that families bought, changed. Even more importantly, we need to know *how much* people spent on *different items*. We call this their *basket of consumables*. We can then decide if the changes that took place in the prices of their basket of consumables was significant.

WAGES

The evidence on wages is fairly clear, although there are problems. One is that in the nineteenth century many families worked as a *family unit* and pooled their wages. Another is that parents often had children working for them and their wages are not shown separately. During the course of the century, the methods of payment changed; it is not always clear how much allowance we should make for payments in kind, or deductions we should make for fines for bad workmanship or being late. Again there is the problem of unemployment, and we do not know how much allowance to make for that.

We have quite a lot of of information about wages from the account books of different companies and the records kept by trades unions, as well as from parliamentary and private enquiries into different trades. Often, however, these are *not* for long periods, and so it is difficult to make *comparisons over time*. What they *do* show is big differences between workers doing the *same job* in the *same factory*, and between *different factories and regions*. Most historians have come to accept that on average, wage rates probably did not become any lower, even if they did not improve, beween 1790 and 1850.

It can be shown that *particular groups of workers* such as the *handloom weavers* in the period 1797–1830 (see Figure 9.1) experienced a substantial *fall* in wage rates; so did farm workers in districts where there was no alternative form of employment. But these groups are exceptional. More of a problem is whether family earnings were reduced significantly because of periods of unemployment.

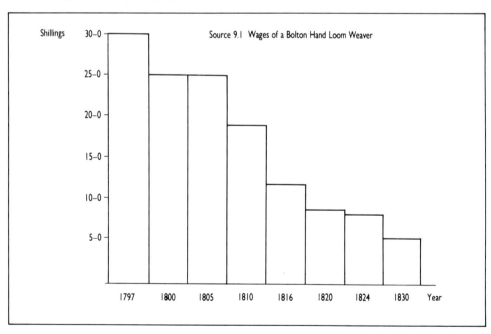

Fig. 9.1 Wages of a Bolton Handloom Weaver

Certain periods were especially severe, for example although the 1840s generally were a good time for black country coal miners, the early years (1842–4) were a period of great distress. Wage rates actually *fell* by about 30%, but the cost of foodstuffs fell by only about 18%. However, there was very high unemployment during this period and if we allow for this, then real incomes (that is what people could actually buy) fell by a massive 70%.

By 1845 employment had recovered, wages had risen and real incomes were about 8 times higher than they had been in 1842. Such *extremes* were probably not unusual in the early nineteenth century. In the long term, however, the position of factory workers did not get significantly worse. Indeed it became better for those groups and individuals who were able to move into more skilled trades. Over the whole period, there was a considerable increase in the demand for all kinds of skilled workers and, by 1850, a larger proportion of workers were in these groups. This means that even if *wage rates* did not go up, *average wages* would rise as there were *more skilled workers* earning *higher wages*. It seems unlikely that there was a *general fall* in either wage rates or weekly earnings.

PURCHASING POWER

Even more important is what will these wages really buy? Today the government collects information on wages and prices, and the television news regularly reports changes in the monthly cost of living index. This information is collected by researchers who *record* the weekly prices of goods that people buy from the supermarkets and use them to show how the average family's *purchasing power* has been affected by such changes. Of course this means that you need to know how much prices have changed *and* what proportion of incomes was spent on different goods.

The government carries out regular surveys of how families in different parts of the country spend their money. From this information an average 'basket of consumables' is produced. This shows the *proportion of income* that is spent on food, clothing, travel, mortgage, rent and so on.

How the cost of living index changes depends not only on how much the *price* of a particular item alters, but also on its *relative importance* in the overall pattern of spending. Clearly, measuring this is a very complicated and difficult task even today. It is hardly surprising that the historian has difficulties undertaking the same exercise from the evidence that has survived from the nineteenth century!

Weekly expenses of a family, consisting of a man and his wife, and five children the eldest eight years of age, the youngest an infant.

	s.	d.
Flour: 7½ gallons at 10d per gallon	6	3
Yeast to make it into bread, 2½d; and salt 1½d		4
Bacon, 1lb boiled at two or three times with greens; the pot-liquor, with bread and potatoes, makes a mess for the children		8
Tea, 1 ounce, 2d. sugar, 6d; ½lb butter or lard, 4d	1	0
Soap, ¼lb at 9d. per week		2½
Candles, ⅓lb per week with another at a medium, at 9d.		3
Thread, thrum, and worsted, for mending apparel, &c		3
TOTAL	8	11½

Weekly earnings of a Man and his Wife, viz

	s.	d.
The man receives the common weekly wages 8 months in the year	7	0
By task work the remaining 4 months he earns something more: his extra earnings, if equally divided among the 52 weeks in the year, would increase the weekly wages about	1	0
The wifes common work is to bake bread for the family, to wash and mend ragged clothes, to look after the children; but at bean setting, and harvest she earns as much as comes one week with another to about		6
TOTAL	8	6
Deficiency of earnings		5½

Fig. 9.2 Labouring people's budgets in the 1780s from David Davies, *The case of Labourers in Husbandry, 1795* quoted in Pamela Horn, *The Rural World.*

However to this had to be added annual outgoings, viz. rent for a cottage and garden, estimated at £2 for a family; fuel, being cut on the common, from 10s to 12s – say 10s; clothing – £3 10s for a man, wife and three children; lying in, one year with another, 10s; casualties, including sickness, loss of time thereby, and burials estimated at 10s. This made a sum of £7. When these items were taken into account the family had a deficiency of earnings amounting to £8 16s 9d per annum. Very few poor people could afford to lay out this sum in clothes; but they should be enabled to do it. Some cottagers breed a few fowls, with which they buy what sheets and blankets they want: but those who live in the old farmhouses are seldom allowed (to use their own words) to keep a pig or a chick.

During the *late eighteenth century*, various enquiries were made by individuals and poor law authorities on how *labourers* spent their wages (see Figure 9.2). In the nineteenth century, several studies were undertaken by researchers interested in poverty and the condition of the urban worker to find out how *families* spent their money. Some evidence is also given by *individuals* to Royal Commissions of enquiry. Sometimes both *Poor Law Commissioners* and *factory inspectors* included in their reports comments on wages, prices and weekly budgets (see Figures 9.3–9.5). The question is, are these family budgets accurate or representative enough for historians to use them in constructing a general cost of living index? Or can we only use them to make vague general statements and very limited deductions?

Consumption by the week, of different articles, by her husband, herself, and five children

	£	s	d
Butter, 1½lb at 10d		1	3
Tea, 1½oz			4½
Bread she makes herself; buys 24lb flour barm salt and baking, cost		4	6
Half a peck of oatmeal			6½
Bacon 1½lb			9
Potatoes, two score a week, at 8d a score		1	4
Milk, a quart a day, at 3d a quart		1	9
Flesh meat on Sunday, about a pound			7
Sugar, 1½lb a week at 6d			9
Pepper, mustard, salt, and extras, say			3
Soap and candles		1	0
Coals		1	6
Rent of house, per week		3	6
Total food, rent and fuel		18	1
Alleged total of weekly income	1	5	0
Leaves for clothing, sickness of seven persons schooling etc, a surplus of		6	11

Fig. 9.3 A Manchester housewife's weekly budget; *Factory Commission Report, 1833;* examination taken by Mr. Cowell, May 26, 1833.

Mrs B, Manchester: This witness was accidently met with, 13th May, 1844. She was waiting for Dr. Hawkins, to consult him about her niece's health. I took her into a room, and examined her about the customs and comforts of operative families. I consider her evidence to be a specimen, somewhat under the average, of the way in which an operative family lives.

Her husband is a fine spinner, at Mr M's where he has been from 1816; has five children. Her eldest daughter, now going 14, has been her fathers piecer for three years at her present age, her labour is worth about 4s 6d a week. At present her husbands earnings and her daughters together amount to about 25s a week – at least she sees no more than 25s a week; and before her daughter could piece for him, and when he had to pay a piecer in her stead, he only brought home 19s or 20s a week. (N.B. Whatever sum her husband may bring home, his earnings as a fine spinner at Mr M's are certainly not less than 28s a week.)

Breakfast is generally a porridge, bread and milk, lined with flour or oatmeal. On Sunday, a cup of tea and bread and butter. Dinner, on week days, potatoes and bacon, and bread, which is generally white. On a Sunday a little flesh meat; no butter, egg, or pudding. Teatime everyday, tea, and bread and butter; nothing extra on Sunday at tea. Supper, oatmeal porridge and milk; sometimes potatoes and milk. Sunday, sometimes a little bread and cheese for supper; never have this on week days. Now and then buys eggs when they are as low as a halfpenny piece, fries them to bacon.

They never taste any other vegetable than potatoes; neve use any beer or spirits; now and then may take a gill of beer when ill, which costs a penny. Perhaps she and her husband may have two gills a week. Her husband never drinks any beer or spirits that she knows of beyond this. . . .

Extracts from the family budgets reported by William Neild, 1841 for Dukinfield. These budgets are all for moderately skilled workers who were asked by Neild to record their earnings and expenditure during 1841. Neild was a Mayor of Manchester and a member of the Manchester Statistical Society. His survey covered nineteen families in Manchester and Dukinfield.

Item	Family No. 4		Family No. 6		Family No. 19	
Rent	4	0	5	0	2	8
Flour or bread	10	0	5	10	5	3
Meat	10	0	4	8	1	6
Bacon	1	0		4	1	0
Oatmeal		—		—		10
Butter	4	0	2	0	1	3
Eggs		—	1	0		—
Milk		—		10	1	6
Potatoes	3	0	1	8		10
Cheese	1	0		9		8
Tea	1	3	1	0		6
Coffee	1	2		6		3
Sugar	2	6	2	0	1	3
Treacle		—		—		6
Tobacco		9		—		—
Soap		9		6		10
Candles		6		6		2
Salt		2		½		1
Coals		—	1	2		10
Yeast		—		½		3½
Total	£2 0s 1d		£1 7s 10d		£1 0s 2½d	

Family No.4: husband a storeman, family of 8, total family income £2 17s.
Family No.6: husband an overlooker, family of 6, total family income £1 14s.
Family No. 19: husband an assistant mechanic, family of 7, total family income £1 7s.

Fig. 9.4 Family budgets in 1841

Summary of diets for the Labouring Classes as Reported by Dr Edward Smith, 1863

	Agricultural Labourers	Indoor workers
Bread	12⅓ lb	9½ lb
Sugar and treacle	7⅓ oz	8 oz
Butter, dripping, suet	5½ oz	5 oz
Bacon and meat	1 lb	13½ oz
Milk	1½ pints	1 pint
Cheese	5½ oz	—
Tea	½ oz	¾ oz

from: Practical Dietary for Families, Schools and the Labouring Classes, Dr. Edward Smith M.D. 1864.

Fig.9.5 Diets in 1863.

Even if we *have* the basket of consumables, do we have accurate *prices* for the different products bought? Well again we do have a lot of information on prices. But much of it is on *wholesale* not *retail* prices, usually recording what institutions like hospitals or Poor Law institutions paid. Wholesale prices are rather like buying in bulk and do not really give a clear idea about the *retail prices paid in shops*. These prices do however give us the *general trend* for important foodstuffs and basic commodities.

The general impression historians have from all the information on prices is that there were very big price differences for given goods between regions, and that prices for basic goods such as bread were very erratic. However, the general trend over the whole period was for the price of *manufactured products* to *fall* as mechanisation improved, leading to lower costs of production and prices. Apart from particular years, the price of food seems to have been static, if not actually falling.

What this suggests overall is that if wage rates stayed about the same, and the prices of many products fell, then many groups of workers were in the long term better off. *Particular groups*, such as the *highly skilled workers* in the traditional and new factory trades, became very much better off; *artisans* who became manufacturers at the times when particular branches of industry expanded could also do very well. It seems very likely that during the period 1760–1850, the wealth created by industrialisation was *not distributed evenly*. The rich became even richer, and although the poor were better off than before, the *gap* between them and the well to do became even wider.

STANDARDS OF LIVING

This view that the material well-being of the labouring classes probably did not worsen, except during relatively short periods of harvest failure or trade failure, does not mean however that the workers were enjoying a high standard of living. Labourers in 1850 might just have been better off than in 1790; but the work of researchers such as Mayhew in the 1840s and 1850s, Dr Edwin Smith in 1860, and Booth and Rowntree in the 1880s, has shown that at least a third of the population could not earn enough to feed themselves adequately. Disease caused by malnutrition was widespread, and another third of the population were sent into regular bouts of poverty by illness and short time working (see Chapter 10). What is also clear from enquiries done by Dr Smith in his 1860 report to the Committee of the Council on Health, is that most of the improvement in diet must have taken place in the second half of the century.

If even limited improvements in wages and real incomes did take place before 1850, why are some historians convinced that the Industrial Revolution caused great distress to many people? The answer is that they believe that the *quality of life* became very much worse for a considerable period of time, the 'cost' of higher wages being the dislocation to home and family life as labourers moved from agriculture into industry. In particular they had to endure appalling living conditions in the factory towns (see Figure 9.6 and Chapter 8).

In respect to physical appearance and development, the cotton operative occupies a sort of middle and negative position. To say they are decidedly stunted, is probably going too far; but they are certainly neither robust nor a well-made generation. They do not look ill, but they have no appearance of what is called rude health. They are spare and certainly undersized . . . there is no sign of weariness or languor in either face or limbs [their faces have] . . . a sort of unpleasant greasy pallor . . . in the country mills . . . the work people look just as rosy as the peasants around them. The inference would seem to be, that the crowded city life is more injurious than the busy factory labour.

One single fact proves our point that – Manchester operative mortality arises from defective domestic, not defective working arrangements . . . In a report . . . by a surgeon of practical experience and great local knowledge, it is shown that the rate of mortality depends upon the class of street and dwelling in which each individual lives.

Fig. 9.6 The conditions of the cotton operative

4 ⟩ WORKING CONDITIONS

The kinds of rapid changes that took place in cotton spinning led to *factory methods of production* (see Chapter 5). These were not always quickly adopted in other parts of the cotton industry or in other industries. In cotton spinning, the new machinery had swept all before it by the 1780s; but even in cotton the new power looms did not come into general use until the 1820s (see Chapter 5). Large scale factories were quite unusual, and in many parts of industry, handicraft methods and small workshops were the norm, even in the second half of the nineteenth century. For a long time factory and handicraft methods of production existed alongside one another. It was the concentration of the cotton industry around Manchester, its extreme mechanisation and the use of steam engines which attracted so much attention and comment.

FACTORIES

Factory work was not liked by labourers in the eighteenth and early nineteenth century. It led to major changes in how they lived and worked. Factory workers had to work to the *fixed routine of the machine and the clock* (see Figure 9.7). Apart from having to leave home to work, it was the discipline of factory hours and routines which was so different. Just like children going to school for the first time, the first generation of factory workers had to *learn* to obey a whole set of new rules. Rules which were determined by the pace and starting time of the machine. For the first time, there was a difference between work and non-work time.

Adjustment to the new routines and the loss of the freedom of traditional patterns of working at home, took time to be accepted. Employers often found it necessary to impose a hard and rigid regime of work, punishing workers for lateness, poor work or rowdiness in the workshop with a system of fines. Fines were high – often 6d to 2s (2½ to 10 p) and in some mills, swearing or singing could lead to fines up to 5s (25p). These may not sound

RULES AND REGULATIONS
to be observed by
The Workmen
in the employ of the
Stockton and Darlington Railway Company
at
NEW SHILDON

I   The Meal Times to be allowed, are from 8 to half past 8 o'clock in the Morning, for Breakfast; and from 12 to 1, for Dinner, at all times of the year.

II   Overtime to be reckoned at the rate of 8 hours for a Day; but no overtime to be entered till a whole Day of regular time has been worked.

III   Every Workman to put on his Timeboard with his Time, the name of the article or articles he has been working at during the day, and what Engine, or other Machinery they are for.

IV   Every workman who is provided with a Drawer for his tools, with Lock and Key, the Key to be numbered, and all his Tools to be marked with the same Number, and the letters SDWRC; the key to be left at the Office every night when the man has left work.

V   Any Workman who is longer than a quarter of an hour after the Bell is rung will lose a Quarter Day.

VI   Any Workman who does not call for his Time board in the Morning, and return it to the Office in the Evening, or when done work, to be fined SIXPENCE.

VII   Any Workman leaving his work without giving notice to the Clerk or to the Foreman, to be fined ONE SHILLING.

VIII   Any workman swearing, or using abusive language to a shopmate, to be fined ONE SHILLING.

IX   Should any one or more send for Beer, Ale or Spirits, into the Works (without leave), to be fined ONE SHILLING.

X   Any Workman introducing a stranger, or any person into the works (without leave), to be fined ONE SHILLING.

XI   Any Workman giving in more time than he has wrought, to have double the time taken off that he has overcharged.

XII   The Company's time-Piece at the Shops, to be the guide to the Workman's time.

XIII   Any Workman taking Tools from the Lathe or other piece of Machinery, to be fined SIXPENCE.

XIV   Any workman not returning Taps or Dies, or any general Tool, to the person, who has charge of them, to be fined SIXPENCE.

XV   Should any Workman leave his place of work for the purpose of Drinking, in working hours, he will be considered as having forfeited his situation.

Fig. 9.7 The discipline of the workplace

much at today's level of incomes, but look at Figures 9.1 and 9.2 and you can see that several fines in the course of a week could lead to big reductions in wages and could eventually result in dismissal. Even in modern times, many factories had the system where being a minute late 'clocking in' for work could lead to a deduction of 15 minutes pay. Some employers did use the 'carrot' as well as the 'stick', by offering special rewards for good work, but these were unusual (see Figure 9.8).

Working hours

In many communities, there was a traditional level of income expected from work, and workers in coal and lead mining would often *only work long enough* to provide themselves with this traditional level of pay. In other industries there was a tradition of long hours, and the twelve hour day from 6 am to 8 pm with breaks was probably the norm; with some others, a ten hour day was usual by about 1800. In the *cotton spinning mills* the government enquiry of 1816 showed that about 16 hours was the norm, with a 40 minute break for lunch. Even humane employers such as Samuel Oldknow expected apprentices to work 13 hours, beginning at 6 am.

Safety

Working in the factory was unhealthy in a number of different ways. Today, factories are regulated by health and safety regulations, but there were none before 1802. In many industries, and not just the factory trade, there were bad conditions of work which led to industrial diseases because dust and particles of fibres in the air got into the lungs and led to asthma, cancers and tuberculosis. All kinds of poisonings resulted from lead and mercury or from the chemicals used in dying cloth. There were injuries caused by unfenced machinery or from working in hazardous conditions in mines, quarries, building sites and iron works. Many factories were damp, cold and ill lit. If you consider all this, together with long hours and poor diets, it was not surprising that it was remarked even in

1782, *before* the widespread use of factory methods, that "while they minister to our needs and please our tastes and fancies, they [the common people] are impairing their health and shortening their days."

These problems were accepted as part of the ordinary way of life. There was no such thing as *compensation* for injuries or illness as a result of a lifetimes' work in a dangerous trade. Workers 'chose' their trade, and they and the well-to-do took it for granted that this was their lot.

Dismissal	353	Kindness	2
Threat of dismissal	48	Promotion/reward	9
Fines	101	Reward payment	23
Corporal punishment	55		
Complaints to parents	13		
Confined to mill	2		
Degrading dress badge etc	3		
Total	575		34

Fig. 9.8 Number of firms using punishments or rewards to influence factory children 1833

From: 1833, *Factories Enquiry Commission Report*

5 FACTORY REFORM

The problem then is why did the factory system lead to such an outcry and stream of criticisms that the government was moved to regulate and control working conditions? Firstly, it should be noted that this change did *not* happen overnight; it was a long slow process that was only partially effective, even by 1914. Attitudes were slowly changed as reformers from a wide variety of backgrounds used a wide variety of publicity methods to bring issues to the attention of the upper and middle classes. Pictures and descriptions were provided of conditions in the factories that were so horrible that nobody with a Christian conscience could allow them to continue, whatever the cost to manufacturers. It was not that the conditions were new, rather that the *developments in printing and communications* allowed the evidence to be brought before the public in a way that was not possible before.

Parliament and factory reform

A most important factor in changing public opinion was the use of *special investigations by Parliament*. These could be either *select committees of enquiry*, in which a small committee of M.Ps. investigated a problem and, after hearing evidence, presented a report to Parliament or a *Royal Commission of Enquiry*. Royal Commissions consisted of M.Ps., peers and others not necessarily from Parliament. The Commission was given a *particular* problem to investigate and it had the powers of a court to call witnesses and to examine them under oath. A report was published that included all the evidence collected, together with recommendations of the actions which Parliament should take.

These enquiries were supposed to be impartial, but there is considerable evidence to show that the government often chose for membership those whose ideas fitted in with their own plans and ideas. We know that in some cases the reports and recommendations (for example the report by the Royal Commission on the Poor Laws) were even being written *before* all the evidence had been heard, and that evidence that was not convenient was often ignored by the Commission.

Very often, even as the Commission was collecting evidence, it was published in newspapers and magazines. The Illustrated London News regularly published reports on the major enquiries when the pictures or facts given in evidence appeared to be particularly dreadful. During the later 1830s and 1840s, another important influence was the evidence collected by the *factory inspectors* and the *Poor Law Commissioners*. They published *annual reports* and were often called as expert witnesses by parliamentary committees. Almost without exception, these inspectors and commissioners, once they became aware of the problems in industry from first hand experience, encouraged Parliament to extend their powers and to widen the industries which were regulated. In a whole number of areas, not just factory legislation, it was the development of an efficient and effective *civil service inspectorate* which became the main agency for change. This was especially the case when inspectors were given discretionary powers, or were allowed to make new rules and regulations without always having to go back to Parliament for approval.

6 THE PROGRESS OF REFORM

The earliest action taken by Parliament was in 1802, when reports of how pauper apprentices were being treated came to public attention. The main terms and effects of the legislation are shown in the summary table Figure 9.9. This was followed by a series of

select committees of enquiry from 1815 to 1825 which made recommendations about the need to improve safety and the working conditions in factories in order to protect women and children. However, although the law was changed, they had little practical effect because nobody was appointed to *ensure that the laws were enforced*.

Fig. 9.9 Summary of Factory Legislation 1802–1908

DATE	ACT	MAIN PROVISIONS	INDUSTRIES COVERED	EFFECTS
1802	Health and Morals of Apprentice	1. Employers to provide some education for working children 2. Maximum working day for children of 12 hours 3. Night work prohibited 4. Annual whitewashing/cleaning of factory	cotton & woollen	almost none
1819	Factory Act	1. Work by children under 9 not allowed 2. Children aged 9–16 restricted to 12 hours	cotton	almost none
Amendments to 1919 Act in 1825 and 1831 raised age of children covered to 18 and abolished nightwork for all persons under 21 years. Lack of paid inspectors meant that still not very effective however.				
1833	Factory Act (Lord Shaftesbury's Act)	1. Work by children under 9 prohibited 2. Children under 9 limited to 9 hours daily or 48 hours per week 3. Children 13-18 limited to 12 hours daily or 69 hours per week 4. Nightwork prohibited for those aged under 18 (except in lace making) 5. 2 hours schooling for factory children 6. Appointment of 4 full time paid inspectors	all textile factories	not fully effective till after 1838. Inspectors gradually increased
1842	Mines Act	1. Employment of children under 10 underground prohibited 2. Only those aged 15+ allowed to operate winding gear	mines	much evasion
1844	Factory Act	1. Employment of children under 8 banned 2. Children aged 6-13 limited to 6½ hours work, plus at least 3 hours daily schooling 3. Machinery to be fenced 4. Females limited to 12 hours daily; prohibited from nightwork	all textile factories	much evasion
1847	Factory Act (10 Hours Act)	1. Limit 10½ hours daily for children 13-18 and women	all textile factories	limited by use of relays
1850	Factory Act	1. Persons covered by 1847 Act could only work between 6 am and 6 pm (2 pm Saturday) 2. Meal allowance to be minimum 1½ hours	all textile factories	stopped use of relays
1853	Employment of Children in Factories Act	Conditions of 1850 Act extended to children 8-13	all textile factories	
1860	Coal Mines Regulation Act	Safety regulations announced in 1850 and 1853 improved	mines	improved
1867	Factory Extension Act	1. Factory Acts applied to other trades 2. Employment children under 8 banned 3. Children 8-13 to be given at least 10 hours schooling per week	non textile trades	covered most industries
1867	Agricultural Gangs Act	1. Employment children under 8 banned 2. Women and children banned from working with men in field gangs	agriculture	first coverage
1872	Mines Regulation Act	1. Full time Employment boys under 12 banned 2. Boys 10-13 to attend school minimum ½ day per week		major fall in use of child labour
1878	Consolidating Act	All previous legislation reorganized into a single Act	all industries	
1908	Coal Mines Act (Eight Hours Act)	Working hours limited to 8 hours daily	coal mines	first Act to control adult hours

In the later 1820s there developed a coalition of working class radicals, humane employers, methodist journalists, conservative Christian peers, and M.Ps., who organised a general campaign to introduce more effective legislation. The campaign began with a series of letters to the Liberal newspaper, the Leeds Mercury, and to other Yorkshire newspapers written by Richard Oastler. Oastler was a Leeds merchant who, although a former Methodist, had become a strong Tory supporter of the Church of England. His fiery letters argued that the same kind of conditions which Parliament had recently banned when it made slavery illegal, were similar to those which applied in the Yorkshire woollen industry (see Figure 9.10).

Richard Oastler though born into a Methodist family became a member of the Church of England and a strong supporter of the Tory Party. After an unsuccessful career as a merchant in Leeds he took over his father's job as a Steward on the estate of the Thornhill family at Fixby Hall near Huddersfield. He became interested in the problems of workers in the Leeds woollen mills and during 1830 he wrote a series of letters to the Leeds Mercury, a leading Liberal newspaper. By 1831 he was actively involved in getting Radicals and Tories to co-operate against factory owners to obtain a reform of working conditions in factories.

YORKSHIRE SLAVERY

To the Editors of the Leeds Mercury

Let truth speak out, appalling as the statement may appear. The fact is true. Thousands of our fellow creatures and fellow subjects, both male and female, the miserable inhabitants of a Yorkshire town, (Yorkshire now represented in Parliament by the giant of anti-slavery principles) are at this very moment existing in a state of slavery, more horrid than are the victims of that hellish system of 'colonial slavery'. These creatures drawl out, unpitied their short but miserable existence, in a place famed for its profession of religious zeal, whose inhabitants are for ever foremost in professing 'temperance' and 'reformation' and are striving to outrun their neighbours in missionary exertions, and would fain to send the Bible to the farthest corner of the globe – aye, in the very place where anti-slavery fever rages most furiously, her apparent charity is not more admired on earth, than her real cruelty is abhorred in Heavan. The very streets which receive the droppings of 'Anti-Slavery Society' are every morning wet by the tears of the innocent victims of the accursed shrine of avarice, who are compelled (not by the cart-whip of the negro slave driver) but by the dread of the equally appalling thong or strap of the over-looker, to hasten, half-dressed, but not half-fed, to those magazines of British infantile slavery – the worsted mills in the town and neighbourhood of Bradford!

Would that I had Brougham's eloquence that I might rouse the hearts of the nation, and make every Briton swear, 'These innocents shall be free!'

Thousands of little children, both male and female, but principally female, from seven to fourteen years of age, are daily compelled to labour from six o'clock in the morning to seven in the evening with only – Britons, blush while you read it! – with only thirty minutes allowed for eating and recreation. Poor infants! Ye are indeed sacrificed at the shrine of avarice, without even the solace of the negro slave; ye are no more than he is, free agents; ye are compelled to work as long as the necessity of your needy parents may require, or as the cold blooded avarice of your worse than barbarian masters may demand! Ye live in the boasted land of freedom, and feel and mourn that ye are slaves, and slaves without the only comfort which the negro has. He knows that it is his sordid mercenary master's interest that he should live, be strong and healthy. Not so with you. Ye are doomed to the labour from morning to night for one who cares not how soon your weak and tender frames are streatched to breaking! You are not mercifully valued at so much per head; this would assure you at least (even with the worst and cruel masters) of the mercy shown to their own labouring beasts. No, no! Your delicate limbs are tired and fagged, and jaded, at only so much per week, and when your joints can act no longer, your emaciated frames are cast aside, the boards on which you so lately toiled and wasted life away, are instantly supplied with other victims, who in this boasted land of liberty are HIRED – not sold – as slaves and daily forced to hear that they are free...

The nation is now most resolutely determined that negroes shall be free. Let them, however, not forget that Britons have some common rights with Afric's sons...

Fig. 9.10 Extracts from Richard Oastler's Letter on Yorkshire Slavery

Oastler's letters received widespread publicity and led to various actions in parliament to improve conditions. One was the attempt by Michael Sadler to introduce a new factory Bill in 1832. This Bill was referred to a select committee, despite Sadler's protests. However this probably worked to his advantage because, together with other M.Ps. sympathetic to the workers, Sadler was able to manipulate the committee. He arranged that *carefully selected witnesses* were financed and coached in the answer to give when committee members asked arranged questions. It is in fact quite clear that there was considerable prompting of witnesses. Nevertheless, the string of crippled children who gave evidence was a clear indication that the callous and immoral treatment in some factories (see Figure 9.11) and by some factory masters (some of whom such as John Marshall of Leeds were M.Ps.) who took their profits without any thought of the cost to their young and defenceless employees.

Extract from First Report of the Factory Commissioners 1833

> One of the great evils to which people employed in factories are exposed is, the danger of receiving serious and even fatal injury from the machinery. It does not seem possible, by any precautions that are practical to remove this danger altogether. There are factories in which every thing is done that seems practicable to reduce this danger to the least possible amount, and with such success that no serious accident happens for years together. By the returns which we have received, however, it appears that there are other factories, and these are by no means few in number, nor confined to the smaller mills, in which serious accidents are continually occurring, and in which, notwithstanding, dangerous parts of machinery are allowed to remain unfenced. The greater the number of the proprietors in neglecting sufficiently to fence their machinery, and the greater the number of accidents, the less their sympathy with the sufferers... it appears in evidence that cases frequently occur in which the workpeople are abandoned from the moment an accident occurs; their wages are stopped, no medical attention is provided, and whatever the extent of the injury no compensation is afforded.

Fig. 9.11 Evidence from the Sadler Committee Report

The *Sadler Report* was published in January 1833, and this was followed by a wave of carefully organised petitions to Parliament from the industrial areas demanding that working hours be reduced to 10. However, Sadler had lost his parliamentary seat during the 1832 elections, and the leadership of the campaign had been taken by Lord Ashley, who introduced proposals for a new factory Bill. It was this Bill which, despite protests, was again referred to a new commission of enquiry. This was on the grounds that the previous enquiry had not given the *factory owners* the opportunity to put their case. The 15 Commissioners of this Royal Commission were mostly men who had already written extensively in opposition to factory legislation and to the reduction of hours. The three leading Commissioners were Edwin Chadwick, Thomas Tooke, and Dr. Southwood-Smith, each one of whom was to appear on many other enquiries. The factory reformers thought the Commission would be a whitewash. But although the Commission heard new evidence and was not generally sympathetic to reform, it could not totally ignore the evidence. The final report was written by Edwin Chadwick, and though it is clear he had already made his mind up about what the recommendation would be *before* all the evidence had been collected, the report *did* make some radical proposals that were in favour of reform. The main demand of the reformers for a general reduction of hours was *not* accepted, and the proposals really only applied to women and young children who, it was said, could not defend themselves.

 Background to the 1833 Factory Act

THE FACTORY ACT

The Act that finally appeared in 1833 was not the same as the Commission's recommendations, but it did include the vital element of *inspection*. The powers and numbers of the inspectors were very limited at first, and the Act only came into effect in stages. Nevertheless by 1838, the experience of the Act and the abuses which the inspectors had come across, led to further enquiries and to the gradual extension of factory regulations to more industries. Finally, in 1847, the number of hours that could be worked by *adults* was limited to 10 hours. It was not however until 1867 that attempts were made to control the hours worked by women and children in *agriculture*, and not until 1878 that the rules and regulations in different industries were brought together in a single set of regulations.

EXAMINATION QUESTIONS

The examination questions in this Chapter consist only of the student's answer type. Tutor's advice to the later parts of the question are also included.

A STUDENT'S ANSWER WITH EXAMINER'S COMMENTS

QUESTION

Evidence based questions aim to test how well you understand and can use information given in the question. You must also expect to show awareness of any bias and contradiction in the sources and to comment upon the reliability of the sources. Examine each of the sources as directed and answer the questions which follow.

Source A Andrew Ure, *The Philosophy of Manufactures*, written after a two month tour of the cotton manufacturing districts of Northern England in 1833 and published in 1835:

" . . . I have visited many factories, both in Manchester and in the surrounding districts, during a period of several months, entering the spinning rooms, unexpectedly and often alone, at different times of the day and I never saw a single instance of corporal chastisement [punishment] inflicted on a child, nor indeed did I ever see children in ill-humour. They seemed to be always cheerful and alert, taking pleasure in the light play of their muscles, enjoying the mobility natural to their age.

It was delightful to observe the nimbleness with which they pieced the broken ends, as the mule carriage began to recede from the fixed roller beam, and to see them at leisure, after a few seconds' exercise of their tiny fingers, to amuse themselves in any attitude they chose, till the stretch and winding-on were once more completed.

The work of these little elves seemed to resemble a sport, in which habit gave them a pleasing dexterity. Conscious of their skill, they were delighted to show it off to any stranger.

As to exhaustion by the day's work, they evinced no trace of it on emerging from the mill in the evening; for they immediately began to skip about any neighbouring play-ground, and to commence their little amusements with the same alacrity as boys issuing from a school . . ."

Source B Evidence of Samuel Coulson to Parliamentary Select Committee on Childrens Labour 1831–2:

Samuel Coulson, tailor at Stanningly, near Leeds, with three daughters working in mills:

Q At what time in the morning in the brisk time did those girls go to the mills?

A In the brisk time, for about six weeks, they have gone at 3 o'clock in the morning, and ended at 10, or nearly half-past, at night.

Q What sort of mills were these?

A Worsted mills.

Q What intervals were allowed for rest or refreshment during those nineteen hours of labour?

A Breakfast a quarter of an hour, and dinner half an hour and drinking a quarter of an hour . . .

Q Had you not great difficulty in awakening your children to this excessive labour?

A Yes; in the early time we had to take them up asleep and shake them when we got them on the floor to dress them before we could get them off to work; but not so in the common hours.

Q What time did you get them up in the morning?

A In general me or my mistress got up at two o'clock to dress them.

Q So they had not above four hours' sleep at this time?

A No they had not.

Q For how long together was it?

A About six weeks it held; it was only when the throng was very much on; it was not often that.

Q The common hours of labour were from 6 in the morning till half past 8 at night?

A Yes. . . .

Q Had any of them an accident in consequence of this labour?

A Yes my daughter when she first went there . . .

Q Did this excessive labour cause much cruelty also?

A Yes, with being so very much fatigued the strap was very frequently used . . .

Source C Evidence of John Hall, a mill overlooker, to Parliamentary Select Committee on Childrens Labour, 1831–2:

Q Do you believe that children can endure the labour you have been describing without injury?

A No, I do not.

Q When your hands have been employed for some time, do you see any alteration in their faces?

A In the course of a few weeks I see a paleness in their faces, and they grow spiritless and tired.

Q Have you remarked that cases of deformity are very common in Bradford?

A They are very common. I have the names of I think, about 200 families I have visited myself that have deformed children, and I have taken particular care not to put down one single case where it might have happened by accident, but only those whom I judged to have been thrown crooked by the practice of piecing . . .

Source D Evidence of William Forster, a mill owner to Parliamentary Select Committee on Children's Labour, 1831–2:

If the hours of child labour were reduced, mills will be unable to work a full twelve-hour day, with a consequent reduction in the earnings of the adult workers as well as the profits of the mill-owners. The youngest child employed by me is never exhausted by 12 hours labour and, which they clearly show by playing and romping when the hours of labour terminate. . . .

Examine Source A above then answer the questions which follow.

1 a) What evidence is there in Source A to explain why manufacturers employed young children?

b) Give three ways in which Source A supports the view that factory work did no harm to children.

c) Why might a historian regard this source as either reliable or unreliable?

Examine Sources B and C.

2 a) List three ways in which Sources B and C disagree with Source A and the view that children were well cared for in factories.

b) Why might a modern historian be more likely to agree with the views expressed in Sources B and C rather than Source A?

c) Do you think that historians would consider Sources B and C to be more or less reliable than Source A? Give reasons for your answer.

3 The chairman of the 1831–2 Parliamentary Select Committee of Enquiry from which Sources B, C, and D above were taken was Michael Sadler who together with Richard Oastler was a well known campaigner against child labour. Using the evidence in the sources above and your own knowledge explain why:

a) factory owners complained that the evidence given before the enquiry and its report were biased;

b) what actions would need to be taken by a modern historian who wished to use the evidence presented in the report by Michael Sadler's committee?

4 Using all these Sources and your own knowledge, outline the different points of view concerning the employment of children in textile factories that might have been expressed at a meeting between employers and a group of workers in 1834.

STUDENT'S ANSWER

1 a) Young children were employed because they were
      cheaper than adults and their small size made it
      easier for them to crawl beneath the machines to
      piece together the broken ends of the threads. They
      were also better than adults at piecing together the
      broken threads with their smaller hands.
   b) Source A says that the children were always cheerful
      and alert and that they enjoyed their work. He also
      says that the children were not exhausted after the
      days work.
   c) This source is one mans point of view after spending
      just a few months visiting the factories. He does not
      say how many factories were visited but it is not
      likely that he could have visited very many over a
      large area. He does say that his visits were
      unexpected and took place at different times but it
      does not seem likely that a manufacturer would let a
      stranger visit his factory without permission. When a
      visitor was about the foreman were likely to be on
      their best behaviour and unlikely to punish children.
      It seems unlikely that this information is telling us
      what mills are really like though it is likely that
      this is what Andrew Ure actually saw.

Examiner's comments

a) The source makes no mention of children being cheaper than adults. The question asks you to use information in the source, so no credit is given for this; otherwise good.

b) Accurate selection of material from source.

c) Excellent opening sentence that uses information in heading to make point. Sensible comments about why source unlikely to be representative and reliable whilst being an accurate record of what Ure himself saw.

2 a) The children had to get up too early and did not have
      much sleep so they were tired and made mistakes or
      fell asleep at work. When they did this they were
      punished and it was not fair because it was not their
      fault they were tired. They also did not have much
      time to eat and they had to start work even before
      they had breakfast.
   b) Sources B and C are by people who worked in the mills
      and had experience over a long time so they are
      likely to be accurate. We also know today that young
      children need to have enough sleep if they are to
      grow properly and that working long hours in poor
      conditions is not good for your health. Source C by a
      factory overlooker in charge of children does say
      that children were deformed and injured because of
      their work in the factory and this is backed up by
      knowledge of 200 families.
   c) Though these people would know more about conditions
      in the factories because they worked there, they
      might be biased and only saying how bad it was
      because they did not want children to work there.

Examiner's comments

a) It would be much better to refer to the sources directly e.g. in Source A it says that there was no corporal punishment and that the children were happy in their work and not punished, but in B it says that the children were strapped for bad work and were exhausted because of the long hours. In Source C it says the children became ill and dispirited.

b) Are B and C likely to be more accurate just because the witnesses had worked in the factory? They could be just as likely to give a biased view or even to tell lies if it made their case stronger, they are not necessarily more accurate than an outside impartial visitor. The reference to modern medical knowledge is a good point as is the cross reference to Source C and why it is likely to be reliable.

c) Sound comments on Sources B and C but omits to mention the circumstances in which Source A came to be written and is therefore less likely to be as accurate as B or C.

TUTOR'S ADVICE TO PART 3

a) Note that the question says from the evidence and your own knowledge, therefore a full answer would be expected to include material not available in the sources.

   Information from the sources includes: the way in which the questions appear to be leading the witnesses in a particular direction, they are encouraging them to make a particular kind of answer. This suggests that only questions and evidence likely to prove the point of view of Michael Sadler was used.

   Other relevant information: the chairman was Michael Sadler a noted campaigner against the factory system, could he be an impartial chairman? It has been shown that Sadler packed his committee with opponents of the factory system and that witnesses were carefully selected and even coached to give particular answers. Factory owners complained that the evidence given was out of date and was not representative of mills and factories generally.

b) Today historians would want to know whether the report and the evidence it contains is accurate and fair. To do this we need to know about the membership of the committee and whether it was a fair cross-section of different views and political parties. Did for example all the members attend and participate or did a few people do all the work? This often happened even with Royal Commissions (most notably in 1832 Royal Commission Report on the Poor Laws), so that the report represents the view of only a few people, sometimes the report was even written before all the evidence was heard or only used carefully selected parts of the evidence that fitted in with the point of view of the chairman. This was said to be the case with the Sadler report but historians can check up on this by looking at all the published evidence and whether the witnesses were a fair cross-section of different groups. In particular historians would need to check up on what the witnesses had said or written beforehand to try and find out whether their evidence was likely to be biased.

TUTOR'S ADVICE TO PART 4

Your answer must show that you are aware not only of the different viewpoints of masters and employees, but of differences between people in each of these groups e.g. Why did some masters believe that child labour was necessary? Why did they say that such long hours had to be worked? Did all masters believe that children had to be treated cruelly and worked for such long hours? What actions were taken by some masters to improve conditions in factories? Why did such factory masters want Parliament to regulate hours and make everyone adopt good working conditions? Did all parents agree that a cut in children's hours was a good thing? What would the attitude of some poor parents have been if this meant a reduction in children's earnings or their own? Why did some parents object to their children working in factories, but still allow their children to work in factories?

GETTING STARTED

Until the twentieth century, it was generally accepted that poverty was the result of personal weakness. The poor were idle, shiftless or lazy; weaknesses in their character led them to waste their time and prevented them from developing good habits of behaviour. The 1834 *Poor Law Amendment Act* introduced a system where the basic objective was to force people to work by only providing relief that was at a *minimal level* and involved the personal disgrace of the poor who asked for it. The way to treat such people was to make them work. It was not until the 1850s and 60s that investigators such as Mayhew and charity workers showed that whilst there were scroungers, the main causes of poverty were low wages, ill health, old age and above all, unemployment.

During the 1870s and 1880s, further 'scientific' research confirmed these views, and slowly changed opinions. Such practical evidence was used by trade unions and the developing Labour Party to put pressure upon the established political parties. The aim was to develop a system of relief which recognised the causes of poverty and to get the government to adopt policies for overcoming these problems.

It gradually came to be accepted that the state had a *responsibility* to remove the weaknesses in the economic system that led to poverty. After 1906, the government adopted a series of measures which introduced the principle of *insurance*; the working classes could, with contributions from employers and government, now protect themselves against a variety of misfortunes, such as unemployment and ill health. There was a grudging acceptance that the state had responsibilities towards its citizens.

Eventually, during the late 1930s, this notion of responsibility came to be seen not as a gift of the state but as a *basic right* of all citizens. This included the right to a decent home, protection from ill health and poverty, and even the right to equality of opportunity and employment. The election of the Labour government in 1945, brought to power a political party which for the first time accepted this notion that everyone had certain basic rights. An attempt was made to develop a 'welfare state' which would protect all citizens from the 'cradle to the grave'.

Candidates should be able to describe and explain:

- How the Old Poor Law worked, i.e. Speenhamland systems etc.
- Why the Old Poor Law was heavily criticised during and after the Napoleonic Wars.
- The recommendations of the 1832 Poor Law report.
- The terms of the 1834 Poor Law Amendment Act and the problems of putting it into effect.
- The increasing criticism of the 1834 Poor Law Amendment Act and how it failed to deal with the causes of poverty 1850–1900.
- The actions by Liberal governments before 1914 to prevent and deal with the social problems arising from poverty.
- The Beveridge Report of 1942 and the introduction of the Welfare State after 1944.

CHAPTER 10

POVERTY AND SOCIAL WELFARE

THE OLD POOR LAW

THE ROYAL COMMISSION ON THE POOR LAWS 1832

THE NEW POOR LAW

CHANGING ATTITUDES TOWARDS POVERTY

THE LIBERAL SOCIAL WELFARE REFORMS

THE PROCESS OF REFORM

BEVERIDGE AND THE WELFARE STATE

ESSENTIAL PRINCIPLES

1 ▶ THE OLD POOR LAW

The 'Old' Poor Law of the *eighteenth century*, was based upon the basic principles developed during the *sixteenth century* and brought together in a single Act of 1601, usually called the *Elizabethan Poor Law*. The principles of the 1601 Act were that each *parish* should be responsible for its own poor. Local taxes (rates) were collected based upon the value of the land and these were distributed to the deserving poor by a committee of local churchwardens or poor law overseers. During the eighteenth century, the Poor Law authorities found that the growth of population, war and occasional harvest failure made it increasingly more expensive and difficult to deal with the requests for help under the Poor Law.

To try and cut costs, churchwardens and overseers sometimes set up *workhouses* in which the poor could be put to work. Often the cost of doing so was more expensive than giving occasional relief in the pauper's own home (*outdoor relief* as it was called). In 1722 Parliament had allowed parishes to *refuse* to give help to the poor *unless* they entered the workhouse. In 1782, Parliament passed *Gilbert's Act* which allowed parishes to group themselves into *unions* and to set up workhouses to be used for the sick and orphans. A year later, in 1783, the justices of Whittlesford in Cambridgeshire met and agreed that 'every man who has a family and behaves himself seemly, shall be allowed the price of five quartern loaves per week with two quartern loaves added for each member of his family'.

This was only one of many schemes which linked relief to the price of food and the size of the family. The most famous is the *Speenhamland System* adopted in 1795 by justices in Berkshire (see Figure 10.1) to give general directions to overseers in their area. During this period it seems that the poor were generally treated with some compassion and understanding, and although scroungers were dealt with severely, the details in church-wardens' account books show the considerable care given to the sick and the elderly, and to the placement of orphaned children (see Figure 10.2). There was also a determination to make the fathers of children born to unmarried mothers pay for the upkeep of their children.

> **❝ The search for new alternatives ❞**

There was a rise in the *cost* of poor relief, as enclosures forced many small landowners into becoming poor, landless labourers. This was made worse by the series of poor harvests during the French wars, which led to high wheat prices. These resulted in a considerable increase in Poor Law taxes. Criticism of the Old Poor Law now increased and there was a search for new methods to deal with the problem of poverty. Some writers suggested leasing *small holdings* to the poor so they could grow their own food; some radicals like Robert Owen suggested *communal farms*, and some developed complicated suggestions for what we today would call social insurance. Such schemes were, however, against the general attitude of the age. Local ratepayers demanded that the churchwardens

The Speenhamland System

During the eighteenth century there developed a number of local poor relief systems that tried to link the amount of relief given to the poor to the prices of basic foodstuffs and the size of the family. The most famous of these systems was devised by the local J.P.s responsible for the operation of the Poor Law at Speenhamland in Berkshire.

> At a general meeting of the Justices of this County on Wednesday May 6th, 1795, it was resolved unanimously:
> that the present state of the poor does require further assistance than has generally been given them...
> The Magistrates make the following calculations and allowances for relief of all industrious men and their families who shall endeavour (as far as they can) for their own support and maintenance.
> That is to say, when the gallon loaf shall cost 1s (5p), then every poor and industrious man shall have for his support 3s (15p) weekly, either produced by his own hand or family's labour, or an allowance from the poor rates; and for the support of his wife and family and every other of his family, 1s 6d (7½p)...
> And as the price of bread rises, for every 1d (½p) which the loaf rises above 1s (5p), an extra 3d (1½p) to the man and 1d (½p) to every other member of the family.

Fig. 10.1 The Speenhamland System

The Accounts of Richard Savage one of the Church-Wardens of the Parish of Wrenbury for the Year. 1711. Deliver'd. August.7.1712.

	£	s	d
For Ringing when I was chosen Warden	0	1	0
At the Visitation for Fees 1s 1d Ordinary's 1£	1	1	1
To Gwen Wilkison for Tabling a Bastard one year ending Feb.2.1711. my Part	1	0	0
May.13. when Mr. Edgley preached here	0	0	6
July.19. At the Taking of the Old Warden's Accounts	0	3	0
Towards mending the Church-Yard-Walls my Part	0	0	6
When Mr. Legh's preach'd here 3 Several Sundays	0	1	6
To Tho.Furbar for a Bastard's Table one Quarter	0	5	0
For this Bastard's Table five Weeks more	0	2	0
Towards clothing him when Set out an Apprentice	0	5	0
The Clerk's Wages my Part	0	8	0
Toi David Hulse and his Man five days Helping Gabriel Smith to set up the new Clock	0	10	0
Toward the new Clock and Boards my Part	5	10	0
Towards Drink when the new Clock was setting up	0	1	6

Fig. 10.2 Wrenbury Village Accounts 1712

or parish overseers become more economical. In many parishes, 'houses of industry' were set up where the 'idle poor', as they were increasingly referred to, should be put to work. Examinations of the poor by churchwardens *before* they would grant relief became increasingly stricter and schemes were adopted for hiring out the poor to local farmers or putting them to work on the roads before any relief was given.

Between 1817 and 1832 there were many parliamentary enquires into aspects of poverty. The ideas of Thomas Malthus were particularly influential. Malthus suggested that because population increased faster than food supply, allowance schemes such as the Speenhamland System made poverty *worse* by encouraging couples to have larger families to qualify for more relief. Some areas began to have *paid overseers* to run workhouses and in general there was a considerable tightening up in the way in which poor relief was given. It was the *labourers' riots* in 1830 and an apparent connection between those counties which adopted allowance systems and the riots which gave the government the opportunity to set up a Commission of enquiry into the operation of the Poor Laws.

2 THE ROYAL COMMISSION ON THE POOR LAWS 1832

It now seems clear that the government had made up its mind about the policy it intended to adopt and only used the Commission of enquiry to remove opposition to its proposals. In 1841, Sir James Graham, in a letter to Sir Robert Peel, said as much: 'A Commission is most useful to pave the way for a measure which is preconcerted; take for example the Poor Law enquiry.' Later, in 1842, he wrote again to Peel, 'the Government which granted the Enquiry [on the Poor Laws] contemplated and sought a specific change, and had the commission as a Pioneer for their measure.'

It seems that even in June 1831, the government had already made up its mind about some course of action because, when a proposal was put in the House of Lords for a bill to deal with agricultural unemployment and relief, Lord Brougham said for the government that he had studied the problem very carefully and that 'at length he believed he saw daylight amidst the darkness which had hitherto enveloped the subject'. He refused to explain what the plan was, but said that before the end of the session a proposal would be made that 'was intended to be preparatory to another measure for the consolidation and simplification of the existing Acts on the subject of the Poor Laws'.

As with the Commission into the Employment of Children (see Chapter 9) the government was very careful in the *membership* of this Commission and it chose as commissioners people who it knew would come up with the recommendations that it wanted. Seven commissioners were appointed, and five of them had been actively involved in either writing about or introducing reforms to the Poor Law. Later, 26 assistant commissioners were appointed, and these too included Edwin Chadwick, a well known supporter of reform, to reduce Poor Law cost. Later Chadwick was made a full commissioner.

HOW THE ENQUIRY WAS CONDUCTED

The published reports suggest that the commissioners carried out an exhaustive scientific enquiry and that their recommendations are based upon this evidence. Certainly the enquiries *were* exhaustive, but it seems that the way these were conducted and the questions asked (see Figure 10.3) were designed to produce evidence of a certain kind that would *support opinions and views already held*. The long list of questions sent to every parish about the cost and methods of relieving the poor was very similar to the enquiries done by one of the commissioners, Sturgess-Bourne, ten years earlier. The assistant commissioners went to every area, collected information and made reports according to a *particular schedule of questions*. They sent in regular weekly reports and these were read by the Commissioners in London.

'In Coggeshall Essex', says Mr Majendie, 'weekly wages are 8s; but by piecework a good labourer may earn 10s. Now, consider the case of labourers with four children, for the subsidence of which family (according to the Chelmsford scale, which is the law of this district) 11s 6d is required. Of this sum the good labourer earns 10s, and receives from the parish 1s 6d. The man who does not work, and whom no one will employ, receives the whole from the parish.

... the gentleman at whose house I was stopping being doubtful of the encouragement offered to early marriage from the mode of administering the Poor Laws proposed to obtain, if possible, the opinion of the first labourers to be met with in the fields; an opportunity soon occurred: four men were working together near a farm house; upon questioning them as to the wages they were earning, who informed us that he was 30 years of age and unmarried, complained much of the lowness of his wages, and added, without a question on the subject being put to him. "That if he were a married man, and had a parcel of children, he would be better off, as he should either have work given him by the piece, or receive an allowance for his children."

The Poor Law Commissioners complained that the generosity and method of giving relief, especially outdoor relief, encouraged an immoral attitude towards work and led to idleness and the belief that charity was a right not a privelege.

...But in the large number of cases, it (the workhouse) is a large almshouse, in which the young are trained in idleness, ignorance and vice; the able-bodied maintained in sluggish indolence; the aged and more respectable exposed to all misery that is incident to dwelling in such society, without government or classification, and the whole body of inmates subsisted on food far exceeding both in kind and amount, not merely the diet of the independent labourer but that of the majority of persons who contribute to their support.

Fig. 10.3 Extracts from the Report of the Poor Law Commissioners 1834 criticising allowance systems

In February 1833 part of the evidence collected by Chadwick on London and Berkshire was printed. Nasseau Senior wrote several articles anonymously which outlined his proposals for reforming the parish system by creating a professional central bureaucracy. These leaks served the purpose of getting the main ideas of the Commissioners known and the public prepared for what was to come in the official recommendations. It is now also clear that much of the report was *already written* before all the evidence was in and that information was carefully selected from the evidence to support particular viewpoints about the weaknesses and failure of the Old Poor Law (see Figure 10.3).

The *Report of the Poor Law Commissioners* was published in 1834. It made major criticisms of the Old Poor Law, it said that:

i) parishes were inefficient in giving relief;

ii) there was corruption in some parishes, especially those which adopted the *Roundsman type system* where large farmers obtained poor law labour at low rates;

iii) *Allowance systems*, such as Speenhamland, not only were expensive but they discouraged workers from moving to areas where there were jobs. They led to increased family size and generally encouraged idleness, creating a class of workers dependent upon relief.

Each of these charges was backed up by evidence from particular parishes. The Report rejected the division into 'deserving' and 'undeserving' poor and showed how it encouraged parents to escape their responsibilities by making the Poor Law pay for the upkeep of their children.

The Report proposed to deal with these problems by:

i) creating a central body to regulate all relief;
ii) creating a professional and efficient administration by forcing parishes to amalgamate into larger groups called *Unions*;
iii) requiring Unions to employ paid professional *Relieving Officers*;
iv) regulating how relief was to be given by requiring all Unions to build workhouses and to abolish outdoor relief, thus forcing paupers into the workhouse (the so called 'workhouse test');
v) making conditions in the workhouse no better and slightly worse than those that the working labourer might expect outside (the principle of 'less eligibility');
vi) encouraging emigration.

THE POOR LAW AMENDMENT ACT

These proposals were discussed in great detail by the Cabinet and several draft Bills were produced. Eventually, the Cabinet accepted a Bill which it believed its supporters would accept and which it could get through Parliament. The basic features of the Commission's recommendations remained in the *1834 Poor Law Amendment Act*. Although the new Poor Law Commission did not have the kind of powers to force its will upon Unions, it did have the power to make such regulations as it thought necessary. It only had to inform the Home Secretary and Parliament of its proposals 40 days before they came into effect.

The Act created a new kind of administration over which Parliament had almost no control. The Commissioners had powers to regulate how poor relief was given and to issue instructions to Unions. However, it had little power to force the elected Boards of Guardians to apply its rules. It could only persuade and disallow money payments to paupers, so that in effect the Act was banning outdoor relief. The only escape from this was on the grounds of emergency which the overseers had to report to the Commissioners within 15 days. Such payments were only supposed to be in food, lodging or clothing.

The Act was put into effect remarkably quickly. By 1835, 112 unions covering 2066 parishes had been organised; by 1836, almost 8000 parishes were covered, and by 1839 almost 14,000. It was not until 1837, that the Commissioner met any serious opposition to the Unionisation of parishes; then there were riots at Todmodern (Lancashire) against the New Poor Law and many districts refused to appoint Boards of Guardians or to build workhouses. In Wales in 1843–4, resistance to the Poor Law finally erupted into the *Rebecca Riots*. Such actions were, however, unusual, though it forced the Commissioners to alter their regulations, sometimes considerably.

For all practicable purposes the process of reorganisation was completed by 1840. By 1838, the Commissioners claimed that savings of £2.3m had been made. Between 1834 and 1865, there was a reduction in expendicture of about £1m a year in terms of what the average rate had been from 1813 to 1834. The Poor Law Amendment Act appeared to have served its purpose, it had massively cut costs. Not only that, but the Commissioners showed that they had been 'more efficient'. They had given prompt and adequate relief to the elderly and sick; pauper children often received education in schools within the workhouse and the habit of work and good moral behaviour was spreading amongst the lower orders.

3 THE NEW POOR LAW

The question is, had the Poor Law Amendment Act done what it was supposed to do or had it merely forced people to find some other means of getting assistance? In many ways the Act *was* successful. Poor people stopped going to the Relieving Officer for relief. Conditions in the workhouse were so bad that people did not apply for relief when they needed it. There were tales of just how bad conditions were and these appear to be confirmed by the scandal at the *Andover Workhouse* in 1845. The paupers were treated so badly that they were eating the gristle and marrow from the bones supplied for crushing. Finally the government had to dismiss several officials and set up a select committee of enquiry. The enquiry criticised Chadwick and Nicholls as Commissioners for their vigour in applying the New Act and the other Commissioners for their slackness. It recommended increasing the number of assistant commissioners to 21. To prevent further complaints, in 1847 the government dismissed the Poor Law Commission and replaced it with a new *Poor Law Board*.

WORKHOUSES

Although conditions were generally not as bad as at Andover, the workhouse did become a place of dread. The Board of Commissioners published detailed regulations on how workhouses should be built, the treatment of inmates and even a set of approved diets (see Figure 10.4).

It seems likely that material conditions were probably better than in the homes of many of the labouring poor, but the stigma of going into the workhouse deterred many from asking for relief. But to what extent the rules and regulations of the Poor Law Commissioners, and later the Board, were *applied*, is difficult to say. It is clear that in the northern industrial districts, such as Leeds and Manchester, many of the old practices continued. To have all poor families in the workhouse was just not practicable, particularly at times of high seasonal unemployment. Outdoor relief continued to be the main relief given. This was recognised by the Board which changed its regulations to permit special 'exceptions' to the rules (see Figure 10.5). In practice these exceptions covered *most* cases of poverty, and by 1854, about 85% of paupers were on outdoor relief.

In 1836, the Poor Law Commission published six diet sheets which were used in different parts of England and boards of guardians were recommended to use the one which 'appears to be best adapted for each particular Union.' The diets were described as being of 'sufficient in quantity, and perfectly unexceptional as to the nature of the provisions specified in each.' Some historians have suggested that these diets may in practice have been slightly better than the standard of food that many very poor labourers were accustomed to live on at this time.

No.1 – Dietary for Able Bodied Men and Women		BREAKFAST.		DINNER.				SUPPER.		
		Bread	Gruel	Cooked Meat	Potatoes	Soup	Suet, or Rice Pudding	Bread	Cheese	Broth
		oz.	pints.	oz.	lbs.	pints.	oz.	oz.	oz.	pints.
Sunday	Men	6	1½	5	½	– –	– –	6	– –	1½
	Women	5	1½	5	½	– –	– –	5	– –	1½
Monday	Men	6	1½	– –	– –	1½	– –	6	2	—
	Women	5	1½	– –	– –	1½	– –	5	2	—
Tuesday	Men	6	1½	5	½	– –	– –	6	– –	1½
	Women	5	1½	5	½	– –	– –	5	– –	1½
Wednesday	Men	6	1½	– –	– –	1½	– –	6	2	—
	Women	5	1½	– –	– –	1½	– –	5	2	—
Thursday	Men	6	1½	5	½	– –	– –	6	– –	1½
	Women	5	1½	5	½	– –	– –	5	– –	1½
Friday	Men	6	1½	– –	– –	– –	14	6	2	—
	Women	5	1½	– –	– –	– –	12	5	2	—
Saturday	Men	6	1½	– –	– –	1½	– –	6	2	—
	Women	5	1½	– –	– –	1½	– –	5	2	—

Old people of 60 years of age and upwards may be allowed one ounce of tea, five ounces of butter and seven ounces of sugar per week, in lieu of gruel for breakfast, if deemed expedient to make this change.

Children under nine years of age to be dieted at discretion; above nine, to be allowed the same quantities as women.

Sick to be dieted by the medical officer.

taken from: Report of the Poor Law Commissioners, 1836.

Fig. 10.4 Workhouse Diets

A major principle of the 1832 Poor Law Amendment Act was to deter scroungers and the idle able-bodied. Poor Law Guardians were expected to apply the Workhouse Test and only to give relief in the workhouse. To try and prevent extensive use of outside relief, each year, the Poor Law Commissioner published a set of Outdoor Relief Prohibition Orders *instructing Guardians on who might be given relief. The fact that these 'Orders' had to be published annually suggests that many people continued to receive outdoor relief; also this extract from what was the strictest 'Order' shows how Guardians could, if they wished, avoid taking into the workhouse most of the people who applied for help. What for example could* not *be covered by the clause on 'account of a sudden and urgent necessity'. The discretion which was given to Guardians meant that very few people who asked for help had to go into the workhouse unless the Guardians wanted them to do so.*

General Order December 1844

Article 1 Every able-bodied person, male or female requiring relief from any parish within any of the said Unions, shall be relieved wholly in the Workhouse of the Union, together with such of the family of every able-bodied person as may be resident with him or her, and may not be in employment, and together with the wife of every such able-bodied male person, if he is a married man; save and except in the following cases:–

1st Where such person shall require relief on account of a sudden and urgent necessity.
2nd Where such person shall require relief on account of any sickness, or bodily or mental infirmity affecting such person, or any of his or her family.
3rd Where such person shall require relief for the purpose of defraying the expenses wholly or in part, of the burial of any of his or her family.
4th Where such person being a widow, shall be in the first six month of her widowhood.

Manchester Guardians: Regulations for Outdoor Relief 1875

1. Out-door relief shall not be granted or allowed by the Relief Committees, except in case of sickness, to applicants of any of the following classes:–
   (a) Single able-bodied men.
   (b) Single able-bodied women.
   (c) Able-bodied widows without children, or having only one child to support
   (d) Married women (with or without families) whose husbands, having been convicted of crime, are undergoing a term of imprisonment.
   (e) Married women (with or without families) deserted by their husbands.
   (f) Married women (with or without families) left destitute through their husbands having joined the militia, and being called up for training.
   (g) Persons residing with relatives, where the united income of the family is sufficient for the support of all its members, whether such relatives are liable by law to support the applicant or not.
2. Out-door relief shall not be granted in any case for longer than thirteen weeks at a time.
3. Out-door relief shall not be granted to any able-bodied person for a longer period than six weeks at a time.
4. Out-door relief shall not be granted, on account of the sickness of the aplicant, or any of his family, for a longer period than two weeks at a time, unless such sickness shall be certified in writing by the district medical officer as being likely to be of long duration, or to be of a permanent character.
5. Where relief is allowed to a parent through the admission of a child or children into the Swinton schools or the workhouse, such relief shall not be granted for a longer period than six months at a time; and if at the expiration of such period a continuance of the relief is required, the relieving officer shall visit and inquire into the circumstances of the parent, and bring the case up for re-consideration by the Relief Committee, on the same manner as if it were a case of out-door relief.

Fig. 10.5 Outdoor Relief Prohibition Orders

4 ▶ CHANGING ATTITUDES TOWARDS POVERTY

The mid nineteenth century saw the beginnings of considerable changes in attitudes towards, and treatment of, the poor. Henry Mayhew and other reporters from the Morning Chronicle undertook what today would be called 'investigative journalism'. They undertook *personal enquiries* into the conditions of the poor in different cities and social classes (Figure 10.6). Mayhew's reports were eventually published as *London Labour* and the *London Poor (1851–52)* but because of his political and religious beliefs, few took any notice of what Mayhew reported.

A piece of even more sensational journalism was James Greenwood's account of *'A Night in a Workhouse'* (Figure 10.7). This was his account of how, disguised as a poor engraver, he spent nights in several different workhouses in London. His accounts comparing the quality of the workhouses were serialised in the Pall Mall Gazette and later in the Daily Telegraph. He also published several pieces on low life in other towns, and his work shocked Victorian readers, as did the novels of Dickens and Charles

In 1849, Mayhew published in the Morning Chronicle a series of 'Letters'. These were accounts of interviews and visits to the homes of poor people in different trades and conditions. The extract below is taken from letter IX, 16 November 1849.

A distressed gentlewoman doing needlework

…I was no sooner in the presence of the poor family than I saw, by the manner of all present, how differently they had once been situated. I could tell by the regularity of her features that her family for many generations past had been unused to labour for their living, and there was that neatness and cleanliness about her costume and appearance which invariably distinguish the lady from the labouring woman. Again, there was a gentleness and a plaintiveness in the tone of her voice that above all things mark the refinement of a woman's nature. The room in which the family lived, though more destitute of every article of furniture and comfort than any I had yet visited, was at least untainted by the atmosphere of poverty. I was no longer sickened by that overpowering smell that hangs about the dwellings of the very poor. The home of the distressed gentlewoman consisted literally of four bare walls. There was no table, and only two chairs in the place. At the foot of the lady was an old travelling trunk, on which lay a few of the nightcaps that she and her daughters were occupied in making. One of the girls stood hemming by the window, and the other was seated in a corner of the room upon another trunk, busily engaged in the same manner. Before the fender was a piece of old carpeting about the size of a napkin. On the mantlepiece was a few balls of cotton, a small tin box of papers, and a Bible and Prayer Book. This was literally all the property in the place.

Fig. 10.6 Extract from Henry Mayhew's letters to the Morning Chronicle

James Greenwood was a journalist who in 1866 dressed as a tramp and obtained temporary accommodation as a 'casual' in several of London's workhouses. He published a record of his exploits in serial form first in the Pall Mall Gazette in 1866 and later in the Daily Telegraph in 1874. This extract comes from his book 'Low Life Deeps' of 1876.

…I lifted the big knocker and knocked; the door was promptly opened, and I entered. Just within, a comfortable clerk sat at a comfortable desk, ledger before him. Indeed the spacious hall was as cheery as cleanliness and great mats and plenty of gaslight could make it.
'What do you want?' asked the man who opened the door.
'I want a lodging.'
'Go and stand before the desk', said the porter; and I obeyed.
'You are late', said the clerk.
'Am I sir?'
'Yes, if you come in you'll have a bath, and you'll have to sleep in the shed.'
'Very well sir'.
'What's your name?'
'Joshua Mason, sir'.
'What are you?'
'An engraver.'…
'Where did you sleep last night?'
'Hammersmith', I answered – as I hope to be forgiven!
'How many times have you been here?'
'Where do you intend to go when you are turned out in the morning?'
'Back to Hammersmith, sir.'
These humble answers being entered in a book, the clerk called the porter, saying, 'Take him through. You may as well take his bread with you.'
[There then follows a detailed account of how 'Mason' was taken and bathed and had his clothes taken away and put in a safe place for the morning. He was then taken across the yard in his bare feet to a room.]
…Imagine a space about thirty feet by thirty enclosed on three sides by a dingy white washed wall, and roofed with naked tiles which were furred with the damp and filth that reeked within. As for the fourth side of the shed, it was boarded in for (say) a third of its breadth; the remaining space was hung with flimsy canvas,…My bed fellows lay amongst the cranks, distributed over the flagstones in a double row, on narrow bags scantily stuffed with hay. At one glance my appalled vision took on thirty of them – thirty men and boys stretched upon shallow pallets which put only six inches of comfortable hay between them and the stony floor.…

Fig. 10.7 Extract from 'A Night in a Workhouse, by James Greenwood 1866

Kingsley. Similar pieces were written by a whole host of writers, including Rider Haggard (more famous for his *King Solomons Mines* and *She*) and Jack London, detailing the horrors of life amongst both the rural and urban worker in the late nineteenth century.

THE CHARITY ORGANISATION SOCIETY

Probably the most important influences which helped to change attitudes towards poverty were the activities of the *Charity Organisation Society* (COS) and respectable groups of Christian charity workers such as Andrew Mearns (*The Bitter Cry of Outcast London*, 1883) or William Booth (*In Darkest England and the Way Out*, 1890). Above all it was the 'scientific' research of Charles Booth (not the William Booth mentioned above, who also founded the Salvation Army) and Seebohm Rowntree which helped to change attitudes.

The COS began in 1869 and intended to organise all major city charities into a *single organisation* so that paupers refused relief by the Poor Law authorities did not go from charity to charity getting assistance, as it was claimed many were doing. The COS was very strict and, before it gave any relief, investigations were carried out into the circumstances of each family. It only gave help to the 'deserving poor'. What it did mean, however, was that the organisation developed a lot of *information* from its 'case notes' about the extent and character of poverty amongst the honest working classes. This, like the journalistic studies, showed just how much poverty was caused by low wages and ill health. The help which it gave was often designed to help the poor become independent and more able to help themselves. For example, widows were often given mangles (to help squeeze water out) so they could take in washing.

THE POVERTY LINE

The work of Charles Booth and Rowntree was important because not only was it full of harrowing details of poverty, but they tried to *assess* both the *extent and causes of poverty* in a way that other writers in England had not done. Booth wanted to undertake an objective study of poverty (see Figure 10.8). He began by calculating a 'poverty line', the level of income needed to keep a man and his family in basic necessities, such as food, clothing, fuel, etc. and then began a series of massive studies into all areas of London. His early pilot studies in 1886/7 in Tower Hamlets showed that about a third of people lived at, or close to, the poverty line and this was confirmed by his other studies. Booth's studies were careful street by street enquiries, which recorded the occupations and family sizes of every household, together with an estimate of incomes and description of the general character of the area.

Booth's investigations into poverty in London were conducted on a street by street basis. He also tried to develop an objective definition of poverty and social class and extracts from these are given below. His classification of classs divided the population into eight categories A to H, according to both their incomes and general lifestyle. Note how neither is truly objective.

By the word 'poor', I mean to describe those who have a fairly regular though bare income, such as 18s [90p] to 21s [£1.05] a week for a moderate family, and by 'very poor' those who fall below this standard, whether from chronic irregularity of work, sickness, or a large number of small children. I do not here introduce any moral question: whatever the cause, those whose means prove to be barely sufficient, or quite insufficient for decent independent life, are counted as 'poor' or 'very poor' respectively; and as it is not always possible to ascertain the exact income, the classification is also based on the general appearance of the home. Cases of large earnings spent in drink are intended to be excluded, as not properly belonging to the poor, but the results of ordinary extravagance in drink on inducing poverty are not considered any more than those of other forms of want of thrift...

Class B (casual earnings)
These people as a class are shiftless, hand to mouth, pleasure loving, and always poor; to work when they like, and play when they like, is their ideal. ...they cannot stand the regularity and dullness of civilised existence and find the excitement they need in a life of the streets, or at home as spectators in some highly coloured domestic scene. There is drunkenness amongst them ... but drink is not their special luxury as with the lowest class...

Fig. 10.8 Charles Booth's Definition of Poverty

The work of Rowntree was similar but was based on a study of families in York. He too developed an 'objective' test of poverty based upon 'the minimum necessaries for the maintenance of physical efficiency'. He developed basic diets and then collected details of actual weekly diets and their cost from working class families. Rowntree's studies confirmed the work of Booth. On his stringent test of primary poverty (see Figure 10.9), at least 10% of York inhabitants fell *below* this line and could not earn enough money; another 20% or so were in poverty for other reasons beyond their control. Rowntree placed great importance upon the distinction between those whose wages were not high enough to keep the family healthy, and those who spent their income unwisely. Rowntree also developed what has become known as the *poverty cycle*. He showed how, at different stages of life, the needs of the family varied and placed them in danger of poverty. He particularly showed the importance of occasional ill health in putting families below the poverty line.

In 1899, B. Seebohm Rowntree, in order to 'throw some light upon the conditions which govern the life of the wage earning classes in provincial towns and especially upon the problem of poverty', undertook a massive study of the working classes in York. His methods of enquiry were a considerable improvement upon Booth's since he obtained information about incomes and expenditure directly from the families themselves by interviews or from the records of employers. He not only developed an objective 'poverty line' based on the retail prices of food, etc, but developed the concepts of primary *and* secondary *poverty.*

from B.S. Rowntree. Poverty. A Study of Town Life (1901)

...the information regarding the number, occupation and housing of the working classes was gained by direct enquiry, which covered practically every working class family in York. In some cases direct information was also obtained regarding earnings, but in the majority of cases these were estimated, the information at the disposal of the writer allowing him to do this with considerable accuracy.

...Families regarded as living in poverty were grouped under two heads.

(a) Families whose total earnings were insufficient to obtain minimum necessaries for the maintenance of merely physical efficiency. Poverty falling under this head was described as 'primary' poverty.

(b) Families whose total earnings would have been sufficient for the maintenance of merely physical efficiency were it not that some portion of it was absorbed by other expenditure, either useful or wasteful. Poverty falling under this head was described as 'secondary' poverty.

...for a family of father, mother and three children, the minimum weekly expenditure upon which physical efficiency can be maintained in York is 21s 8d, (£1.09p), which is made up as follows

	s	d
Food	12	9
Rent	4	0
Clothing, light, fuel etc	4	11
	21	8

... this estimate was based upon the assumptions that the diet is selected with a careful regard to the nutritive values of various foodstuffs, and that these are all purchased at the lowest possible current prices. It only allows for a diet less generous as regards variety than that supplied to able-bodied paupers in workhouses. It further assumes that no clothing is purchased which is not absolutely necessary for health, and assumes too that it is of the plainest and most economical description.

In this way 20,302 persons, or 27.84 per cent of the total population, were returned as living in poverty. Subtracting those whose poverty is 'primary' we arrive at the number living on 'secondary' poverty, viz. 13,073 or 17.93 per cent of the total population.

...we are faced with the startling probability that from 25 to 30 per cent of the town populations of the United Kingdom are living in poverty.

Fig. 10.9 Rowntree's Study of Poverty in York

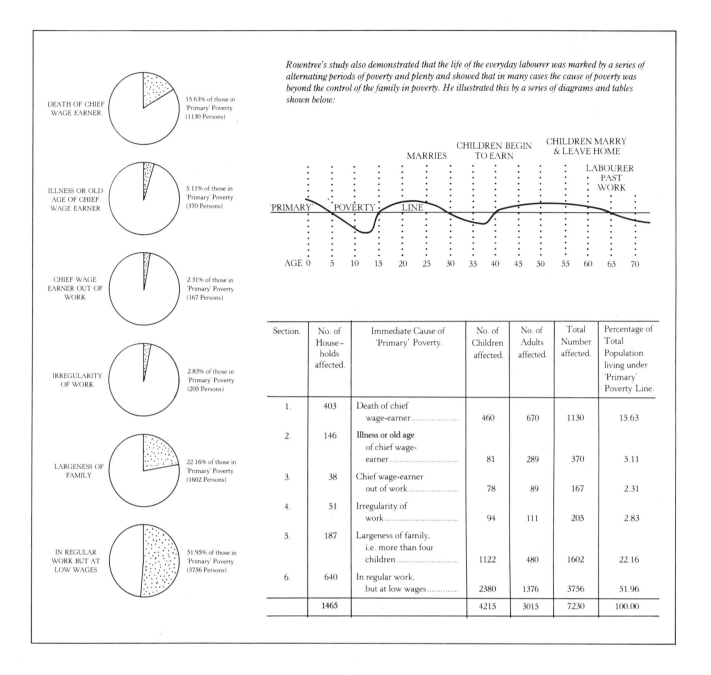

Rowntree's study also demonstrated that the life of the everyday labourer was marked by a series of alternating periods of poverty and plenty and showed that in many cases the cause of poverty was beyond the control of the family in poverty. He illustrated this by a series of diagrams and tables shown below:

DEATH OF CHIEF WAGE EARNER — 15.63% of those in 'Primary' Poverty (1130 Persons)

ILLNESS OR OLD AGE OF CHIEF WAGE EARNER — 5.11% of those in 'Primary' Poverty (370 Persons)

CHIEF WAGE EARNER OUT OF WORK — 2.31% of those in 'Primary' Poverty (167 Persons)

IRREGULARITY OF WORK — 2.83% of those in 'Primary' Poverty (205 Persons)

LARGENESS OF FAMILY — 22.16% of those in 'Primary' Poverty (1602 Persons)

IN REGULAR WORK BUT AT LOW WAGES — 51.95% of those in 'Primary' Poverty (3756 Persons)

Section.	No. of House-holds affected.	Immediate Cause of 'Primary' Poverty.	No. of Children affected.	No. of Adults affected.	Total Number affected.	Percentage of Total Population living under 'Primary' Poverty Line.
1.	403	Death of chief wage-earner......................	460	670	1130	15.63
2.	146	Illness or old age of chief wage-earner..............................	81	289	370	5.11
3.	38	Chief wage-earner out of work......................	78	89	167	2.31
4.	51	Irregularity of work	94	111	205	2.83
5.	187	Largeness of family, i.e. more than four children	1122	480	1602	22.16
6.	640	In regular work, but at low wages..............	2380	1376	3756	51.96
	1465		4215	3015	7230	100.00

Fig. 10.9 (contd.) Rowntree's Study of Poverty in York

SOCIAL AWARENESS

These studies, and many others, began to develop a new awareness that poverty was not always the fault of the individual. Some of these attitudes were already being shown in the operation of the Poor Law. There was a gradual extension of services in the workhouses with the development of basic schooling, dispensaries and the provision of basic hospital services. (Some of the NHS hospitals of today began as workhouses and gradually changed their use.) But as George Lansbury, who spent part of his early years in Poplar Workhouse, has vividly shown in his autobiography, 'Although the place was clean . . . brass knobs and floors were polished, but of goodwill, kindness, there was none . . . everything possible was done to inflict mental and moral degradation'.

These studies, and the appalling results of the recruitment campaign for the Boer War when large numbers of recruits were *not fit enough* to enter the army, began a major debate on the 'Condition of England Question'. Finally, in 1905, the government appointed a new *Royal Commission on the Poor Laws*. However, even before this Commission had reported in 1909, the new Liberal government had already taken steps to introduce reforms in several areas of social welfare.

Though some historians have suggested that the social policies of the Liberals during 1906–14 amount to the beginning of the welfare state, it is quite clear that most Liberals did *not* view them in this way; certainly not Lloyd George and Churchill, who were leading campaigners for the reform measures. The Liberals did not have a coherent policy or strategy on social reform and the principal element in their election victory in 1906, was opposition to the protectionism proposed by Chamberlain and others in the Tory party. It is not even clear whether the Liberals themselves *wanted* to introduce all the measures they actually did or whether they were forced into some of the measures in an attempt to head off the growth of the developing Labour Party. The legislation which had emerged by 1914 was often the result of many different pressures upon the government (Figure 10.10).

Key persons in the reform measures were Lloyd George and Winston Churchill who were on the radical wing of the Liberal Party and often described as New Liberals. Lloyd George had been an active campaigner for improvements in housing and social welfare to bring about a greater sense of social justice, if only to head off the emergence of the Labour Party. There was also pressure from a variety of groups who took up the evidence provided by the social researchers. Although there were powerful groups, such as the friendly societies, who *opposed* increased government intervention because it affected their areas of business, on balance there were probably more pressures for greater government action than ever before. There were also many civil servants who had become convinced of the need for change and who used their position as government advisers to point policy in particular directions, even when groups such as the Poor Law Board opposed easier relief. In 1908, Lloyd George himself even went to Germany to see how the system of social benefits operated.

Year	Act	Effects
1906	Trade Disputes Act	Gave unions protection from employer claims for damages as a result of strikes.
1906	Education Act	Provided cheap school meals for needy children.
1906	Workman's Compensation Act	Extended 1897 Act which made employers insure employees for accidents at work.
1907	Notification of Births Act	Led to fuller details on causes of infant deaths.
1907	Matrimonial Causes Act	Consolidated earlier Acts on divorce into single Act, but payments to women still needed to be enforced by a court order.
1907	Education Act	Introduced medical inspection in schools.
1907	Probation Act	Permitted probation instead of prison for young offenders.
1908	Children Act (Children's Charter)	Brought together all previous legislation into single Act, introduced separate juvenile courts for children under 16 no longer sent to prison, remand homes for child criminals.
1908	Coal Mines Act	Introduced 8 hour day.
1908	Old Age Pensions Act	Non-contributory pensions of between 1s (5p) and 5s (25p) per week to the deserving poor (not criminals, wives of aliens, drunkards, or those who had not worked or those whose income was £21 to £31-10s (£31.50) per year. Payment began 1909.
1909	Labour Exchanges Act	Introduction of Labour Exhanges (i.e. Job Centre)
1909	Trade Boards Act	Set minimum wages in 'sweated trades' i.e. mostly non-unionised jobs such as tailoring, lace making, cardboard-box making where mostly women workers.
1909	Housing and Town Planning Act	Allowed local authorities to control new building developments, affected working class housing.
1911	Insurance Act	Act in 2 parts. Part I health insurance weekly payments from worker (4d) employer (3d) government (2d) (i.e. 9d for 4d), which gave sick pay 10s (50p) per week and free medical treatment to insured male workers (7s 6d or 37½p to women workers). Part II gave unemployment insurance to most workers in a few major sections of industry subject to fluctuations e.g. shipbuilding, employees and employers paid 2½d each, government gave about 1½d this gave benefit of 7s- (35p) for 15 weeks.
1911	Shops Act	Gave all shop workers half-day holiday.

Fig. 10.10 Summary of Liberal Social Reforms 1906–14

6 > THE PROCESS OF REFORM

The table (Figure 10.10) outlines the broad measures adopted by the Liberals. The early reforms dealt with issues that were not especially controversial, such as the care of children, but the proposal for old-age pensions certainly was controversial. This not only attacked the basic belief of the New Poor Law, namely that people should be responsible for their own actions, but proposed to use tax payers' money to pay for the pensions.

The developments in employment policy had begun with the Conservative government's *1905 Unemployed Workmen Act*. This had tried to provide temporary work for respectable, able-bodied men, but it did not work very well. In 1909 the Liberals had tried to create minimum basic conditions in the sweated industries and in other industries with the *Trade Boards Act*. This set minimum rates of pay and maximum hours. But the really big change came with what Lloyd George himself described as his 'war budget' of 1909. This budget for the first time tried to use government taxation as a *tool of social policy*. It was proposed to raise taxes on beer, tobacco and petrol, and to increase income tax with a *graduated tax* that increased with income, as well as to bring in a totally new tax on the value of land. The increased revenue was to be used to pay for the new social policies.

Although Lloyd George had to back down on a number of issues, the constitutional crises that developed when the House of Lords refused to pass his Budget led to the powers of the House of Lords being limited in the *1911 Parliament Act*. This gave the House of Commons total control over finance. It was this which allowed Lloyd George to introduce the radical *1911 National Insurance Bill*, which provided the basic framework of unemployment and health insurance used up to 1945. Though the scheme was enlarged to cover more groups, the principle of contributions from general taxation, the employer and the employee remained throughout.

During the inter-war years the financial problems of governments sometimes forced them to vary the provisions of unemployment and health insurance. Nevertheless, there was never any possibility of returning to the notion of deserving and undeserving poor that had been the basis of the 1834 Act. What is also clear however is that the 1911 Act was not really part of a programme towards a socialist state; in fact it was quite the opposite. By insisting upon the insurance principle, the government was making the point that it was the efforts of *individuals* that paid for the benefits they received. The Liberal governments of 1906–14 did not lay the foundations of the welfare state; they created a social service state in which everyone was expected to contribute towards the benefits that they deserved in times of need.

7 > BEVERIDGE AND THE WELFARE STATE

At one time, historians and social scientists believed that the experience of war during 1939–45 led to major new developments in social and economic policy, and a complete break with earlier policies and attitudes. It was suggested that the experience of war helped to break down social barriers, making the middle classes more aware of the extent of the social evils affecting the working classes, and again, that the experience of managing the war economy had given governments an appreciation of the advantages of intervention and collectivism.

The government began, from about 1941, to plan wide ranging policies of social and economic reconstruction to be put into effect when the war ended. It was these ideas which were apparent in the *Beveridge Report* of 1942. It was the Labour Party, because of its victory in the 1945 elections, that was able to put these plans into effect between 1945 and 1951, and create the welfare state. Today, most historians are not so certain that the changes were either so overwhelming or so sudden.

THE BEVERIDGE REPORT

There is no doubt that the Beveridge Report, or more properly, the *Report of the Committee on Social Insurance and Allied Services*, did introduce some new ideas and did help to change the climate of political opinion, making it certain that *whichever* party won the first post-war election, substantial changes would be introduced. The belief that social welfare programmes should apply *universally*, rather than selectively, to *all* social groups and classes was also probably taken up more enthusiastically by the Labour Party than the Conservative Party. However, there was a great deal in the report and the recommendations for change that was really a *continuation* of ideas and practices that had been present in the 1930s. It could be that rather than leading to comprehensive changes, the war simply *speeded up* the introduction of reforms in areas of health, social security, family allowances and even town planning. In other areas, such as education, the policies introduced by the coalition government and carried through by Labour were in fact *already well established ideas and proposals* suggested before the war.

The only real development was in *finance*. The government introduced a rapidly *progressive* system of taxation, in which the rich paid a much higher level of taxes than the poor, and this helped to redistribute incomes. However, this was done because of financial problems after the war and was not really part of an overall strategy to bring about social change.

The Beveridge Report was clearly very influential and became a best seller with the public. But it only dealt with a limited area of social policy, namely social and health insurance, although it did have implications for other areas. It did not deal with education or with many other areas. The report was produced by a committee of civil servants, with William Beveridge as the chairman, called the Inter-departmental Committee on Social Insurance and Allied Subjects, set up in 1941. When it became clear to the minister that the recommendations of the committee were likely to be very controversial, the report appeared under Beveridge's name.

The report had three guiding principles:

i) it was a time for revolutionary changes and policy should not be limited by past experience;

ii) social insurance should be part of a comprehensive scheme to tackle what Beveridge had earlier (June 1942) described as the five giants: **Want, Disease, Ignorance, Squalor, Idleness**;

iii) any policy should be a partnership of the state and individual action which would not stifle individual initiative.

NATIONAL INSURANCE

The report only dealt with the problem of **want** and was really a development of the ideas Beveridge had gradually evolved over 30 years of concern with unemployment and health insurance. Although the emphasis upon insurance and the responsibility of individuals to help to protect themselves was not radical, his idea of a *comprehensive universal social policy* involving family allowances, health and unemployment, certainly was.

His scheme proposed a *single payment* which would cover *all risks* and *everybody in the family*; it was to be universal. By regular planned payments, everyone would be covered for adequate, minimum levels of benefit, irrespective of the level of payment. Flat rate payments and flat rate benefits were part of the plan to abandon the selectivity that was the feature of the earlier schemes. Coverage was from the cradle to the grave, including benefits for sickness, medical treatment for all, unemployment, maternity, widows, old-age, and death. All benefits were to be dealt with by a single comprehensive administrative agency, a *Ministry of Social Security*.

However a close look at the proposals shows that they are not really so revolutionary. The basic principle of the scheme was still insurance, and Beveridge *rejected* the socialist idea of paying for social benefits out of *general taxation*. Beveridge was actually opposed to many areas of socialist principles and policy. He believed not in free allowances, but in State benefits arising as a right from a properly organised scheme of insurance. Perhaps even more significantly, the scheme was really only *bringing together* many of the existing schemes into a single and more efficient organisation. What *was* revolutionary about the Beveridge plan was that it made the link between the 'five giants' and emphasised the need to plan a *coherent policy* of social reform across several different areas, rather than to deal with each problem in isolation from one another. Perhaps even more importantly, the scheme caught the public imagination, particularly the idea that everyone should be treated the same way. This attitude was helped by the publicity given to the proposals and by the promise of a better life to come after the war ended.

THE NATIONAL HEALTH SERVICE

The proposals did become something of a political football, whose principles all parties had to accept. The Ministry of Reconstruction White Paper (a document that outlines proposals for government future policy), *A National Health Service*, published in 1944, accepted the need for 'a comprehensive service covering every branch of medical and allied activity'. How far the Conservative Party would have made this a priority, given the opposition of groups such as the British Medical Association (BMA) and the high costs involved, is difficult to say, but the Labour Party were fully committed to the idea.

UNEMPLOYMENT

An essential element in the Beveridge proposals was the *level of unemployment*; the scheme would only work if this was no higher than 8½%. The problem of *how to achieve this* was covered by another White Paper, *Full Employment*. This accepted many of the ideas which had been developed by an economist, John M. Keynes, showing how the government could maintain full employment by controlling both taxation and government expenditure. It also suggested how the problems of the old industries and areas with high unemployment should be tackled.

EDUCATION

The 1944 Education Act

In September 1944, the government published a third White Paper, *Social Insurance*, which showed how it intended to *implement* the Beveridge proposals. This was followed by other reports which showed how *particular policies* were to be implemented. Almost the final act of the coalition government was to introduce an educational reform that had been outlined in a 1943 White Paper, *Educational Reconstruction*, produced by R. A. Butler and his deputy Chuter Ede. Of all the proposals for reform this was the least controversial and the *1944 Education Act* was approved almost without any major dissent. The reason for this is that the proposals were *not* radically different from anything that had been proposed in a whole host of reports and commissions of enquiry written in the 1930s, but not put into effect, largely because of the economic situation. Like the Beveridge proposals, the aim was to create a system of education that covered *all types* of schools and ages in a *single system* of administration which offered 'parity of esteem and equality of education'. As one historian put it, the Butler Act was 'the most fitting gesture towards democracy made in the twentieth century, a fitting product of the People's War'. The difficulties of actually introducing a system which *did* meet the needs of all pupils were, however, not fully appreciated. The end of the war marked a time of hope, the opportunity for a new beginning. The *practical implementation* of these hopes was to be a problem for the new government, and it was the Labour Party which, after its landslide victory in 1945, had gained this responsibility.

In a series of documents, the Labour Party had outlined its plans for a programme of social and economic reform based upon the proposals developed during the war. Although Clement Atlee had a large majority in Parliament (150 over all other parties), the financial situation which the government inherited, made it difficult to do all the things which had been intended. Perhaps even more significantly, the financial problems became worse through developments beyond the government's control. For example, the terrible weather conditions of 1947/8 and the vast military expense arising from the development of the 'Cold War' with Russia. In addition, many of its proposals were very controversial and were opposed strongly by other parties, both in the House of Commons and the House of Lords. There were also many groups *outside Parliament* who believed their interests were not served by the reforms in health care, e.g. the doctors and the BMA, and the insurance companies. Even amongst its own supporters, there were disagreements about the *best way* to do things or what should be done first.

Though the Labour Government was *not* re-elected in 1951, it had clearly brought about a major change in the character of government and particularly in attitudes towards the role of government. No matter how much later governments would modify particular aspects of social policies, the *general character* of the welfare state had been established. Political parties might disagree about the importance of specific aspects of policy, but there was a general acceptance by government throughout the period 1951 to 1979 of its responsibility to maintain full employment, have steady growth and rising real incomes, and a commitment to the idea of social responsibility and social justice towards all groups in society. There were to be significant differences about *how* these were to be achieved, but the need for governments to *intervene directly* in the economy and to develop a coherent social and economic strategy to achieve these objectives, was never in doubt.

EXAMINATION QUESTIONS

a) What part was played in improving social conditions in Britain by:
    i) Lloyd George; ii) William Beveridge; iii) the 1945–51 Labour governments?

TUTOR'S ADVICE

Remember that what is expected is a good factual knowledge of each of these person's career and how they influenced social policy. This means that you should also try to comment not just upon what they did but how their ideas were important in developing social policy in a particular way. For example, Lloyd George did many things before he was a Cabinet Minister but this does not need to be covered in any detail, neither do his actions in economic and military affairs. What should be commented upon is the way his plans for OAPs, social insurance etc. influenced later policies and how they were new developments concerning the role of government.

a) Outline the main proposals for social reform between 1940 and 1945.
b) What, if anything, was 'revolutionary' about these proposals.

TUTOR'S ADVICE

Part a) expects a good basic description of developments, what was suggested, by whom and when. Most marks would be for b) which expects some comment about how the proposals in Beveridge and other reports were significantly different from what had gone before i.e. what was new? In what ways did the proposal bring about changes in the principles on which policies were based, the way in which they were put into effect by developing new forms of administration and perhaps even whether the part played by government was any different? To get a really good mark, comment upon the fact that many of the proposals had developed out of plans suggested in the 1930s.

A STUDENT'S ANSWERS WITH EXAMINER'S COMMENTS

A structured essay question.

a) Briefly describe how the Old Poor Law was organised between about 1790 and 1830.
b) What were the major criticisms made of the Old Poor Law?
c) What proposals for reform were adopted in 1834?

a) The Old Poor Law was organised by churchwardens in each parish. They were responsible for collecting the poor law rate which was used to look after people who were too old to work or who could not work because they were ill. When children were orphaned they were the ones who apprenticed them to a farmer or tradesman. The increase in population and the enclosures in agriculture meant that there was an increasing number of poor people in the countryside and the poor harvests and Napoleonic wars meant that food prices increased so much that many people could not get jobs or afford to buy food.
In 1795 a group of churchwardens and magistrates from Speenhamland in Berkshire decided that the fairest way to treat the poor was to give each

unemployed or poor person money to buy food depending upon the size of their family and the price of bread. This system was used in many parts of southern England. Some parishes had workhouses where people were given jobs to do before they were given food and sometimes the churchwardens would make the poor go to work for a farmer or work repairing the roads.

b) Farmers who had to pay the poor rates complained that their taxes were going up because there were too many people who were scroungers. They got so much money from poor relief that they were better off than working. Malthus also said that the Speenhamland system encouraged people to have bigger families because how much they got depended on how many children they had. It was said that people got poor relief to easily and became lazy and did not bother to look for work.

c) The reform in 1834 was the Poor Law Amendment Act. A Royal Commission in 1832 said that the parish system was inefficient and had to be changed. Parishes were put together to form Unions told to be much stricter when giving relief. They were told to stop outdoor relief. They were to build workhouses and only give relief to people who went into the workhouse. Conditions in the workhouse were to be pretty awful so that only people who were desperate would go in. This would act as a deterrent to the scroungers and force people to look for work.

Examiner's comments

Well informed and organised answers, though some points missed out e.g. could have mentioned word outdoor relief and referred to the other systems used such as Roundsman. Point needs to be made that the system of poor relief was a local system solely the responsibility of the local parish officers, each did what they thought best in their district. Could also have referred to settlement laws that meant that only people born in a parish were entitled to relief.

In b) reference to Malthus is a good point about people becoming scroungers, would have been better if reference made to outdoor relief and complaint that people were given too much and not encouraged to be thrifty. Could perhaps have said that by 1820s some parishes already becoming very strict in giving relief. In c) forgets to mention that government appointed a Central Board to oversee the Unions and had a team of inspectors to ensure that the Unions did the job properly and adopted the rule recommended by the Central Board. The officers for each Union were to be elected and they were supposed to appoint a professional paid overseer to run the workhouses. Could also have mentioned the principle of "less eligibility" and the "workhouse test".

QUESTION

a) How did the Poor Law Amendment Act work and why was it so bitterly resented by the poor?

b) Why and by whom did the operation of the Poor Laws come under increasing attack between about 1850 and 1890?

a) Poor people did not like the Act because it treated them like criminals. Even when they were poor because of no fault of their own, they were forced to go into the workhouse. Here they were treated badly. Their clothes were taken away and they were put into a uniform, families were split up and put into different rooms. The food was terrible and they had to work breaking rocks or picking oakum just like in prison. At Andover workhouse the food was so bad that people even used to fight for scraps from the bones that were supposed to be breaking up to be made into glue.

b) The Poor Law was attacked by different groups. The
well off people were disgusted when they heard how
badly old people and children who could not help
being sent to the workhouse were treated. Because of
scandals like that at Andover, improvements were
gradually made and some workhouses had hospitals and
schools where children were taught to read and write
or learn a trade. It was also shown that because
people did not like to go to the workhouse private
charities ended up dealing with most poor people. The
people who ran these charities began to realise that
most people who were poor could not help it. They
were poor because there was no work or they were ill
or widowed or were old and could not work any more.
The enquiries by Henry Mayhew were published in
newspapers and helped to change ideas later William
Booth and Rowntree did surveys in London and York
that showed that most people were poor not because
they were lazy or scroungers but because their wages
were too low for them to save for when they became
old or ill.

Examiner's comments

Again no mistakes but things missed out. In a) good on pointing out how bad workhouses
could be so that people were ashamed to go into the workhouse but does not point out that
in fact most people who needed help still received outdoor relief. The Central Board was
never able to stop it. The workhouses were used mostly for old people and children and
those people whom the Guardians regarded as workshy. Guardians pointed out that it
would cost too much to build new workhouses to deal with all the people who were
temporarily unemployed and it was cheaper to use short term outdoor relief.

Much the same for b), it needs to be made clearer that people who worked with the poor
and applied the Poor Laws came to realise that the deterrent effect did not work because
most people could not help being poor. The work of the social investigators slowly made it
clear that the only way to help people was to give them the chance to get better paid jobs
or to bring in schemes for social insurance such as was happening in Germany in the 1880s.
More detail could be given on the work of Booth and Rowntree.

QUESTION

a)   What were the major social reforms introduced between 1900 and 1914?
b)   Why were such reforms adopted?

a) The years 1900—1914 was one when Conservative and
Liberal governments introduced major social reforms
in education, and treatment of poor children, the
care of old people and actions to improve health and
the problems of poverty in old age. Some historians
have said that the Liberal governments 1906—14 even
laid the basis of the welfare state.
   In education, the Conservatives introduced the 1902
Balfour Act which placed elementary schools under the
control of LEAs and allowed them to start secondary
schools. After their election in 1906, the Liberals
acted on the report about physical deterioration and
allowed LEAs to give cheap school meals and later in
1907 to have school medical inspection. This meant
that children from poor homes were likely to be
better fed and for illness and disease to be dealt
with. In 1908, Parliament passed the Children's
Charter which brought together a lot of different
Acts affecting children and introduced better ways to
deal with young criminals as well as allowing the
development of child welfare and maternity clinics.
   The main changes though were in the Poor Laws and
the treatment of old people. In 1908 Lloyd George
introduced old age pensions in his budget so that

from Jan 1 1909, OAPs who were deserving would get
5/— a week at 70 or 7/6 if married. Because these
pensions were paid at the Post Office people did not
feel ashamed to collect them as they did with Poor
Law relief. In 1909 the Royal Commission on the Poor
Laws reported and although the members could not
agree and published two reports, Lloyd George had
already decided to introduce a scheme of national
health insurance like that in Germany which meant
that many people would no longer have to go to the
Poor Law when they were ill. The 1911 National
Insurance Act meant that workers, employers and the
government paid in money so that it was an insurance
policy for people who would not have been able to
have afforded one. This meant they could now afford
to go to a doctor and would get money when they were
off ill from work or temporarily unemployed. Only a
few groups of workers were included at first but
during and after the war it was expanded to include
almost everyone.

Examiner's comments

a)   Detailed and accurate answer, very good introduction that outlines the basic points to
come. Might perhaps have included a bit more detail on the 1911 Insurance Act and
some comment on the 1909 People's Budget or what Lloyd George described as a
"War Budget . . . against poverty and squalidness" with the proposal to pay for
welfare services by increasing taxation on the rich and landowners. There could also
be some comment on unemployment exchanges and more detail on the limited
coverage of the Insurance Act 1911 and minimum wages legislation and regulation of
the sweated industries.

b)   The Liberal government was not elected on a policy
of social reform but because they opposed the
introduction of import taxes on food. Once in
office they acted to improve social conditions for
poor people because they were frightened by the
growth of the Labour Party and the spread of
socialist ideas. Also there were some reformers
like Lloyd George and Churchill who honestly felt a
responsibility towards the poor and used the
reports by Booth and Rowntree to show that many
problems of poor people were a result of the
economic system that they could not control and not
because they were lazy or scroungers. The Liberals
did not have a carefully thought out policy, they
dealt with particular problems as they came up.
They did not believe in giving people something for
nothing. People should be helped to help themselves
as much as possible but governments ought to protect
people who could not always help themselves.

Examiner's comments

b)   Excellent understanding of the different pressures put upon the Liberals. Ought to
have mentioned the majority and minority Poor Law reports 1909 and that this was a
society in which attitudes were beginning to change but it was not yet accepted that
the state had much more responsibility for those unable to help themselves.

11

TRADE UNIONS AND THE LABOUR MOVEMENT

GETTING STARTED

As has already been shown, the changes that took place in British industry before 1850 led to many changes in people's lives. Although, in the long run, everybody became very much better off, at times particular groups of workers were very badly affected by the *technological changes* taking place in industry and agriculture. Working conditions changed, some jobs disappeared as they were replaced by machines, and workers had to move from rural areas into over crowded and often unpleasant towns.

There were also changes in society, some people were able to take advantage of these opportunities and became part of a new wealthy industrial elite. As society became more clearly separated into different social and economic groups, so these groups came to develop different life styles and cultures.

As society became more industrialised in the late eighteenth and early nineteenth centuries, the manufacturing class acquired more political power and a share in deciding how the government ran the country. Since the right to vote was decided largely upon wealth and landownership, the vast majority of the working classes did not have the right to vote or have any direct influence upon government. They had few ways to protest about the conditions in mines or factories and little opportunity to explain their point of view to M.Ps. Much of the history of the nineteenth and twentieth centuries is concerned with how ordinary people gained the right to vote, to participate in politics and to bargain with employers over wages and conditions of employment. These 'privileges' were not won easily; there were violent and sometimes bloody struggles with authority. There were gains and losses, but gradually the working classes gained the legal right to join a trade union, to strike in support of a wage claim and to vote.

The examination syllabuses tend to concentrate upon one or more of the following periods and problems:

- The difficulties of forming general trades unions before about 1840 and the Chartists.
- The development of New Model Unions for the skilled worker 1850–70.
- The development of New Unionism for unskilled workers 1870–1914.
- The legal and political problems of trades unions 1872–1914.
- The General Strike 1926 and union problems in the inter-war years.

For each of these topics, candidates must not only know the basic facts, but should be able to explain why the events happened as they did and the consequences of developments.

ESSENTIAL PRINCIPLES

Many textbooks suggest that the development of trade unions is relatively modern, in the sense of organisations of workers which pressed for higher wages, better conditions of work and generally looked after members' interests by providing a variety of services. Many see this development as being the *result of industrialisation*. Modern research has shown that this is *not* the case. Certainly, as the economy became industrialised, an increasing proportion of the population was directly involved in manufacture on a regular and permanent basis. And again new technology has changed the scale, character and location of industry, causing changes in working practices. So workers' organisations have indeed faced new problems. There were also changes in the attitudes of employers, governments and the law which, initially at least, made it more difficult for labour organisations to exist and to operate legally.

There were, however, well-organised and long-established unions in some towns and crafts *long before* the industrial revolution. Workers in the traditional skilled crafts, such as printers, carpenters, masons, and watchmakers for example, were very well organised. So also were weavers and especially the shearmen or croppers and combers who did skilled jobs that had not yet been replaced by machines. These trade *clubs* or unions had arrangements with masters about fixing wages and conditions of employment. In 1800, at least 50 trade unions existed in different trades. Some had been in existence for many years, but often only came to public notice during a dispute. In London, the tailors had a union which had lasted for over a century, and was so effective that as early as 1720 the masters persuaded the government to pass a law making it illegal. It is also likely that the hatters' union went back as far as the tailors'.

The eighteenth century is littered with attempts by masters to get Parliament to outlaw the activities of particular unions. In his book the *Wealth of Nations* (1776), Adam Smith shows that he thought it natural for workers to combine to achieve higher wages and better conditions.

During the Revolutionary and Napoleonic Wars, the fear of industrial and social unrest spreading to England increased the hostility of landowners and manufacturers to unions and other radical organisations. This was especially the case because of the increased use by unions of violent tactics to intimidate others into joining a protest. 'Blacklegs', strike breakers or 'unfair' men were often attacked and sometimes even killed by mobs of workers. During a strike, groups of workers would go from mine to mine, or factory to factory persuading others to join them. These kinds of tactics were used by mobs in America during the 1760s and 1770s, as well as in France during the Revolution to overthrow the government.

THE COMBINATION LAWS

In 1799 and 1800, Parliament passed the *Combination Laws* which made it illegal for workers to band together in unions. These laws were only part of a general campaign of intimidation against unions; it only made *general* a ban which had previously applied to particular unions. It does not seem as if the Combination Laws were effective in stopping the development of unions. There were very few prosecutions under the Combination Acts proper. Also, before the laws were repealed in 1824, there were some long and largely successful strikes organised by workers in London, such as printers, carpenters, shipwrights, coopers and tailors, amongst others. Some historians even suggest that unions became *stronger* during the years 1790 to 1815, as they were forced into actions to oppose the legislation. Certainly we have evidence that the tramping artisans, the skilled craftsmen who moved from place to place, helped to form strong links between workers in different parts of the country. Notice though that it was the *skilled workers* who had unions and it was these workers for whom demand increased as factories expanded and incomes grew.

By the middle of the 1820s, there were links between at least 27 trades in different towns, and we know that the steam engine makers had branches in at least 28 towns. Some of the unions in London even developed regular newspapers and journals and were well organised, with regular subscriptions and funds to pay the families of strikers.

In the new industrial regions of the north, and especially the newly-developed factory trades in cotton, employers were especially hostile. However, even here the Combination

Laws were not used very often. In Lancashire between 1818–22, we only know of 7 convictions under the Combination Acts. Employers used older legislation relating to conspiracy and leaving work without permission to break unions. Employers generally found it impossible to *enforce* the Combination Acts and it was partly because of this that Francis Place was able to convince Parliament in 1824 that unions should be permitted, so that workers would learn by experience that they could *not* force up wages beyond the natural market level. In many instances the authorities had used troops to try and break up strikes and demonstrations, and by the 1830s over 30,000 were permanently on garrison duty to be used whenever necessary against strikers. Troops often caused more problems than they solved and were not very effective. During a strike in Oldham in 1826, a garrison of about 200 troops was surrounded by strikers, and stoned. Also the military found that even when rioters were caught, they could not break the organisation as a whole. Often local people and the police refused to give evidence or to enforce the law.

GENERAL UNIONS

The repeal of the Combination Acts in 1825 did, however, help the formation of *semi and unskilled groups of workers* in the new factory trades. However, the formation of *large general unions* was not successful. The older, skilled craft unions had partially succeeded because the workers possessed skills in short supply. This did *not* apply to unskilled workers. To try and increase wages, they had to stop employers getting labourers from elsewhere when they went on strike. The only way to do this was to get all the workers in a district into a single *general union* covering all trades and crafts. It was the failure of strikes in Manchester which led John Doherty to try and organise all the Manchester and Stockport mule spinners (a skilled group of workers) in the 1820s with his *General Union of Operative Spinners*. A national conference was held on the Isle of Man in September 1829 and plans laid for a central organisation to form a national strike fund and to link the activities of branches so that strikes only took place one at a time in each area. But when the union failed to prevent reductions in wages in 1830, and the support given to some strikers by those still at work was not very good, the union collapsed. At the same time, Doherty tried to form a more general union of all cotton and related trades workers.

The *National Association of United Trades for the Protection of Labour* (NAPL) was formed in September 1829. Its first meeting included 1000 workers from 20 trades and it quickly spread throughout Lancashire and Cheshire where, by 1831, it had about 60–70,000 members; but there was little success elsewhere. By 1831, Doherty had organised a newspaper, *The Voice of the People* and was actively campaigning for political reforms. The NAPL was not successful and Doherty even formed links with Robert Owen who was at the same time forming his own general union, the *Grand National Consolidated Trades Union*. Formed in 1833, this existed more on paper and in the mind of Robert Owen than in practice. Full of grand schemes and plans for amalgamating all workers into a single organisation, the GNCTU had a constitution and some links with trade unions, in particular trades, but little effective organisation. Though it claimed 800,000 members, it probably had no more than 16,000 paid-up members and became famous largely because of its organiser, Robert Owen, and its links with the case of the 'Tolpuddle Martyrs'. Its effective power was very limited. By 1834, the GNCTU had disappeared and in effect had been rather less important than hosts of other local unions which organised workers in particular trades.

THE FAILURE OF GENERAL UNIONS

The failure of general unions like the GNCTU was almost inevitable, but it was speeded up by the incompetence of the organisers. The 1830s were a time of difficulty for labour generally; trade was bad and employment limited. There were more workers than jobs. The attempt to create a *single general union* covering all trades required *administrative skills* which the organisers did not have. The problem of trying to get agreement amongst groups of workers, friendly societies and individual artisans, whose particular interests often *conflicted* with one another, was made worse by the problem of creating an organisation which had very little money. Few workers had cash to spare on union subscriptions and if the union could *not* provide strike benefits, there was little hope of keeping workers out on strike whilst their families starved. The failure of the GNCTU and other unions to beat the employers and to prevent them from reducing wages or only employing non-union labour, meant that there was little point to being a member. Robert Owen was not in favour of strikes and wanted to transform society by peaceful means. It was however the fiasco of the Tolpuddle Martyrs which spelt the end of the general unions.

3 ▷ THE TOLPUDDLE MARTYRS

The problem for the *Tolpuddle Martyrs* was that they were unlucky. The six men, led by George Loveless, formed the union in Dorset where there were memories of the Swing riots 1828–30 and farmers were determined to prevent any repeat. The local magistrate, James Frampton, was particularly hostile to unions and the government took no action to curb the zeal of the magistrates' prosecution. The judge who finally tried them was also convinced of the need to make an example of union leaders. In forming a union to oppose the reduction in their wages from 7 shillings (35p) to 6 shillings (30p), they committed no crime, they planned no strike, they did not even withdraw their labour and issued no threats to farmers or other workers who did not join. Their crime was to be foolish enough to adopt a silly initiation ceremony using hoods and oaths of loyalty to the union, which was against the law passed in 1797 to prevent oaths of loyalty amongst mutineers in the navy and which aimed at preventing rebellion. There was clearly no such intent by the labourers, but despite this they were sentenced to transportation for 7 years.

The injustice and severity of the treatment led to protests, but within a month of the trial they were in Bombay, already on their way to Australia. Eventually, after a long campaign, their sentences were reduced in 1836 but they did not return to England for another two years. The Dorset labourers were unlucky in that other union activists, both before and after their case, accused of similar crimes generally got off. Informers were persuaded to retract their statements or often went away and could not testify at the trial. It was yet another example of the GNCTU being badly organised.

4 ▷ TRADE UNIONISM AFTER 1835

The collapse of general trade unions did not mean the end of unions. Many unions were formed in particular trades and amongst the skilled craftsmen, so unions remained active and effective. There were also unions amongst groups such as coal miners and in 1842, the Miners Association of Britain had at least 60,000 members and was active in every major coalfield. In Northumberland and Durham, the miners employed a lawyer, W.P. Roberts, who was very successful in using the courts against mine owners following accidents and in defending miners accused of breaking contracts. However during 1844, when the miners went on strike, the mine owners were successful in using blacklegs and in turning striking miners out of the cottages they rented from mine owners. This led to defeat, and similar action by employers elsewhere meant that the union had ceased to be effective, especially when employers refused to employ the leaders of the strikes. In London, Henry Mayhew in the late 1840s and 1850s also found numerous examples of well-regulated trade unions amongst the skilled craftsmen. However, the 1840s was really the period of the *Chartists*.

5 ▷ CHARTISM

Many historians believe *Chartism* was the most important working class movement of the 1840s. A national movement, strong in most cities but especially the northern industrial towns, it had a working class leadership and aimed at political reform as a means of achieving economic changes. It grew rapidly during the years of trade depression from 1839–42, and with its marches, riots and petitions, seemed to be a major threat to the established order. It faded during the economic revival of the middle 1840s and reappeared briefly in 1848. It seems to have achieved none of its political or economic objectives and though there was a general support for many of its ideals later in the century, its activists became involved in a host of other labour organisations, including the co-operative movement as well as trade unions.

The organisation arose out of the *London Working Men's Association* formed by William Lovett and other radicals in 1836. The following year Lovett, with others, produced the *Charter*. This included six demands for political reform which were distributed in pamphlets and often presented as a discussion about the meaning of a Chartist, as in the case below between Mr. Doubtful and a Radical.

Radical: [a Chartist] is one who is an advocate of the People's Charter.
Mr. Doubtful: The People's Charter, pray what is that?
Radical: It is an outline of an Act of Parliament drawn up by the London Working Men's Association and six members of Parliament; it embraces the six cardinal points of radical Reform.
Mr. Doubtful: What are these points?
Radical: They are as follows: 1. Universal suffrage 2. Annual Parliaments 3. Vote by Ballot 4. Equal Representation 5. Payment of members 6. No property qualification.

Although some of these demands were introduced by 1914, this was *not* the result of Chartist action. Thomas Attwood's proposal in 1838 that the Charter be presented to Parliament as a petition, led to tremendous activity to collect signatures in support, and was eventually signed by 1.2m people. Parliament rejected it by 235 votes to 46. Proposals were made for a general strike or 'Sacred Month', but this failed because of poor organisation. In Newport, in November 1839, John Frost led an uprising with the probable intention of freeing Chartist supporters from prison, but the authorities were well prepared and 14 rioters were killed. At the subsequent trial, John Frost, a respectable draper and former mayor and magistrate, was sentenced to death.

In 1842, a further National Petition was presented to Parliament and again after violent riots and unrest, it was rejected. Chartism as a political organisation did not reappear until 1844, when the third National Petition was organised. After a mass rally at Kennington Common, a large procession made its way to Parliament. But again the government, fearing disorder, had organised over 150,000 special constables, 8,000 soldiers and thousands of regular police. It even had cannon, armed civil servants, the Chelsea pensioners and the aged Duke of Wellington to defend Parliament. The rally at Kennington varied in size according to contemporary estimates. Fergus O'Connor, who addressed the meeting, said the crowd was 4–500,000; *The Times* newspaper said 20,000, but the Prime Minister only 12–15,000. The government also said that the petition was a fraud with many of the 1,975,496 signatures being clear forgeries including 'Victoria Rex', Peel and sixteen signatures by the Duke of Wellington. The petition was ridiculed and thrown out by 222 to 17 votes. Chartism never again was able to mount a large scale campaign.

WHY DID CHARTISM FAIL?

J. R. Stephens a Chartist leader said that:

> 'The question of universal suffrage is a knife and fork question . . . a bread and cheese question . . . and if any man asks me what I mean by universal suffrage, I would answer: that every working man in the land has a right to have a good coat on his back, a comfortable abode in which to shelter himself and his family, a good dinner upon his table, and no more work than is necessary for keeping him in good health and as much wages for that work as would keep him in plenty . . .'

By the middle 1840s the general improvements taking place in the economy meant that there was less depression and so fewer people were interested in Chartism. Chartist leaders had shown themselves to be incapable of uniting together or of developing a coherent policy. The leaders from different regions were divided amongst themselves and with the development of physical force under Fergus O'Connor, many Chartist moderates started to look elsewhere. It also convinced the government of the need to make plans to crush any attempts at revolution. Chartist support gradually melted away and became devoted to more practical and peaceful activities, such as the co-operative movement or other trade union activities.

Although in many ways Chartism was a revolutionary organisation it never really developed a national working class character. In some areas, especially the northern industrial towns such as Oldham, Stockport and Manchester, it probably was important in developing a *class consciousness* amongst the working classes that might not have been so well developed without the experience of Chartism. It also provided opportunities for individuals to gain experience and to learn the lessons of protest activities.

6 NEW MODEL UNIONISM

The collapse of Chartism and many of the unions of the unskilled has led some historians to emphasise the importance of the development of *New Model Unionism* amongst the skilled craft unions. Particular importance has been given to the formation of the *Amalgamated Society of Engineers* (1851) and its leader, William Allen. It is suggested that this union, along with other craft unions such as the *Carpenters and Joiners* (led by Robert Applegarth), provided a model which other unions were to follow. By moderate policies it convinced both employers and government that respectable unionism was one way to prevent revolutionary activities. As a result they were able to get the government to remove most of the legal restrictions upon unions. This picture almost certainly exaggerates the successes of New Model Unionism and ignores the extent to which later unions did *not* follow their example.

The strength of the New Model Unions was that, as the demand for skilled labour increased, they were able to assert the traditional advantages of the *apprenticeship system* for training labour in order to limit entry into the trade. This allowed them to maintain high wages and to ensure that it was in the employers' interests to negotiate and reach agreements on conditions of employment. The skilled craft unions during the 1850s gradually developed, so that tradesmen in different cities and regions were organised into *national* associations. Their high wages allowed them to make regular subscriptions, often as high as one shilling a week (5p), which enabled the unions to employ full time secretaries and officials. These officials not only co-ordinated activities between different branches of the union but established *national scales for wages* that each branch used as a minimum. If a particular employer *failed* to pay the correct wages, he would find that his factory was blacklisted by the workers. Also employers found it useful to avoid competition amongst themselves for scarce labour if their associations negotiated directly with local unions branches and national officials. The unions generally had rules that *limited* the authority of local branches to strike without national approval, and so it was possible to avoid direct confrontation, except in a few circumstances. The absence of numerous strikes probably indicates the strength of the union at a time when the skills of their members were in tremendous demand (the ASE in 1852, did in fact lose its largest strike).

By the later 1850s, the secretaries of these unions had formed themselves into a small group later called the *Junta*. This consisted of:

Robert Applegarth; Amalgamated Carpenters
William Allen; ASE
Edwin Coulson; Operative Bricklayers
David Guile; Ironmongers
George Odger; Secretary of the London Trades Council

THE TRADES UNION CONGRESS

This group used their influence to develop links between unions and eventually, in 1867, the *London Trades Council* developed into the *Trades Union Congress* (TUC). Unions at last had a national organisation to act on the behalf of all unions.

The Junta was particularly active in 1866. Following the Sheffield Outrages when, during a strike, non-union members were attacked, the government set up a Royal Commission. The Commission showed that the secretary of the grinders union had paid £20 to have an employer murdered, and to arrange for the blowing up of a blackleg's house. The extent of the violence shocked everyone, but the Junta were able to present evidence to the Commission which showed that such acts of violence would *not* have happened in a well regulated union. In 1867, unions also received good publicity in the Hornby v Close case. It was shown that when the secretary of the Bradford Boilermakers Society refused to repay £24 from the unions Friendly Society funds, and the union was itself registered as a Friendly Society, it was still not protected by the 1855 Friendly Society Act. The judges ruled that the trade unions did not have a legal status and could not therefore sue in a court of law.

THE LEGALISATION OF UNIONS

As a result of these developments, and especially since the *1867 Franchise Act* had extended the vote to many working men, pressure was put on the government to reform the law and to legalise unions. The first Bill proposed by the government disappointed the unions, and the TUC set up a Parliamentary Committee to alter the Bill. Eventually, in 1871, Parliament passed two Acts: *The Trade Union Act* (1871), which made unions legal institutions, and the *Criminal Law Amendment Act* (1871). This act was disliked by unions because it prohibited picketing. Without picketing unions had effectively lost the power to strike. At the 1874 elections, the unions encouraged members to vote for Conservatives who supported their proposal for reforming picketing. In 1875, the new Conservative government repealed the Criminal Law Amendment Act after another Royal Commission report. In the same year the government repealed the 1867 Employers and Workmen Act which allowed for the imprisonment of workers who went on strike and broke their contracts. Picketing was now once more legal, striking could not come under the law of conspiracy and workers were now on the same legal footing as employers.

From the 1870s, historians have noted how changes in the law and the changing character of employment in industry created opportunities for the development of new forms of union organisation. The *New Model Unions* had really only dealt with a small portion of the workforce, the *skilled craft unions*. By 1900 there had developed a number of very large *general* and *industrial* unions which organised the great mass of semi- and unskilled workers. These have been called *New Unions* and some historians have suggested that 'new unionism' was radically different from what had gone before. Besides adopting a different form of organisation, the unskilled union leaders were said to be more radical or revolutionary. Many were politically active as socialists and wanted to change society through Parliamentary reforms or, if this failed, by revolution. They are said to have adopted more militant strike tactics and to have developed class consciousness amongst the workforce. Again, whilst some of this is true, the differences between New Model and New Unionism can be exaggerated, and it is not true that the unions for the semi and unskilled workers disappeared between 1844 and 1880.

The rise of incomes with the development of mechanisation led to a wide range of service industries, such as transportation, shops and offices. This created an increased demand for labour just at the time when the slow down in the rate of population growth meant that the surplus of labourers was beginning to disappear. The appalling conditions of work in some industries were becoming more widely known, so that attempts to organise particular groups of female and casual workers began to be successful. In a number of very well publicised strikes, e.g. the *Match Girls*, 1888, journalists such as Annie Besant helped the workers to form unions and to improve their conditions of work. The horror stories of women deformed by working with phosphorus and earning 1d (less than ½p) per hour, when shareholders received 23% on their investments, helped the Bryant and Mays match girls to win better conditions in 1888. Similar publicity in 1889 helped the London Dockers to raise their wages from 5d to 6d (2½p) per hour. The leader of the tea warehousemen who campaigned for the 'dockers tanner' was Ben Tillett and when he brought his men out on strike, other dockers followed. The success of this strike led to the formation of the *Dock, Wharf, Riverside and General Workers Union*. Similarly, Will Thorne was able to use the 1889 London gas workers' strike to form a national union, and the same happened in the lower paid and semi-skilled *General Railway Workers Union*.

RISING MEMBERSHIP

Between 1888 and 1914, trade union membership increased from about 0.75m to 4.2m, and during the 1880s and 1890s there was a general spread of union activity to industries where it had never been successful before. The New Unions tended to be of two broad types. Some were *general unions*, covering particular groups of workers in a number of different industries. Gradually they managed to recruit workers from different sectors or to amalgamate with other unions. Others tended to be *industrial unions*, organising all the semi- and unskilled workers in a particular industry.

During this period, the *craft unions* similarly expanded their membership by as much as, if not more than, the general labour unions. Under threat from new technologies, many of them changed and recruited *less skilled* groups of workers. The net result of this growth in membership was that the *percentage* of the labour force in unions rose from about 5% in 1888, to 25% in 1913. At the same time, New Unions began to offer a *wider range of benefits and services* to their members and the differences between the two groups generally narrowed. Unions also became more acceptable to the establishment and union officials were increasingly consulted by government on issues affecting workers. Some even participated as witnesses and members of official enquiries, especially the massive 1892–4 report by the Royal Commission on Labour. This acceptance of unions was however shattered by new legal interpretations which appeared to fundamentally alter the legal status of unions and their rights to picket. Partly in response to this, even the moderate craft unions began to seek parliamentary representation by M.Ps. who would represent the interests of labourers. Eventually, in 1900, the TUC was encouraged to give active support to the *Labour Representation Committee* (LRC) and in 1906 the name was formally changed to the *Labour Party*.

8 > TRADE UNIONS AND THE LAW

It was generally believed that the 1871–5 Acts provided unions with a legal framework within which they could work without leading to claims for damages as a result of their actions. Once claims for damages by employers began to be brought before the courts, however, it appeared that this was *not* strictly the case. In a series of cases beginning in 1891, the courts took the view that the officers and members of a union could, in certain circumstances, *be liable* for charges of intimidation and therefore damages. It was however the *Taff Vale* decision of July 1901 which appeared to destroy the protection to damages from picketing which trade unions believed they had. In 1900, railwaymen in South Wales went on strike for higher pay during the Boer War. Despite opposition from some members of the union, the action by the railwaymen was declared official. But instead of coming to negotiations with the union, the railway company tried to obtain alternative labour and used the services of Collisons Free Labour Association to try and break the strike. When damage was done to railway property, the railway company offered rewards and two union members were convicted. This led the railway company to obtain an injunction from the court ordering the officials of the union to prevent unlawful picketing. After mediation, the railwaymen returned to work but when the strike was over, the courts granted an injunction against named union officials as private individuals and allowed the company to put a claim against the union because of damages caused to the company by the actions of its officials which had been illegal under the laws on peaceful picketing. In 1902, the railway was awarded £23,000 to cover the losses incurred and £19,000 costs. It now seemed that if any actions during a strike were declared illegal, e.g. the strikers did not picket peacefully, the *union* could be held responsible for the actions of its members and officials, and would be forced to pay damages from their funds and property. This effectively meant that unions would be unable to mount a successful picket during a strike.

Some conservative unions were actually pleased that the unreasonable actions of radical unionists were curbed by the courts. But the general view was that this was an attack upon trade unions and the law had to be changed to give them equal opportunity with the employers. In 1906, after considerable debate and discussion between the unions, the Labour Party M.Ps. and the Liberal government, the *Trade Disputes Act* was passed. This gave trade unions *immunity from damages* as a result of losses incurred by an employer during a strike.

In 1909, the trade unions were again in trouble with the courts, this time over their connection with *political parties* and in particular because most unions paid sums into a political fund that went to the Labour Party. In 1909, the case brought by W.V. Osborne against the *Railway Servant Union* was decided in favour of Osborne. Osborne, who was a Liberal, had objected to the union imposing a compulsory political levy on members. This meant that the new Labour Party, which was almost totally dependent upon unions for funds, lost its main source of income and that Labour Party M.Ps. were in financial difficulty, since at this time M.Ps. received no parliamentary salary. The Liberals took no action in this matter until 1911 when, in order to obtain the support of the Labour Party M.Ps., a payment of £400 was provided for M.Ps. In 1913 *another* Trade Union Act allowed unions to have political funds, but gave members the right to contract out.

9 > THE GENERAL STRIKE 1926

During the war period, the government had found it very convenient to use the unions to encourage increased production and to get labour to accept new methods of production. As part of the process of directly involving workers, it had been the government which had encouraged the development of shop stewards in each factory to meet with management on behalf of the workers. The return to peace began, however, to bring major problems, especially in the *staple industries* where new techniques had brought radical changes to the position of skilled workers, and in the *coal industry* which had effectively been nationalised during the war. When in 1919 the miners had demanded a 30% increase in wages, Lloyd George had quickly appointed a Coal Industry Commission to enquire into wages, hours and nationalisation. Several reports were issued and the final one by Sir John Sankey had recommended nationalisation, with the support of 6 out of the remaining 12 members of the Commission. The government decided, however, to return the industry to private ownership. The Miners Federation of Great Britain, the main miners' union, opposed this, fearing that private ownership would mean a return to the conflicts that had been a feature of the industry before the war.

As the world economy returned to normal, so coal prices began to drop from the artificially high levels of 1920, when they had risen to over 125 shillings (£6.25p) a ton. As prices continued to fall so owners, faced with the high wage levels from the war, tried to reduce wages and increase hours. The miners called upon the transport workers and dockers to support them. There had been an agreement signed in 1911 called the *Triple Alliance* by which they would help one another. However the railway men and dockers refused to support the miners. On *Black Friday* April 15, after a bitter strike without any support, the miners went back to work. During 1925, as coal prices continued to fall, so owners *again* sought to cut wages. This time the other unions in the Triple Alliance agreed to support the miners and faced with united union opposition, the government, led by Stanley Baldwin, agreed to give a temporary subsidy to mine owners whilst an enquiry was carried out by Sir Herbert Samuel. This was the so called *Red Friday*.

Whilst the Samuel Commission was meeting, the government began to make preparations for future strikes. It set up a private organisation the *Organisation for the Maintenance of Supplies* (OMS) and prepared plans for an emergency. The TUC and other unions did nothing. When the Samuel Commission reported, it recommended the removal of the subsidy and the reorganisation of the coal industry, but with no changes in pay or hours of work. During the negotiations between miners, mine owners and government which followed, substantial cuts in wages were proposed. When the mine owners issued lockout notices, the General Council of the TUC took over negotiations with the government. On May 2, 1926, Baldwin suddenly stopped negotiations, claiming that the unions had already issued notices for a general strike. Also Baldwin claimed that printers' unions had taken actions to interfere with the freedom of the press. Apparently a printer at the *Daily Mail* had refused to set up an article claiming that a General Strike was an act of revolution. When the TUC returned to Downing Street, Baldwin refused to see them as he had gone to bed. The *General Strike* began the following day.

During the nine days that the strike lasted, the government used all its resources to break the strike. It used troops to protect convoys and volunteers to operate buses and distribute food, etc. Generally the belief was held by many sections of the upper classes that the unions wished to bring about a revolution. They saw the strike as a challenge to democracy and to the elected government. In fact, despite this revolutionary hysteria, the strike was remarkably peaceful, though the aggressive views expressed both in the official government newspaper, the *British Gazette*, and that run by the unions, the *British Worker*, make this seem unlikely. The unions did not see the General Strike as a challenge to the government; they generally believed that it was an *industrial dispute*, not the first stage in a Russian-type revolution, which is what the Cabinet believed it to be. Baldwin refused to see the TUC until the strike was called off, but on his return from holiday, Sir Herbert Samuel acted as go-between for the two sides. Once the TUC saw that the government had no intention of giving in, most of its members were prepared to surrender, whatever the price. On May 12, despite protests from the miners, the TUC called off the strike. The miners held out for a while longer, but eventually they too went back to work.

Following the strike, the miners were forced to accept the return to an eight hour day, and reduced wages based on local conditions. Though some leaders were victimised and never found work in the industry, the overall feeling by the miners was one of betrayal by the TUC and by other unions. The final humiliation for the unions was that in 1927, the government passed the *Trade Disputes Act*, which banned sympathy strikes and changed contracting *out* of the political levy to contracting *in*. This greatly reduced the income of the Labour Party, and was generally regarded as a vindictive action to further reduce the political power of the unions. At the same time, the Act made picketing even more difficult and prohibited civil servants from joining unions that had any links with the TUC.

66 Breaking the
strike 99

EXAMINATION QUESTIONS

QUESTION 1 Study Sources A, B, C and D below and then answer questions a) to e) which follow:

Source A (Taken from *The Combination Act*, 1799):

Any workmen who shall at any time enter into any combination to obtain an advance of wages, or to lessen the hours, of working, or who shall persuade, intimidate, influence or force any workmen to leave his work; or who shall hinder any manufacturer from employing such workmen as he shall think proper; or who shall refuse to work with any other workmen . . . shall be committed to and confined in the common Gaol or House of Correction.

Source B (Taken from *The Poor Mans Guardian*):

Article 6: That the main aim of the Masters' Union shall be by all legitimate means to separate their workmen from the Unions to which they belong, and give encouragement and protection to those who have persisted in refusing to enter into such combinations. Article 7: That a register shall be kept of all the names and addresses of all workmen, distinguishing the members of the union from others, recording the character of each for industry, honesty and skill.

Source C (From A. Watson's, *The Life of Thomas Burt*):

There was no eagerness for a strike, for there were no defensive resources. The tommy shops, the only shops where the miners' families had been able to obtain food, would close. There were no co-operative societies with little saved up balances to the name of each member. The union had no reserve funds. So methods of conciliation were resorted to. On March 20, 1844, the men sent a letter to the owners asking them to receive a deputation from the Miners' Association. There was no reply of any sort.

Source D (*Punch* cartoon of 1852):

EFFECTS OF A STRIKE
UPON THE CAPITALIST AND UPON THE WORKING MAN

a) Study Source A.
   i) What light does Source A throw upon the relations between workers and their employers in the period before 1800? (2)
   ii) What circumstances in the late 1790s made the government consider it necessary to pass the Combination Act in 1799? (1)

b)   Study Source B.
i) Why did employers in Source B want to keep a register of workers (line 4)?   *(2)*
ii) Explain why the employers' desire to create such a Masters' Union (line 1) would have been less great in 1799.   *(1)*

c)   Study Source C.
i) What were the tommy shops referred to (line 2) in Source C?   *(1)*
ii) What evidence is there in Source D to support the evidence of Source C?   *(2)*

d)   Study Source D and C
i) How far does the view expressed in Source D support the evidence of Source C?   *(2)*
ii) How far does Source D represent an accurate view of the success of strikes and labour disputes during the period 1760–1852?   *(5)*

e)   To what extent did some unions during the years 1851–70 overcome the problems referred to in Sources C and D?   *(4)*

(LEAG; 1988)

QUESTION 2

a)   Why and how did the government attempt to prevent combinations of workers between 1790 and 1820?
b)   How did changes in the law 1824–7 affect trade unions?
c)   Explain why the GNCTU was not a successful union.

QUESTION 3

a)   What were the main demands made by the Chartists for the reform of Parliament?
b)   How did the Chartists try to influence Parliament? Explain why these actions were not successful.
c)   Why did many workers turn away from Chartism and give their support to the co-operative movement instead?

QUESTION 4

a)   In what ways were the New Model Unions of the 1850s different from the GNCTU?
b)   How did changes in the law 1865–75 affect the position of trade unions?

QUESTION 5

a)   In what ways was the period 1888/9 a successful one for trade unionists?
b)   In what ways does the period 1880–1900 see major changes in the organisation and part that trade unions played in society?
c)   Describe what happened in the Taff Vale and Osborne Judgements. How did these affect the position of trade unions?
d)   What actions did the TUC take to overcome these problems?

TUTOR'S ADVICE

It is likely that there will be questions asking you to compare one period or event with another. It is important in such questions that you do not just describe what happened in each event but point out clearly the differences. Explain why these occur and their importance to the historian. In this question you should be able to show in a) knowledge of the Dock and Match Girl strikes in London and explain why these were a victory for unskilled workers e.g. not only were they reasonably successful in getting their claim but they showed the value of support and sympathy from members of the public who otherwise would have opposed trade unions. Trade unions learned the importance of good publicity. New Unions were unions for the lower paid unskilled workers. The increase in demand and job opportunities for the unskilled worker in trade, transport and power industries provided better opportunities for them to form trade unions. Some were general labour unions organising workers of the same kind across different industries whilst others organised different groups of worker in the same industry. Their leaders were sometimes socialists who wanted changes in the political system so that the worker would be better represented in Parliament. At the same time unions almost become accepted as part of the system and both Liberal and Conservative governments tended to take note of what the respectable union leaders said and involved them in government enquiries into industrial and social problems. Part c) requires an account of how the interpretation of the law by judges in the Taff Vale case placed trade unions at some risk from civil action for damages and in the Osborne Judgement restricted their political funds. In d) explain how the Liberal government under pressure from trade unions and in return for support from Labour Party M.Ps. on other issues, altered the law in 1906 and 1913.

| QUESTION 6 | How might a trade unionist have defended the actions of the TUC in 1926 against the criticisms of those who opposed the General Strike and those who said that the TUC had betrayed the working classes? |

TUTOR'S ADVICE

An empathetic response is expected here. You do not need to give a long description of the events of the strike. You need to show awareness of different attitudes not just between the employer and trade unionist but also why the calling off of the Strike was regarded by some but especially coal miners as a betrayal. Most employers thought that the miners' actions in striking against a reduction in pay were ignoring the realities of the world market for coal and many people and especially Churchill, believed that the sympathy strike by the TUC would lead to revolution and a breakdown of democratic government. Many people blamed their defeat on the TUC for their incompetence in organising the strike and others said they were cowards for backing down. Many workers however said that the TUC acted sensibly to avoid a civil war once the government had shown that it was prepared to use the army. *It is important to be historically accurate when explaining how different groups of people felt, this is not fiction!*

MIGRATION AND PROBLEMS OF DISCRIMINATION

INWARD MIGRATION

OUTWARD MIGRATION

IMMIGRANT AND EMIGRANT TREATMENT

MIGRATION AND EMIGRATION SINCE 1945

SOURCES OF DATA

BRITAIN – A MULTICULTURAL SOCIETY?

GETTING STARTED

Walk down any city centre street today and you are certain to meet a wide range of people of different colours and with faces which some would describe a non-English. Whilst many of these people will be tourists, the likelihood is that most will be English and very often they, and their parents, were born in England. A hundred, or even fifty, years ago such a variety of peoples would have been less common. Britain today has become, or rather is trying to become, a multi-cultural society. Whether this is really true we will examine later in this chapter, but why have people from other countries and cultures come to settle in Britain?

Generally the answer is an *economic* one. Britain has been an attraction to people from other countries because it has offered better opportunities for employment, education and economic improvement than in the places they were living before. Indeed in the years after World War II Britain encouraged such immigration to help solve a labour shortage. Some possibly came because social and economic conditions in their homeland were so bad that they faced starvation and/or political and religious oppression. They were driven to find somewhere else to live. Today we are aware of this because people from so many different countries have come to Britain. Many of these countries were previously part of the Empire or Commonwealth and therefore it was perhaps natural that they should want to come to Britain. However the migration of people to Britain is not a new development; neither is it always the case that Britain has received more people than have left to settle in other countries.

Students will be expected to:

- Describe the extent and character of immigration into and emigration from Britain.
- Explain the reasons for population movements and the changing character of these movements.
- Describe the reaction of British society to immigrants.
- Describe the development of government policies to prevent discrimination and comment upon their effectiveness.

ESSENTIAL PRINCIPLES

1 > **INWARD MIGRATION**

Population movements are a common feature throughout history. The most obvious development from the seventeenth century has been the movement of people *into* Britain. As was shown in Chapter 2, the growth of population since the eighteenth century has been accompanied by changes in the geographical distribution of population, as the location of industries and job opportunities have changed.

Since the eighteenth century, an increasing proportion of the population have come to live in England. The growth of England's population has been *greater* than would have been expected from natural causes. Similarly, the growth of population in Ireland, Scotland and Wales has at times been much *slower than* would be expected from our knowledge about birth and death rates. The same could be said of *regions within England*. The explanation is *inward migration*.

During the eighteenth and nineteenth centuries, population growth in many *rural areas* was *faster than* the increase in jobs. Although employment in agriculture increased until about 1860, developments in agricultural technology and practices often meant that labour efficiency was improved. From the 1870s, as we showed in Chapter 4, foreign imports of cereals meant that many farmers stopped producing cereals, with the result that even at harvest time few jobs were available. It is normally the case that if the labour force grows faster than available jobs, not only will this lead to unemployment, but competition for jobs may well drive down wages, making it difficult for people to earn an adequate wage to live on.

URBAN MIGRATION

At the same time, developments in industry were creating more employment in *urban areas*. A combination of higher wages, better job opportunities in areas where labour was in demand, and the appalling consequences of poverty if they stayed where they were, meant that many rural workers and their families were attracted/forced to move into the towns. We know that this happened because the Census included questions on birthplace.

These and many other details about population were published for the main administrative areas such as counties and towns in the printed Census returns. Historians are also able to refer to the manuscript records and it often becomes clear from the birthplaces of the children that the family has moved about quite considerably. At first it was usual for workers to move into the nearest town but, as communications improved or workers obtained sufficient money, longer moves of fifty or a hundred miles became more common to larger, more industrial towns.

IRISH MIGRANTS

In times of exceptionally bad harvests or particular social problems (such as the Irish Famine 1842–6) numbers of people were forced out of their homes and often made their way to England in search of work. Exactly how many Irish and Scots moved to England will never be known for certain, but we estimate that the Irish population fell from a peak of 8.3m in 1845 to 6.5m in 1851. The population continued to fall throughout the rest of the century. Population did grow more slowly in Ireland because the poor economic conditions discouraged marriage. The Irish marriage rate fell throughout the nineteenth century. It was only about 55% of England's rate in the 1870s and 80s and birthrate was much lower than in England and Scotland. This reflected the fact that so many men, particularly young unmarried men, had left Ireland in search of work. Some Irish villages in the nineteenth century were like parts of Sicily and Turkey today, villages of mostly old men and women. The extent of the migration from Ireland is shown by the fall in population to 5.4m in 1871, 4.5m in 1901, and 4.3m in 1914.

The problems of adjustment to an urban, industrial life style faced by these Irish immigrants when they came to England will be dealt with later in this chapter. It is important to note however that this Irish movement was not really very different from that of agricultural workers from other parts of Britain. It was just bigger in terms of the Irish population and involved movement across the Irish Channel to England and later to America.

2 > OUTWARD MIGRATION

We now know that *outward migration* from England to other parts of Britain or overseas in search of work was quite common, even *before* industrialisation. Between 1585 and 1780 about 350,000 left England to work as servants in America (and at least 1.5m slaves were imported to America). The development of colonies in America and Australasia during the eighteenth and nineteenth centuries, provided alternative places for labourers and skilled craftsmen to settle if they were not satisfied with Britain. These areas had a climate which was more acceptable than Africa or Asia and the land was not intensively cultivated by local people. Many in Britain considered that the development of colonies would provide an outlet for what they considered Britain's excess population. If enough people were to migrate, they would help to remove excess labour and to improve wages and conditions for workers in Britain. Also, by cultivating the land overseas, Britain would obtain raw materials and an expanding market for manufacturers. During times of distress in Britain, both rural landlords and trade unionists often helped those who wanted to migrate with loans or subsidies to help pay for their passage (see Figure 12.1).

We cannot be certain exactly how many did migrate, but the figures we do have of passengers who left British ports after 1853 suggest that, excluding Ireland, about 5½m people left Britain between 1853 and 1900, and just over this number between 1900 and 1930.

HERE   AND   THERE;

OR, EMIGRATION A REMEDY.

Fig. 12.1 Punch Cartoon 1840

MOVEMENT OF THE LABOUR FORCE

This migration from Britain was really only part of an international movement of labour in the nineteenth century that saw massive population movements within *Europe*. Under-exploited farm land was brought into cultivation and progressive urbanisation took place as European countries industrialised. It was the tremendous demand by Europeans for foodstuffs and raw materials that led in part to the substantial movement of peoples not only within Europe, but to America, Africa and Australasia.

As the prices of raw materials and foodstuffs rose, so new sources of supply were looked for. This encouraged improvements in communications both on land and at sea. Improvements in technology made it cheaper and easer to transport even bulky goods over very long distances (see Chapters 4 and 7). The need to invest in new methods of transportation and production encouraged the *export of capital* from Britain, and the increase in the volume of world trade provided the opportunities for some countries to industrialise. The expansion of the American economy in particular brought about *labour shortages*, and this led to high wages, which were a further stimulus to Europeans to migrate. There was, therefore, a close connection between the development of certain regions, improvements in communications, the movement of capital, increases in trade and international migration.

ORGANISED MIGRATION

Population and capital tended *to go* to those areas where the profits to be made were highest. Such international migration was not however easy, though as early as 1830 it had become lucrative and well organised. At first, the only kinds of ships were ordinary sailing ships. Because Britain imported more from America than she exported, there was usually space on the *outward* journey from Britain for a few passengers. It was an easy matter to set up a temporary deck above the cargo with rough pine berths for sleeping that could be removed afterwards. Conditions on these ships could be dreadful and as early as 1803 and 1828, the British government had tried to control conditions with *Passenger Acts* that set minimum conditions for space and food that should be provided by the captains. At first, passengers were only given food that they had to cook themselves, and often men and women were sleeping together.

As a result of investigations by both the American and British authorities in 1848 and 1851 new regulations were introduced. However as the inquiries by Parliament showed in 1854, even these new regulations were often ignored. The main criticisms were about the amount of space provided and the practice of mixed berths. Food provided was often inadequate and still uncooked, except on the long distance routes to Australia. Passengers complained of favouritism by the cooks and extortion by the captain and officers. These complaints occurred even though American and British companies specialised in emigrant traffic and had large new ships specially built for the purpose.

During the later 1840s with the enormous increase in passengers escaping from the effects of the Irish famine, conditions on ships were especially bad. Overcrowding, poor food and water made worse by bad sea conditions, could result in disease and epidemics on board ships. The overcrowding and bad weather could also lead to accidents on board ship, especially fire. The overcrowding and inadequate safety precautions could lead to high loss of life when a ship foundered (see Figure 12.2 for illustrations of these various problems). Though some of these problems were eventually remedied by Parliament and the American Congress, safety precautions for passengers were still inadequate. This was shown by the tremendous loss of life amongst the immigrants on board the Titanic in 1912, when the ship did not have enough lifeboats for everyone on board.

(a) 1817, comments by Rev. William Bell, passenger on the Rothiemurchus from Leith to Quebec.

Our water has for some time past been very bad. When it was drawn out of the casks, it was no cleaner than that of a dirty kennel after a shower of rain, so that its appearance alone was enough to sicken one. But its dirty appearance was not its worst quality. It had such a rancid smell that to be in the same neighbourhood was enough to turn one's stomach.

(b) Thomas Littledale describing the fire on board the Ocean Monarch, August 1848. The ship belonged to the White Diamond line. The fire possibly began when a passenger lit a fire in a ventilator shortly after the ship left Liverpool en route to Boston. The ship was still in sight of land.

...the flames were bursting with immense fury from the stern and centre of the vessel. So great was the heat in these parts that the passengers, men, women and children, crowded to the fore part of the vessel. In their maddened despair women jumped overboard; a few minutes more and the mainmast shared the same fate. There yet remained the foremast. As the fire was making its way to the fore part of the vessel, the passengers and crew, of course, crowded still further foreward. To the jib-boom they clung in clusters as thick as they could pack – even one lying over another. At length the foremast went overboard, snapping the fastenings of the jib-boom which with its load of human beings dropped into the water amidst the most heartrending screams both of those on board and those who were falling into the water. Some of the poor creatures were enabled again to reach the vessel, others floated away on spars but many met with a watery grave... We must not omit to mention an act of heroism exhibited towards the close of this melancholy scene. When only a dozen helpless women and children remained on the burning wreck, paralysed with fear and totally incapable of helping themselves... an Englishman, Frederick Jerome... a seaman of the American ship the New World, stripping himself naked, made his way through the sea and the wreck, and with a line in his hand succeeded in lowering the helpless victims safely into the boats, being the last man to leave the wreck.

Fig. 12.2 Extracts about the problems of passage on an immigrant ship.

(c) Petition by New York Commissioners of Emigration 1860

> The frequent complaints made by female emigrants arriving [at New York] of illtreatment and abuse from ships captains... caused us to investigate this subject; and from investigation we regret to say that... after reaching the high seas... the captain frequently selects some unprotected female from among the passengers, induces her to visit his cabin, and when there, abusing his position as a commander, partly by threats, and partly by promises of marriage, accomplishes her ruin, and retains her in his cabin for the rest of the voyage, for the indulgence of his viscious passions and the purposes of prostitution; some other officers of the ship... often imitate the example of their superior, and when the poor friendless women, thus seduced, arrive at this port, they are thrust upon the shore and abandoned to their fate, without any remedy for the past wrong which has been done upon them; that such occurrences have become so frequent that it is our duty to ask for legislative interposition...

NB. An Act was passed with punishment up to a year's imprisonment or a fine up to $1000 but there is no record of any conviction!!

(d) William Smith, An Emigrants Narrative; Or A Voice from the Steerage, recording his passage in the India from Liverpool to New York, winter 1847–8. Smith was a power loom weaver and during the voyage fever broke out on the ship within a week of leaving Liverpool. The captain and 26 passengers died. On arriving at Staten Island 122 were taken to hospital including Smith.

> ...the scenes I witnessed daily were awful; to hear the heartrending cries of the wives at the loss of their husbands, the agonies of husbands at the sight of the corpses of their wives, and the lamentations of fatherless and motherless children; brothers and sisters dying, leaving their aged parents without means of support in their declining years. These were the sights to melt a heart of stone. I saw the tear of sympathy run down the cheek of many a hardened sailor.

Fig. 12.2 (contd.) Extracts about the problems of passage on an immigrant ship.

NB. Such problems were not confined to ships and death was due less to poor food than pestilence at port of embarkation and poor health of the passengers; this was especially true for cholera. As in cities, cholera was spread by an intestinal microbe found in contaminated water. Normally on board ship water was carried in wooden barrels which easily became contaminated.

Emigrants were cheated by tricksters at the ports of embarkation, such as Liverpool, who convinced emigrants that their English money was no good in America and changed it into American money at an unfair rate. Or they got them to buy unnecessary items for the voyage, and earned excessive commissions from captains and ticket agents.

A lot of attention was also given to the migration of pauper children and others to Australasia, and there were numerous scandals about the appalling conditions on board migrant ships. In general, British colonies in the Caribbean, Africa and Australia were desperately short of labour because America was a much more attractive and easier/cheaper place to go. From the 1830s, because of the difficulties of getting cheap farm labour, some colonies began to import 'coolie' labour. This was free Indians, Africans, and Chinese who went to work as 'indentured servants'. They were employed on plantations, farms and mines throughout the Empire, but especially the Caribbean sugar plantations and later the African gold mines and tobacco and coffee plantations. Like the British servants to America in the seventeenth and eighteenth centuries, they had to work for four or more years at very low wages to pay off their passage money and in many ways were treated just like slaves. This even happened in America in the late nineteenth century.

3 ▶ IMMIGRANT AND EMIGRANT TREATMENT

The reaction of the host country population to new immigrants was rarely favourable. The Irish who came to Britain from the late seventeenth century were blamed for a whole variety of problems (Figure 12.3). The main accusations were that immigrants were loafers who only came to Britain to become scroungers and to live on the Poor Law. Many, it was said, were criminals. Little of this appears to be true. At least in time Irish immigrants could become absorbed into English culture if they wanted. Also, as time passed and more settled in England, there developed in certain districts of the main cities distinctive Irish communities. In time the Irish became accepted into the community. This was not quite so true of other immigrants who came to Britain.

(a) Extracts from the Poor Law Enquiry (Ireland) 1835

(i) ... the Irish immigration into Britain is an example of a less civilised population spreading themselves, as a kind of substratum, beneath a more civilised community, and, without excelling in any branch of industry, obtaining possession of all the lowest departments of manual labour.

Evidence of Dr Duncan from Liverpool

(ii) the Irish seem to be as contended amidst dirt and filth and close, confined air, as in clean and airy situations. What other people would consider comforts they appear to have no desire for; they merely seem to care for that which will support animal existence.

Evidence of Mr. Houldsworth, Glasgow cotton manufacturer

(iii) . . . Wages in the spinning department of the cotton trade have been kept down by the Irish, or rather they have been prevented from rising. If wages were raised, I doubt whether we could meet foreign competition; even now there is great difficulty, as the Americans export a great deal of cotton goods, and meet us successfully in the Indian and South American markets.

(b) Extract from Dr. J.B. Kay (later Kay-Shuttleworth); The Moral and Physical Condition of the Working Class of Manchester in 1832

Fig. 12.3 English reaction to Irish Immigrants in the Nineteenth Century

The contagious example which the Irish have exhibited of barbarious habits and savage want of economy, united with the necessarily debasing consequences of uninterrupted toil, have demoralised the people. ... the habitations of the Irish are most destitute. They can scarcely be said to be furnished. They contain one or two chairs, a mean table, the most scanty culinary apparatus, and one or two beds, loathsome with filth. A whole family is often accommodated on a single bed.

THE JEWISH IMMIGRANTS

One of the by-products of social and political changes in Eastern Europe was a substantial exodus of eastern European Jews. Again precise numbers entering Britain are impossible to obtain, because many just came to Britain as a staging post on their way to America. But in 1911, the number of people born in eastern Europe and living in Britain was just less than 300,000, which was about 0.8% of the total population.

Though Britain had a well-established Jewish community, the new Jewish immigrants were very different. Many came from rural regions and apart from having a distinctive religion they spoke different languages and were culturally distinctive. There was considerable hostility towards them, even from some English Jews. Like the Irish immigrants earlier in the century, they were accused of creating all kinds of social problems. Like the Irish they tended to settle in the major cities, and to congregate in particular areas of the city creating a distinctive Jewish community.

IMMIGRANT CONTROL

The accusations levelled at these new Jewish immigrants indicate a level of prejudice and ill feeling that persisted, despite the fact that most could not be substantiated (see Figure 12.4). Such fears about an alien invasion and in particular a distrust of peoples from Mediterranean and eastern European countries, was also a familiar concern in the USA at this time. Both Britain and the USA took measures to control and limit such immigration. Parliament passed the *1905 Aliens Act*, but this really cannot be justified in terms of the numbers of people who came to Britain. Just as reformers had used the newspapers to get parliament to introduce reforms, so they could be used to encourage racial prejudice and immigration controls.

Surprisingly, perhaps, despite the concern about immigration into Britain, the overall balance was almost certainly a *net outward flow* as British people migrated overseas. This emigration from Britain, seems to have varied with economic conditions in Britain. In the 1880s the net loss varied between about 110,000 and 195,000, after 1895, it fell to about 50,000 but after 1901 it rose once more to between 102,000 and 270,000.

During World War I and the inter-war years, international migration was greatly reduced. America imposed very strict immigration controls and the economic difficulties of

The increased number of Jewish immigrants to Britain before 1914 led to an often violent outburst of anti-semitic feeling, especially in London and other major towns where they settled in any numbers. Such attitudes were not however confined to any one section or class of society as the extracts below show and extreme anti-immigrant views were even expressed as evidence to a Royal Commission.

(a) White A, The Destitute Aliens in Great Britain, 1892

... The alien, not withstanding many virtues, seems to bring a sort of social contagion with him, which has the effect of seriously deteriorating the life of those of our own people who are compelled to be his neighbour. It is a painful thing to write, but truth compels the statement, that wherever the foreigner comes in any number, the district in which he settles speedily drops in tone, in character and morals. It can be seen most distinctly in those districts in London where the alien is to be found in large numbers.

... the presence, especially in London, of thousands of foreign faced men and women crowding into dense parts of the poorer quarters of the great city does not so much anger our own people as it saddens them. Quite apart from other questions, their alien looks, habits and language, combined with their remarkable fecundity [birth rate], tenacity and money-getting gift, make them a ceaseless weight upon the poor amongst whom they live."

(b) Earl of Meath during debate in House of Lords 1890

If you desire to improve the condition of the working classes of this country... we must... do something to prevent this country from becoming the dust heap of Europe. ...that those working classes would become, to a great extent non-English in character and, that both in physique and in moral and social customs, they have fallen below present by no means elevated standard.

(c) Evidence from 1902-3 Royal Commission on Alien Immigration

Samuel Street... used to be a street occupied by poor English and Irish. In the afternoons you would see the steps inside cleaned and the women in their clean white aprons sit in summer time beside the doors, perhaps at needlework with their little children about. Now it is a seething mass of refuse and filth... and the stench from the refuse and filth is disgraceful.

These men come over here and they save a little money and they live in the worst style imaginable, and they get these houses and let them in tenements, and they buy the property and get £100 or £50, and they mortgage it. They do not pay the mortgage... it is the incoming tenant who has to pay the mortgage... people cannot afford to pay the exorbitant rates that very many of these foreign landlords charge. ...it is significant that some East End landlords, and not Jewish ones only, have publicly announced that they will not accept Christian tenants.

There is a street in Mile End... the houses of which were... put up for sale... the rents when sold were 7s 6d per week, after the purchase.. the rents were raised to 15s per week. The mother of a gentleman I know well went for one... she was informed, We do not want English, these are all for the foreigners.

Fig. 12.4 Extracts on English Reaction to Immigrants before 1914

the underdeveloped agricultural regions led many migrants to return to Britain. This was especially true after 1929 when many returned to Britain from Canada and the USA because of the Depression.

4 **MIGRATION AND EMIGRATION SINCE 1945**

The ending of World War II and the recovery of the international economy led to a revival in international migration. Improved economic conditions in Australasia, South Africa and America saw a return of large-scale migration from Britain to these regions. This movement was undoubtedly increased by the financial encouragement and preferential treatment which the governments of the 'white dominions' gave to migrants from the 'home country'. The economic difficulties experienced in Britain throughout the 1950s may also have encouraged many to try their luck elsewhere. As Figure 12.5 indicates, however, since the 1920s there has been a long term *fall* in the number of people leaving Britain. This decline has been interrupted by sharp increases, as from 1972–4 which was undoubtedly linked to economic problems in Britain. Part of the reason for this fall in migration from Britain is undoubtedly the political situation in South Africa and the gradual withdrawal of incentives and preferential treatment for British migrants to Australasia. Australia now does *not* give preferential treatment to British migrants.

Year	Emigrants	Immigrants
1900–1909	4404	2287
1910–1919	3526	2224
1920–1929	3960	2492
1930–1939	2273	2361
1940–1949	590	240
1950–1959	1327	676
1960–1969	1916	1243
1970–1979	2079	1440

Fig. 12.5 People leaving and coming into Britain, 1900–1979 (thousands)

IMMIGRATION FROM THE COMMONWEALTH

The post war period has however seen the most dramatic changes in immigration. Without exception these changes have been the result of the introduction of immigration controls. The *1905 Aliens Act* was linked to the hysteria and fears arising from Jewish immigration in the 1890s. This Act only dealt with aliens, i.e. foreigners from other countries. There was no attempt to regulate immigration from the British Empire and colonies. Since 1962, however, there *has* been a policy of progressive restrictions on immigrants from the Commonwealth and former colonies which is undoubtedly linked to concerns about the increased numbers of non-white immigrants taking up their right to settle in the 'mother country'.

Throughout the period of colonial rule, British colonies were effectively ruled from Britain and the populations overseas were regarded as British citizens. Their populations owed allegiance to the King or Queen and throughout the twentieth century this loyalty has been displayed by their support to Britain in the two World Wars. Once Britain began to decolonialise and to grant independence, this led to changes in the rights of citizenship. In 1948, Britain passed the *British Nationality Act* which distinguished between citizens of newly independent colonies and citizens of the UK and Colonies. Though the authors of this Act had intended to guarantee continued freedom of entry to Britain for Commonwealth citizens, since 1962 the basis of immigration controls upon members of the Commonwealth as well as aliens has been the distinction between different kinds of *citizenship*.

There is no doubt that the development of immigration controls was a direct response to the belief that Britain was being swamped by large numbers of non-white immigrants from the New Commonwealth. The campaigns of fear and alarm about the social and economic consequences of unrestricted immigration which developed in the 1960s was similar to the anti-Jewish hysteria of the 1890s or the anti-Irish feelings in the middle of the nineteenth century.

British attitudes and policies have changed. In 1967 it was said that Britain was the centre of a vast Commonwealth, "the greatest multi-cultural association the world has ever seen," (July 1967 Labour Party, Working Party, Race Relations). But by 1969, Duncan Sandys, a Conservative Party M.P. said in his speech in the House of Commons (11 Feb 1969), when introducing his private members Bill to make the status of Commonwealth citizens the same as aliens, "Our first duty is to consider the interests of our own people". A position which has now developed to the stage where visitors from certain Commonwealth countries now require visas to be obtained before they can visit Britain. Why and how did this position develop?

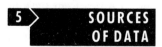

5 SOURCES OF DATA

Accurate figures on Commonwealth immigration into Britain are not really available before 1962. There was no government agency to prevent entry and no attempt to produce definitive figures. In June 1948, 492 immigrants came to Britain on the German cruise ship the *Empire Windrush* as the first party of organised immigrants from Kingston, Jamaica. Throughout the 1950s similar groups came to Britain, often in response to attempts by British agencies actively attracting labour for employers in the public services. The wide publicity given to such arrivals and the absence of accurate figures gave plenty of opportunity to opponents of immigration to raise fears about a black invasion. Even the Census figures did not help, because it only recorded birthplace and almost certainly underestimated the numbers of new Commonwealth immigrants by about 20%. The best estimates we have suggest the following pattern up to the mid 1960s.

BIRTHPLACES OF COMMONWEALTH RESIDENTS IN BRITAIN			
	Irish Republic	*Old Commonwealth*	*New Commonwealth*
1951	533,000	93,000	695,000
1961	726,000	110,000	844,000
1966	739,000	125,000	887,000

Source: Simmons, J., in *Population Policies in Developed Countries*, ed. B. Berelson, 1974 (McGraw Hill).

NET MIGRATION FIGURES

The various estimates of *net migration* into Britain during 1955–60, before controls were passed in 1961, show that most came from the Caribbean with only a few coming from India and Pakistan. The debate about controls and the fears of imminent restrictions led to a substantial increase in numbers entering in the 18 months prior to the introduction of *work vouchers* in 1962. The *1962 Commonwealth Immigrants Act* marked not only a change in government policy but also the beginnings of a change in immigrant composition. Individuals could only enter Britain if they had a work permit from the Ministry of Labour, or were their dependants, i.e. wife, children or aged relatives. The 'voucher system' not only substantially reduced the numbers but also marked the shift in 'non white' migration away from the Caribbean to Asia. Although the number of vouchers issued was reduced, the overall number of immigrants rose because of the large number of dependants. Even these figures do not show a true overall picture, however, because they only show immigrants and give no indication of the numbers returning to these countries. After 1970 the number returning to the Caribbean exceeds those coming to Britain. Even in the case of Asian countries, the level of return is quite high. This in fact fits in with what we know of nineteenth century migration from Europe to America, when perhaps as many as a third of all emigrants returned to their country of birth.

THE RACE RELATIONS ACT

The fall in immigration also reflects the fact that, despite its opposition to the 1962 Act, the Labour Party on coming into power in 1964, accepted the need for immigration controls. The Home Secretary, Sir Frank Soskice in his speech in Parliament on the renewal of the Commonwealth Immigrants Act in November 1964 said, "We are firmly convinced that an effective control is indispensable." Although the government passed the *1965 Race Relations Act*, set up a Race Relations Board and took various measures to improve racial harmony and integration, it actually introduced stricter controls by reducing the number of vouchers to 8,500 and improved measures to stop illegal entry.

THE IMMIGRATION ACT

The *1968 Immigration Act*, introduced by the Labour government specifically limited the entry of British passport holders from Kenya who did not have a substantial personal connection with Britain (born in Britain or descendants of British born parents or grandparents) to 1,500. This was because they feared that the anti-Asian policies of the Kenyan government would be adopted by other African states and they did not want to create a precedent that would lead to a flood of Asian British passport holders coming to Britain. This Act was clearly *racially discriminatory*, with its use of the grandfather clause and was a clear denial of the undertakings given at the time of independence to East African Asians who were the descendants of indentured servants taken to Africa from India by British merchants to work on the coffee and tobacco plantations.

The Conservative government of Edward Heath may have dismissed Enoch Powell for his outrageously racially inflammable speeches, but it went further than Labour in curbing non-white immigration. The *1971 Act* created 8 categories for immigration which made it even more difficult for non-white Commonwealth citizens to come to Britain. British entry to the EEC led to further refinement of nationality because of the EEC laws on freedom of movement. By 1971 the government had the legal power to prohibit all black Commonwealth citizens and even UK passport holders from coming to Britain. The Uganda Asian Crisis of 1972 also showed the lengths it would go to discourage non-whites.

When Idi Amin gave all Asians in Uganda holding British passports three months to leave, the government, afraid of a massive influx, tried to get other countries to accept some of the refugees but in the end had to accept 28,000. To prevent such an occurrence again the government introduced new rules to the 1971 Act in January 1972. The 1971 categories were refined further with detailed rules for putting the Act into effect by adding the Grandfather Clause. These rules limited free entry only to those members of the Commonwealth whose parents or grandparents were born in Britain.

This not only denied practically all non-whites but actually extended entry to many whites such as Zola Budd who had been denied automatic entry since 1962. As Robert Carr, the Home Secretary, made clear in his press release, the government was determined that it would not be held responsible for similar refugees in the future. Government attitudes to such problems is clearly shown in the press release (see Figure 12.6).

> When Asians resident in Uganda were summarily expelled last year the government immediately accepted its obligation to our passport holders who had nowhere else to go and the people of this country responded with characteristic generosity to the plight of the refugees. The Government considers that to have a similar burden thrust upon us again would impose unacceptable strains and stresses... the Government therefore thinks it right... to make it clear that while we shall continue to accept our responsibility to UK passport holders by admitting them in a controlled and orderly manner through the special voucher scheme, this is as much as it is reasonable and realistic for us to do if good community relations are to be maintained in Britain.

Fig. 12.6 Press release by Robert Carr, Home Secretary, Jan 25 1973

Since 1972, further modifications and controls have been introduced but these have really been concerned with matters of detail rather than principle. The surprising fact is that despite all the time spent dealing with immigration since 1962, the actual number of non-whites in the British population is really quite small. Probably no more than 2.5% in 1971. The reason seems to be that despite the small numbers, what is really at issue is the fears which a substantial minority of white British people have towards non-whites. As has already been shown above, English attitudes towards Irish and Jewish immigrants in the nineteenth century demonstrated racial prejudice throughout all sections of society; such prejudice was also a significant element in the pressure brought to bear upon governments in the 1960s. There is also no doubt that, despite the existence of legislation and actions to reduce discrimination in Britain, it still exists.

6 ▷ BRITAIN – A MULTICULTURAL SOCIETY?

Britain today is often described as a *muticultural society*, but what do people mean when they use this phrase? One obvious meaning is that today's British society includes many people who were not born in Britain, or whose ancestors originally came from other countries. We are aware of this today partly because there are many more people from the West Indies, Asia and Africa, whose colour and physical characteristics are clearly different from 'English' people. During the 1950s and 60s, when large numbers of such immigrants began to settle in Britain, many sections of British society found it difficult to accept these people, as is shown in Figure 12.7.

As we have shown above, such discrimination was not new. For many hundreds of years, people who were different from the majority population have experienced discrimination. Until the nineteenth century certain religious groups such as Roman Catholics, were actually *deprived* of basic rights of citizenship *by law*. A lack of toleration and a tendency to blame a wide range of social problems upon people who came from other countries or other parts of England has been a common feature of English society. Many would suggest that dislike and mistrust of minority groups who were distinct from the majority has been a common feature of most societies. What has been new, however, is the *widespread extent* of such discrimination and the fact that today we have in Britain large numbers of non-white English born.

Various governments have taken action to reduce the intake of further non-white immigrants but natural increase will inevitably mean that the total numbers of non-white English, and perhaps even the proportion of non-whites, in the population will continue to increase. We must learn to develop positive attitudes which respect the rights of all

Non-white Commonwealth immigrants to Britain have in general encountered the same kind of hostility and active discrimination as was previously experienced by Irish and Jewish immigrants in the nineteenth century. They have been accused – often without any real evidence – of being the reason for a whole variety of social problems from poor housing, ill health, to loss of employment and increased crime. Perhaps most worrying has been the manner in which during the 1970s and early 1980s non-whites were treated by some police officers.

(a) *Comments by Smethwick Housewife 1961 at a meeting of the Birmingham Immigration Control Association*

Edgbaston Road used to be a lovely road... you used to have nannies up that way, you know. Really good class people used to live there, and it was a pleasure to walk in that area. Now they've taken over and the place is a slum. It's horrible... their habits are terrible. They use the front garden as a rubbish dump, and heaven knows what they do in the toilets.

(b) *Comments by a police officer to Maureen Cain as reported in Society and the Policeman's Role 1973*

There was this enormous negro and we kept batting him over the head with our sticks and he didn't even seem to feel it... I hit him hard where it hurts most and in the stomach and as I went past – just happened to knock against him with my foot, and he went down like a light... we had to take him for assault on police or we could never have accounted for all those knocks.

(c) *Extract from P. Fryer, Staying Power: The History of Black People in Britain 1984*

Every encounter with people was a fresh hazard. Typical was the experience of Wallace Collins, a Jamaican who came to Britain in 1954 at the age of 22. On his first Saturday night in London he was abused by "a big fellow with side-burns", who shouted "You blacks, you niggers, why don't you go back to the jungle?" then lunged at him with a knife.

(d) *Bhiku Parekh, Asians in Britain: Problem or Opportunity? 1978*

The first generation of Asian immigrants in Britain... was not used to the mores (values) and practices of an industrialised society, his presence was resented, and he suffered racialist insults and indignities. He was denied a decent house and a job commensurate with his abilities. He was often not promoted to a higher position...
The Asian immigrants are predictably frightened and bewildered. They are haunted by a sense of impending tragedy.

Fig. 12.7 Attitudes to Commonwealth Immigration since 1945

members of society to play their full role in society and to have exactly the same opportunties as any other member of society. This applies not only to peoples of different colours and religions, but also to both women and men and those who suffer from some physical or other disability.

RACIAL INTEGRATION

As part of its immigration controls, the Labour government and particularly Roy Jenkins when he was Home Secretary, introduced legislation to prevent discrimination and to encourage 'integration'. In May 1966 he said, "I define integration. . . . not as a flattening process of assimilation but as equal opportunity, accompanied by cultural diversity, in an atmosphere of mutal tolerance. This is the goal".

How far these objectives have been achieved today is a matter of dispute. What governments have done since 1964 to promote these objectives has involved two aspects to policy:

1   The promotion of racial harmony and improved race relations.
2   The prevention of racial discrimination.

Since 1962, there has been the establishment of various bodies to reduce racial tension in Britain and to advise the government on racial issues. The *Commonwealth Immigrants Advisory Council* (CIAC) was set up in 1962 to advise the Home Secretary and in 1964 the *National Committee for Commonwealth Immigrants* (NCCI) was established to co-ordinate the activities of statutory and voluntary agencies concerned with race relations and immigrants' welfare. This body was reorganised in 1965 and finally in 1968 the Race

Relations Act created a new organisation – the Community Relations Commission (CRC). This organisation was given two main responsibilities:

1 To encourage the establishment of, and to assist others to take steps to secure the establishment of, harmonious community relations and to co-ordinate on a national basis the measures adopted for that purpose by others.

2 To advise the Secretary of State on any matter referred to the Commission by him and to make recommendations to him on any matter which the Commission should consider should be brought to his attention.

This latter power marks a major development, since the Commission was effectively given the authority to initiate discussion on policy.

ANTI-DISCRIMINATION LEGISLATION

The 1965 Race Relations Act

Anti-discrimination legislation began with the 1965 Race Relations Act. The Act was severely limited, it only made it unlawful to 'practice discrimination' by refusing to serve people in public accommodation such as pubs, restaurants and hotels, and prohibited 'incitement to racial hatred'.

This change in the law was an important point of principle, since it positively *outlawed* certain practices. The Act made no attempt to deal with important areas of personal life such as housing, jobs, or personal finance. Yet as public enquiries such as the 1967 *Street Report on Anti-Discrimination Legislation* and private reports such as the 1967 *PEP Report on Racial Discrimination* were to show, these were all areas of living in which discrimination was widespread in the 1960s. Despite the clear hopes of Mark Bonham-Carter, Chairman of the newly appointed *Race Relations Board* (RRB), for powers to act in these areas, the government was reluctant to take further action. The RRB showed in its reports that most of the complaints it received were outside its authority, since they concerned employment, housing and publications. From February, 1966 until March, 1967 there were 327 complaints, 89 within the Act, 101 on employment, 37 on housing and 24 on publications.

These weaknesses were largely dealt with by the 1968 Race Relations Act, which also gave the RRB greater authority and increased membership. At last, the RRB could initiate *investigations* into discrimination rather than waiting for complaints to be made. It is doubtful if the public at large supported such an active interventionist policy. The policy also reflected Jenkins' views on integration quoted above. Such a policy also must be taken into account with the actively discriminatory action being taken by the government to restrict immigration. In this way, it would seem that the government was trying to satisfy two different elements of public opinion – those who wanted *controls* on immigration and even repatriation if possible, and the 'progressives' who sought *racial harmony*.

From the later 1960s, although both political parties had effectively reached agreement on immigration controls there emerged clear differences on integration. The Labour Party began to favour positive actions to remove discrimination, as well as negative action to outlaw racial discrimination. The Conservative Party doubted that the law was the correct way to deal with the problem as shown by the following statement:

No government can legislate on integration. It depends on individual effort . . . We can help with education, on housing and with the social services . . . but, in the end, it comes down to the individual . . . In conclusion I quote some words of Samuel Goldwyn . . . " the greatest security a person can have comes from within himself and not from the outside. Nothing anyone can do for you can begin to match what you can do for yourself."

This difference in philosophy is best illustrated by the actions of central and local government when under the control of different parties. Perhaps concerned at the appalling race riots in America in Watts, Tampa and Chicago, the Labour government in 1966 gave additional financial support to local authorities which had above average concentrations of Commonwealth immigrants and this was followed from 1967 by reports such as the *Plowden Report on Primary Schools* which advocated additional money for Educational Priority Areas and the *Milner Holland Report* which advocated Housing Priority Areas. The *Urban Programme* announced in May 1968 seemed to promise further aid to offset the disadvantages and deprivation which seemed to be endemic in inner city areas. How effective these programmes have been in dealing both with discrimination and the particular problems of race prejudice and social deprivation which characterise many of the areas where non-whites predominate is a matter of judgement. The fact that non-whites are the majority of people living in many inner city areas and that high unemployment, low educational achievement, poverty and high crime rates are a feature of these areas suggests that the policies have not been very effective. It seems to many that there is a cycle of deprivation and discrimination which is a result of institutional discrimination. The deprivation and social problems of inner city areas make it difficult for the people who live there to break out of their situation, perhaps to obtain the educational and other qualifications which would allow them to gain access to more highly skilled and therefore better paid jobs.

RACIAL EQUALITY

Certainly the government considered it necessary in 1976 to introduce a new Act which replaced the RRB and CRC with a new body – the *Commission for Racial Equality*. This it was hoped would be able to deal more effectively with these problems by identifying discriminatory practices in industry, business and other institutions. In addition it would help to prevent any racial, ethnic or national group from being at a disadvantage. That even this has not been very effective is suggested by the continued problems in many inner city areas.

There has now developed an increasing appreciation that the policy of integration is in fact a denial of the legitimate rights and aspirations of many sections within the immigrant community. Instead of trying to encourage immigrants to conform to English values and cultural patterns we are increasingly coming to recognise the right of immigrant communities to maintain and indeed promote their own cultural values and traditions. This means that *cultural diversity* is seen as a strength rather than a weakness. The contribution which past immigrants have made to British society is considerable; the contribution of recent immigrants to Britain is also substantial. The abandonment of a policy of assimilation is something which many white English people still find difficult to accept but perhaps this is the only way to promote racial harmony and to give real meaning to the idea of a multicultural society.

EXAMINATION QUESTIONS

| QUESTION 1 | Study Sources A, B, C and D below and then answer questions a) to d) which follow:

Source A (Taken from a newspaper article of 1958):

No. 1: INTRODUCING TO YOU...

THE BOYS FROM JAMAICA

They were born in Jamaica. Do you recognise the uniform?

● People are human beings even though they come in different colours. The main reason for race riots is plain IGNORANCE of this simple truth.

This is the first of a series which Keith Waterhouse is writing to give people the facts about the coloured people. Today — meet the Jamaicans:

Smiling Percival Bennett works on a co-operative farm in Jamaica.

① WHERE THEY COME FROM..

HALF the 200,000 coloured people in Britain come from the West Indies, a sunny chain of islands in the Caribbean, between North and South America.

About 70,000 of those are from Surrey, Middlesex and Cornwall, the three counties of Jamaica. British for 300 years.

By the cheapest route, it costs £75 for them to come to Britain — on a British passport.

Jamaicans have been leaving home to look for work since 1884. They helped to build the Panama Canal.

They emigrated to the U.S.A. to Cuba, to South America. After the war, they began to come here.

② WHAT THEY DO AT HOME..

JAMAICA makes the sunshine things: Sugar, Bananas, Coffee, Cocoa, Rum, Tobacco.

About half the workers are in these jobs. And about half its produce comes to Britain.

Jamaica exports £49,000,000 of goods a year. Yet unemployment is still one of its big problems.

To keep in world markets, the country that desperately needs to create labour is obliged to import labour-saving machinery from Britain.

Jamaicans come here for jobs—but Jamaica helps to keep Britain in jobs. We make their machinery. And we provide 40 per cent. of their imports.

③ WHY THEY ARE HERE..

JAMAICA is the big-money island where jobs are few and pay is poor. The £30,000,000 bauxite industry employs fewer than 5,000 people.

The luxury tourist business, earning £10,000,000 a year, has jobs for only 5,700.

One out of every five Jamaican workers is permanently out of a job. And there is big seasonal unemployment among those who do have a job. Pay is as low as this: An unskilled hand in the cigar business earns £2 11s 6d for a fifty-three-hour week. A van driver gets £4 15s. A grade one railway fireman gets £5 10s.

Unemployment pay does not exist. The Jamaicans come here for work.

─────WHEN WAR CAME...─────

● During the war, 10,000 Jamaicans came voluntarily to this country to fight for Britain.
● Eight thousand of them went into the Armed Forces, and 2,000 into munitions work.

F A C T S

● ARE THEY WASTERS? In three years, Jamaicans in Britain have sent home £10,000,000 in postal orders to their dependants.

● ARE THEY CRIMINALS? No Jamaican can leave the island without police clearance. Those with criminal records are not allowed to come.

● ARE THEY HEATHENS? Three out of every five Jamaicans are members of a Christian church or group. In Britain, the churches they attend are packed.

● ARE THEY STEALING OUR WOMEN? After the war, all the Jamaicans who came here were men. Nowadays, half of them are wives and children—coming to rejoin their husbands.

● ARE THEY STEALING OUR HOUSES? Many Jamaicans here live in decrepit houses which white people would not take. Some have done renovations themselves.

● ARE THEY STEALING OUR JOBS? Jamaicans today are in steel, coal, Lancashire cotton and public transport. Colour bar or no, there are still few jobs that employers will give to coloured people if they can get white workers instead.

Twenty-two per cent. of the Jamaicans coming to Britain were in white-collar jobs in the West Indies.

But only four per cent. can get office jobs here. Most become transport workers.

And that—according to West Indian welfare workers—accounts for the good manners of Jamaican bus conductors.

F A C T S

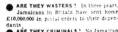
TOMORROW: Meet the West Africans...

Source B (A cartoon from *The Black Worker in Britain*):

JANUARY

JUNE...

Source C (Proportion of household heads unemployed, 1979):

| | London | | Birmingham | |
	Inner %	Outer %	Inner %	Outer %
White	5.6	2.5	6.6	4.0
West Indian	9.5	7.1	14.3	15.4

Source D (Taken from a speech by Alan Beith M.P., 1976):

'Anti-discrimination laws in themselves are not enough. Action must be taken to combat the disadvantage experienced by many people in minority communities, wider disadvantages, not merely discrimination. The new body (The Commission for Racial Equality) needs the resources to combat this'.

a) Study Source A.
   i) What evidence is there in Source A to suggest the existence of racial prejudice and tension in 1958? *(3)*
   ii) In what ways is this newspaper article valuable to someone studying race relations? *(3)*
b) Study Sources A and B.
   i) What evidence in Source A would support the view suggested in Source B? *(2)*
   ii) In what ways might Sources A and B be considered biased? *(3)*
c) Study Source C.
   i) In which area is the highest proportion of West Indian household heads unemployed? *(1)*
   ii) Why do you think this survey gives separate figures for inner and outer city areas? *(2)*
d) Study Source D.
   i) Explain what is meant by *anti-discrimination laws* (line 1). *(2)*
   ii) During the years since this statement was made, how successful has the *Commission for Racial Equality* been (line 3) in dealing with the problems indicated in Sources A, B and C? *(4)*

(LEAG; 1988)

TUTOR'S ANSWER

a)   i) The six questions in 'Facts' that are answered would seem to be questions that many people in Britain would answer 'yes' to in 1958. It is because of this that the writer of the article feels it necessary to explain why the *true* answer to each question is 'no'. Many people must have *thought* of Jamaicans as 'wasters', 'criminals', 'heathens,' and so on in 1958, and so need to be challenged by the facts.

  ii) The newspaper article provides *evidence* of the way people thought in 1958. It shows how prejudice was common then, as it is today, and how such prejudice is often based on an ignorance of the true facts.

b)   i) The view suggested in Source B is that black workers will be the ones still out of a job, even when the demand for labour increases in summer (June). In Source A it says that 22% of West Indians are in office type jobs at home, but only 4% here in England. So although they are capable of *doing* such jobs, they do not get the same chance as white workers in England. So most go into jobs where there are not enough local white people to fill the places needed – e.g. bus conductors, steel, coal, cotton.

  ii) Bias can work *against* people and in *favour* of people. Bias is a view that is not really in accord with the facts – often it is a view that only takes one side into account. Source A is written to counter popular prejudice – but it may take *too rosy* a picture of the Jamaican – i.e. be *biased* in their favour. Source B may *overstate* the true picture – not *all* white persons would have been chosen in preference to a black person by every employer. It is perhaps biased against actual employers.

c)   i) Outer Birmingham, with 15.4% of household heads unemployed.

  ii) It helps show that the situation in inner cities is often different to that in the outer suburbs. Usually inner city unemployment is *highest*, except for Birmingham West Indians.

d)   i) Laws to stop people treating coloured people unfairly, i.e. giving them less opportunity than white people.

  ii) Here you must apply your knowledge to events and situations *since* 1976. Can you *name* any cases where the Commission has helped to prosecute offenders, or to get the law changed in a way which helps the coloured person to have a more equal opportunity?

INDEX